THE INNOVATION MAZE

4 ROUTES TO A SUCCESSFUL NEW BUSINESS CASE

Published in 2016 by BIS Publishers

Building Het Sieraad
Postjesweg 1, 1057 DT Amsterdam
T +31 (0)20 515 02 30
bis@bispublishers.com
www.bispublishers.com

Design
studio frederik de wal

Editing
Christine Boekholt DeLucia

ISBN 978 90 6369 410 4

THE INNOVATION MAZE

4 ROUTES TO A SUCCESSFUL NEW BUSINESS CASE

GIJS VAN WULFEN

BIS PUBLISHERS

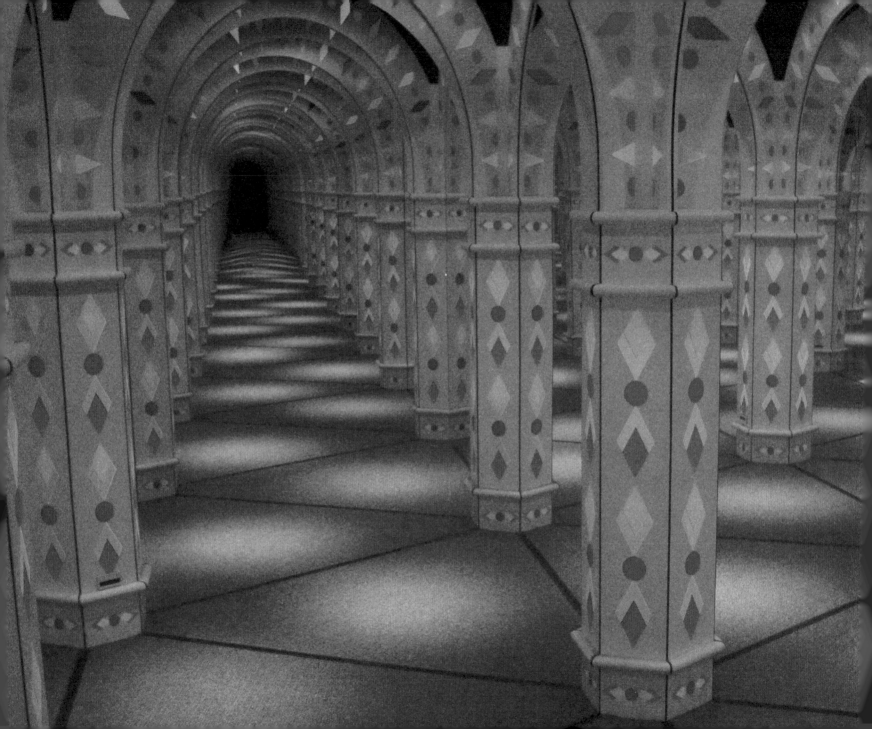

THIS BOOK IS A PRACTICAL GUIDE ON HOW YOU CAN BEST NAVIGATE THE INNOVATION MAZE. IT SHOWS FOUR CLEAR ROUTES FROM DIFFERENT NATURAL INNOVATION STARTING POINTS AND GUIDES YOU PAST ANY OBSTACLES THAT COULD PREVENT YOU FROM SUCCESSFULLY DELIVERING NEW BUSINESS CASES FOR PRODUCTS, SERVICES, EXPERIENCES AND BUSINESS MODELS. IT IS STRUCTURED INTO 20 SECTIONS WITH 34 CHARTS OF GRAPHICS, EXAMPLES, TEMPLATES AND CASES.

ACKNOWLEDGEMENTS

"This is a breakthrough book. Think of it as a cutting-edge GPS system for navigating the innovation maze and producing exciting new growth opportunities. I can't recommend it enough!"

Rowan Gibson,
Innovation thought leader
and bestselling author.

"Innovation starts with 100% uncertainty! This book is a practical guide on HOW to navigate the fuzzy front-end of innovation towards successful new business cases for products, services and business models".

Geovanny Romero,
Managing Director,
NPD Strategy - Andean
Region, Latin America.

"Though all roads may lead to Rome, innovators know that only a few tracks lead to innovation success! Gijs van Wulfen lights up our way with 4 practical routes, depending on your starting point: idea, technology, customer issue, or business challenge. These 4 cardinal points make our navigation more straight-forward, and fruitful: we can now turn every creative experience into an innovation capital."

Nicolas Bry,
Innovation Senior Vice-
President at Orange Vallée -
Orange.

"Innovation isn't always easy! There are many obstacles that need to be overcome including lack of internal support, sufficient resources, time and inspiration. In this book, Gijs van Wulfen guides you through the "innovation maze" using case studies from companies such as Airbnb, Google and LEGO to increase the chances of success for your own innovation projects."

Iain Bitran,
Executive Director, ISPIM –
International Society for
Professional Innovation
Management.

"If you need or want to innovate you are always faced with uncertainty. Innovation becomes increasingly a challenge full of puzzles. Navigating the Innovation Maze by applying the insights within this book, you do have the perfect companion to help. I certainly recommend reading."

Paul Hobcraft,
Innovation author,
blogger and consultant.

"Innovation really is messy business and a dangerous one too for corporate leaders. The chances of failure are extremely high. First with the Innovation Expedition and now with the Innovation Maze, Gijs van Wulfen is like a Sherpa on the Himalayas guiding you safely to the summit through the fog of distraction and confusion. Take this book and apply its methodology as prescribed. No more, no less. There's no guarantee you'll innovate but your chances of success will have grown exponentially."

Gene Browne,
CEO and Founder
of the City Bin Co.

"The Innovation process can be very fuzzy. The Innovation Maze will help you to structure and enhance your Innovation process."

André Groeneveld,
Director of Innovation at
FrieslandCampina Domo

THE INNOVATION MAZE

Eighty percent of innovation projects never reach the market. Many have a false start. It's no wonder that people experience innovation as a maze. In their journey, they either get lost or caught up in obstacles such as a lack of internal support, resources, time, insights or inspiration. As a keynote speaker traveling around the world and giving workshops everywhere from Canada to Cape Town and from Turkey to Tokyo I have encountered innovators all struggling alike with exactly the same issues at the start of innovation. My role here is to help guide you through the maze following along the most effective routes.

This book is a practical guide on how you can best navigate this innovation maze. It shows four clear routes from different natural innovation starting points and guides you past any obstacles that could prevent you from successfully delivering new business cases for products, services, experiences and business models.

Your four innovation routes:
1. The idea route: You are starting with a new idea.
2. The technology route: You have discovered a new technology.
3. The customer issue route: You have identified an unsolved customer pain point.
4. The business challenge route: Your business needs to innovate.

For each of the four innovation routes you will be given practical insights, tools and checklists to answer vital questions like, "How do I know if there's a need for it?", "How do I know if it is technologically do-able?" and "How do I know if I can realize a profit?"

The Innovation Maze simplifies innovation; delivering a coherent approach to the creation of new business cases. I have written it for startups, entrepreneurs, intrapreneurs, managers, consultants and those who are looking for practical real-life advice to successfully navigate the innovation maze.

One of the many important lessons you should take from this book is that innovation is a team effort. Likewise, The Innovation Maze could not have been written alone and without support at each stage of development. First of all, I'd like to thank the many innovators from all over the world whom I have met over the last 15 years while giving lectures, trainings and workshops on the FORTH innovation method. I'm indebted to them for openly sharing their innovation struggles with me. The inspiration for the maze metaphor came to me from meeting with innovators and hearing their stories of how they struggle from the start of their innovation journey.

Next, there are a few people I'd like to thank specifically: André Groeneveld for being an inspiring sparring partner in shaping the innovation maze and for his advice on more technical related issues, Gene Browne and Oscar Dekkers for the approval of publishing their cases, Siemen Eijkemans for his desk research, Christine Boekholt for her excellent advice on textual content, maze designer Martin van der Gaag for designing an amazing maze, book designer Frederik de Wal for co-creating another book with me in a wonderful style and publishers Bionda Dias and Rudolf van Wezel for their support making The Innovation Maze a reality.

Gijs van Wulfen

CONTENTS

THE INNOVATION MAZE

USE THE FOLLOWING FOUR ROUTES TO NAVIGATE THROUGH THE INNOVATION MAZE LEADING YOU TO A WELL-FOUNDED CONVINCING NEW BUSINESS CASE.

DOWNLOAD THE MAZE AND THE 4 INNOVATION ROUTES FOR FREE AT WWW.GIJSVANWULFEN.COM/BOOKS

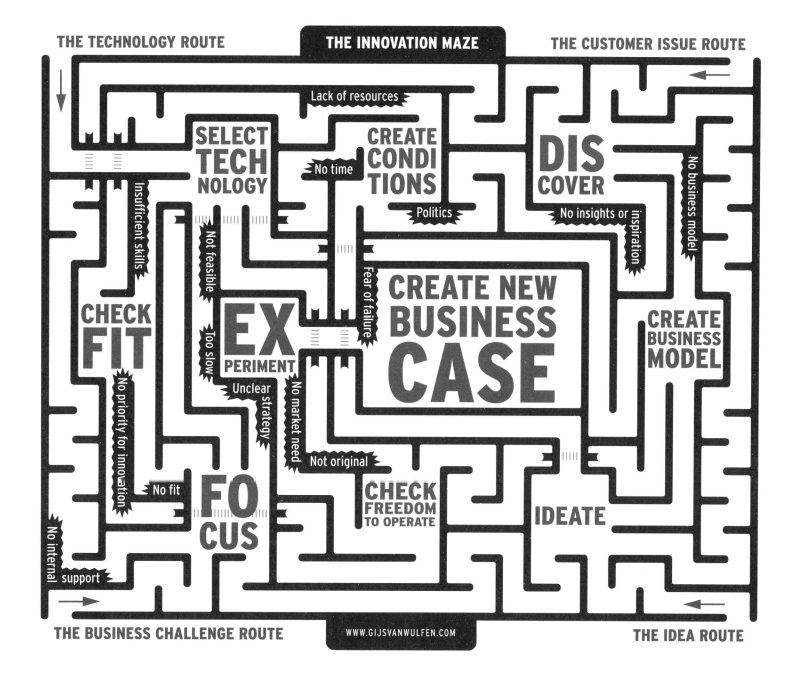

THE TECHNOLOGY ROUTE

THE INNOVATION MAZE

THE CUSTOMER ISSUE ROUTE

Lack of resources

SELECT TECH NOLOGY

CREATE CONDI TIONS

No time

DIS COVER

Politics

No insights or inspiration

No business model

Insufficient skills

Not feasible

Fear of failure

CHECK FIT

EX PERIMENT

CREATE NEW BUSINESS CASE

CREATE BUSINESS MODEL

Too slow

Unclear strategy

No market need

No priority for innovation

No fit

Not original

FO CUS

CHECK FREEDOM TO OPERATE

IDEATE

No internal support

THE BUSINESS CHALLENGE ROUTE

WWW.GIJSVANWULFEN.COM

THE IDEA ROUTE

THE IDEA ROUTE

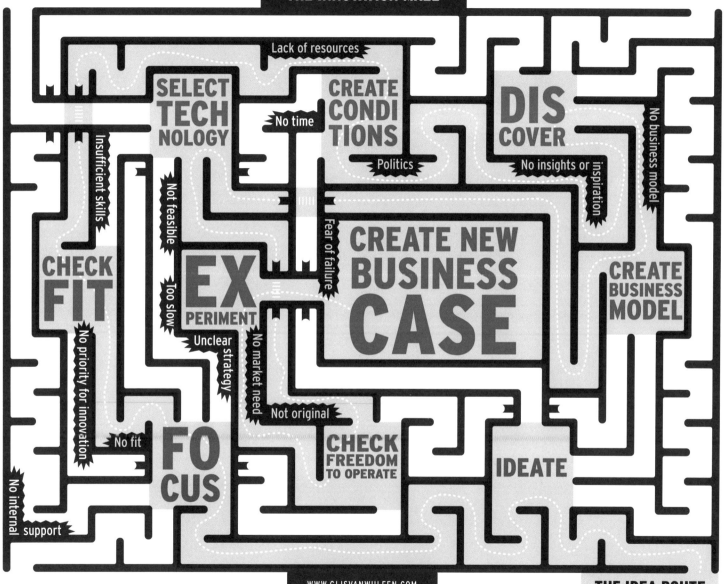

THE INNOVATION MAZE

Lack of resources

SELECT TECHNOLOGY

No time

CREATE CONDITIONS

Politics

DISCOVER

No business model

Insufficient skills

No insights or inspiration

Not feasible

Fear of failure

CREATE NEW BUSINESS CASE

CHECK FIT

EXPERIMENT

CREATE BUSINESS MODEL

Too slow

Unclear strategy

No market need

No priority for innovation

No fit

FOCUS

Not original

CHECK FREEDOM TO OPERATE

IDEATE

No internal support

WWW.GIJSVANWULFEN.COM

THE IDEA ROUTE

THE TECHNOLOGY ROUTE

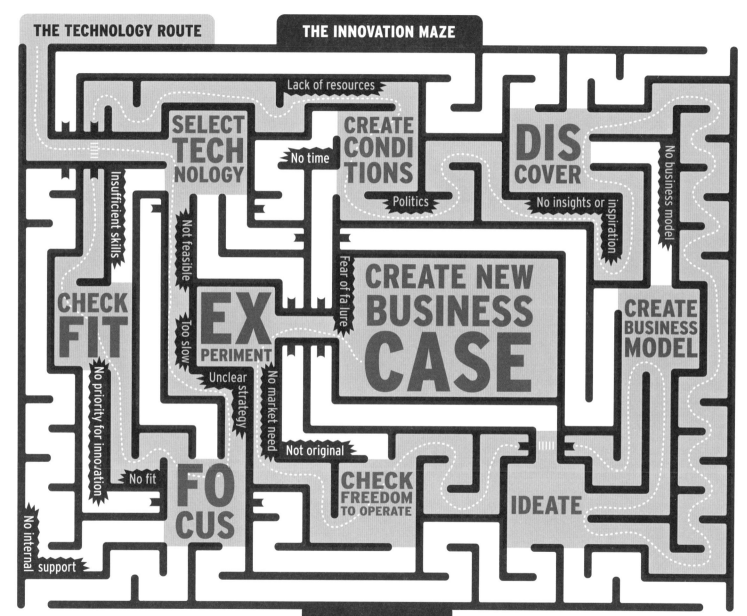

THE CUSTOMER ISSUE ROUTE

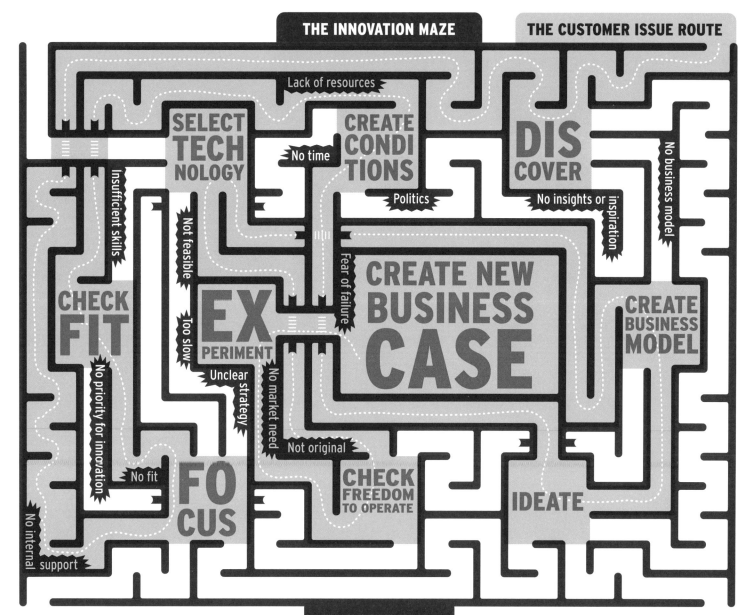

THE INNOVATION MAZE

THE CUSTOMER ISSUE ROUTE

Lack of resources

SELECT TECHNOLOGY

CREATE CONDITIONS

No time

DISCOVER

No business model

Politics

No insights or inspiration

Insufficient skills

Not feasible

Fear of failure

CREATE NEW BUSINESS CASE

CREATE BUSINESS MODEL

CHECK FIT

EXPERIMENT

Too slow

No priority for innovation

Unclear strategy

No market need

No fit

FOCUS

Not original

CHECK FREEDOM TO OPERATE

IDEATE

No internal support

WWW.GIJSVANWULFEN.COM

THE BUSINESS CHALLENGE ROUTE

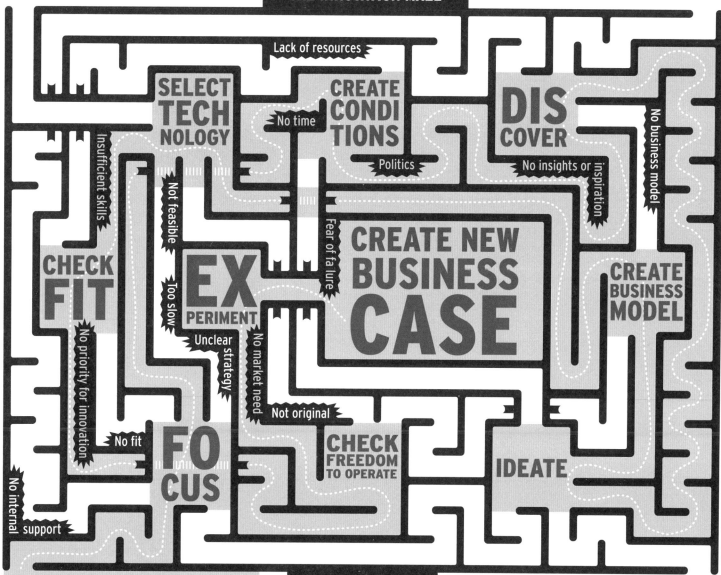

THE INNOVATION MAZE

SELECT TECHNOLOGY

CREATE CONDITIONS

DISCOVER

CHECK FIT

EXPERIMENT

CREATE NEW BUSINESS CASE

CREATE BUSINESS MODEL

FOCUS

CHECK FREEDOM TO OPERATE

IDEATE

Lack of resources
No time
Politics
No insights or inspiration
No business model
Insufficient skills
Not feasible
Fear of failure
Too slow
Unclear strategy
No market need
No priority for innovation
No fit
Not original
No internal support

THE BUSINESS CHALLENGE ROUTE

WWW.GIJSVANWULFEN.COM

The reasonable man adapts himself to the world; the unreasonable one persists in trying to adapt the world to himself. Therefore all progress depends on the unreasonable man.

George Bernard Shaw

INNOVATION IS A MESSY BUSINESS

BUSINESS CONDITIONS CHANGE SPECTACULARLY FAST

Today's pace of change in business conditions is surely spectacular as we live in an age of technological acceleration (artificial limbs that respond to brain impulses, driverless cars, 3D printing, new business models enabled by increasing connectivity). It's also why innovation is such a popular theme. It gets 400 million hits on Google and 70,000 hits on book titles on Amazon.

It took color TV ten years to move from novelty to mainstream. And two generations later it took HDTV just as long to achieve mass success. In the twentieth century it took a decade to build this new HDTV platform and a decade for it to find a mass audience. Steve Johnson, author of *Where Good Ideas Come From* calls it the 10/10 rule.[1] Compare that to the launch of YouTube founded in 2005. Chad Hurley, Steve Chen and Jawed Karim, all ex-employees of PayPal decided to upgrade the role of video on the Web. Using less than $ 10 million of venture capital and two dozen people, YouTube was streaming more than 30 million videos a day within sixteen months. YouTube took the 10/10 rule of the twentieth century and made it 1/1 in this century.[2] As a consequence of this acceleration, the time that companies can count on to hold their leading market positions is shrinking. Did you know that nearly 40% of the companies listed in the Fortune 500 in 1999 were no longer there 10 years later?[3]

YOUR INNOVATIONS HAVE TO BE RELEVANT, FEASIBLE AND VIABLE

Before moving on, let's clarify what I mean by innovation as the term has been defined in so many ways over the last decades. Therefore, I have compiled a list of ten definitions in chart 1, each highlighting a different perspective that resonates with me.[4] In my view,

> "An innovation is a feasible relevant offering such as a product, service, process or experience with a viable business model that is perceived as new and is adopted by customers."

Let me exemplify the keywords in this definition:

Feasible. Feasibility is a precondition for a new product, service, process or experience to be launched. If it's not feasible, it's just a dream. Although dreams are a great source of inspiration they will not provide continuity to your organization.

Relevant. Your customers have to change their present behavior. They will only adopt your innovation when it brings value to them. Most often it's a solution for a customer pain point. In other cases your innovation might even be fulfilling a long cherished wish. It has to be relevant.

Offering. I like to define innovation in much broader terms than mere product innovation such as the smartphone. That's why I use the word 'offering', which was coined by Larry Keeley in his book *Ten Types of Innovation*. An offering can be any form of a product, service, process or experience. As early as 1934, the famous economist Schumpeter proposed a broad definition of innovation as he distinguished: new products, new methods of production, new markets, new supply sources and new ways of organizing enterprises.[5]

Viable Business Model. Every organization needs to secure its future. That's why every innovation should provide a viable business model which contributes to the goals of the organization. This applies to companies, non-profit organizations and even governmental organizations.

Perceived as new. Innovation comes from the Latin word 'innovat', which means to renew or alter. The combination of 'in' and 'novare' suggests 'to come up with something entirely new.'[6] The question is...new for whom? New for you? New for your company? New for your market? New for the world? These days, everybody tends to label everything as 'NEW'. In my view, it's only new when the customer perceives a product, service, process or experience as new.

Adopted. An innovation is only successful when it's adopted by customers, users, clients, or whatever you may call them. Adoption distinguishes the tops from the flops and is one of the biggest challenges for every innovator. So, be relevant!

ACTIVE INNOVATORS WANT TO INNOVATE – REACTIVE INNOVATORS NEED TO INNOVATE

Not innovating is no longer an option for an organization that wants to be in good shape the day after tomorrow. Innovation is moving forward in every sector; whether or not your company moves with it. The world is rapidly changing, as you can see in chart 2 where seven top futurists make some pretty amazing predictions for 2025. Dr. Michio Kaku, professor of theoretical physics at the City University of New York and author of *The Future of the Mind*, predicts for example that, "In the next 10 years, we will see the gradual transition from an Internet to a brain-net, in which thoughts, emotions, feelings, and memories might be transmitted instantly across the planet." Can you imagine how this might impact your organization?

In practice, I see organizations approach innovation in two different ways: those who want to innovate and those who need to innovate. I call those who want to innovate the active innovators and the ones who need to innovate the passive innovators. As you can see in chart 3 their roles are defined by the moments they really innovate their business. Every company, business unit or product has its lifecycle of introduction, growth, maturity and decline. Active innovators, who want to innovate, give innovation priority at the end of the growth stage. Before they reach maturity they want to innovate, often for several reasons simultaneously:

- ▸ To keep their revenue stream growing;
- ▸ To maintain an innovative mindset;
- ▸ To boost internal entrepreneurship (intrapreneurship);
- ▸ To address changing needs and wants of customers;
- ▸ To lead in technology;
- ▸ To expand their business by new business models, distribution channels and customer groups;
- ▸ To anticipate on new governmental regulations or a market liberalization.

Reactive innovators, on the contrary, wait. They wait until they get hit by a crisis, their markets saturate or get disrupted by new technologies and/or business models. They reorganize, lay-off people and prioritize innovation only at the start of their decline stage when they need to innovate. They need to innovate most often with only one goal in mind: to stop revenues and profits from falling and build a new future for their organization.

Both types of innovators have their own challenges. The good news for active innovators is that there are plenty of resources available as the company is doing well at the end of the growth stage. Their challenge is to cope with a lack of urgency at the operational level of the organization: "Why should we innovate? We're damn busy and doing great!" The good news for the reactive innovators is that there's great urgency also at the operational level of the organization, as there's often been a collective layoff due to the business slow-down. Their challenge is compounded by both a lack of resources and a lack of time, as they will have to move quickly.

Are you an active innovator or a reactive one? And what about your organization? We all hear and read a lot of the top innovative companies in the world, like Apple, Google, Samsung, Amazon, Tesla Motors, IBM, Facebook, Starbucks and many more. They dominate the news. But there are more than 200 million companies worldwide. And you better believe the vast majority can be classified as reactive innovators. So, if your organization waits until not innovating is no longer an option, just remember that you will be accompanied by millions of other businesses.

The central question is not if you should innovate. It's HOW you can start and lead innovation effectively.

OUR DISLIKE FOR RISKS MEANS INCREMENTAL INNOVATIONS DOMINATE

Take a look at how companies spend their innovation budgets: 58% of R&D spending is directed at incremental or renewal innovations, 28% at new or substantial innovations, and only 14% at breakthrough or radical innovations.[7] Companies tend to prefer incremental innovations in small steps over breakthrough innovations in big jumps as they can be implemented faster with less perceived risk and fewer resources needed. The share of breakthrough new products has been halved in the last decades from 20.4% in the mid-1990s to only 11.5% in 2010 as you can see in Chart 4.

Incremental innovation fuels the revenues of companies today and tomorrow, while breakthrough innovations might pay off the day after tomorrow. I like to quote the CEO of BMW AG, the German luxury car producer, Dr. Ing. Norbert Reithofer. When asked why BMW started the risky E-car project with the BMWi-3 and i-8 he responded very openly: "Because doing nothing was an even bigger risk."[8]

In *The Innovation Paradox*, Tony Davila and Marc Epstein describe a paradox for managers: "The benefits of pursuing operational excellence and incremental innovation can be liabilities for breakthrough innovation. Efforts to execute better often have the unintended consequence of reducing the likelihood of breakthrough innovation. In other words, the same organizational design that is good for improving operational excellence and developing incremental innovation can get in the way of breakthrough innovation many leaders want."[9]

They further state that, "operational excellence and incremental innovation succeed as long as an industry follows the predicted path. All industries experience breakthrough changes that makes existing strategies obsolete. At these points, what made companies great can become their largest liability".[10]

A great example of this is the story of Nokia, the market leader in mobile phones. They saw the smart phone coming. They even had a prototype of it. Yet, their customers wanted a better mobile phone and that's what Nokia focused on; until the smart phone took away all their customers.

BOTH STARTUPS AND CORPORATE INNOVATORS ALIKE FAIL MOST OF THE TIME

Innovation is seen by a lot of corporate executives and venture capitalists as a black hole, where large sums of money go in and very seldom really innovative products or services come out. And most of the time they are right. The facts are quite depressing. Of the approximately 12,000 new introductions in fast moving consumer goods to Western European markets between 2011 and 2013, only seven generated more than € 10 million in the first year, and an even smaller amount maintained similar performance through year two. On top of that, 76% of all so-called innovations did not even achieve 52 weeks of sales (and barely half achieved even 26 weeks of sales).[11] Market Research Company Nielsen states that new fast moving consumer goods have only a 10% chance of succeeding. Booz & Company reports that 66% of new products fail within 2 years. And Doblin Group reported in a 2012 study that 96% of all innovations fail to return their cost of capital.[12] Financial giant Morgan Stanley estimates that, of the $ 2.7 trillion that companies pour into technology each year, more than $ 500 billion is wasted, in large part due to implementation failure of new innovations.[13]

High failure rates of innovation don't start at market launch. The innovation process from idea to market itself is full of pitfalls and inefficiencies too. Stage-Gate founder, Robert Cooper, shows that for every seven new product ideas about 4 enter development, 1.5 are launched, and only one succeeds.[14] A study of Stevens and Burley gives even more disastrous ratios. Their study shows it takes 3,000 raw ideas to come up with 1 successful product as you can see in Chart 5. This means that enormous amounts of enthusiasm, energy, time and financial resources of organizations are spent in the innovation process without direct returns. Innovation of course is a learning process full of experimenting and trial and error, where you can't expect to always get it right the first time. You learn an awful lot from all the iterations in a new concept, which pays off in other projects or in your daily business. But do you accept wasting more than 85% of your time and money in innovation, because it's so risky? Well, I don't! I see an enormous potential for improvement.

Startups are not doing much better by the way. Eric Ries, author of *The Lean Startup*, defines a startup as "a human institution designed to create a new product or service under conditions of extreme uncertainty." And the facts reflect the extreme uncertainty mentioned. A US study among 2,000 startups financed with venture capital between 2004 and 2010 reveals that more than 95% of the startups fail to see the projected return on investment. An estimated 30% to 40% of high potential US startups liquidate all assets, with investors losing all their money. Of all startups, about 60% of the companies survive to age three and roughly 35% survive to age ten, according to the US Bureau of Labor Statistics.[15] Startups fail according to Ries because the old management methods of a good plan, a solid strategy and thorough market research don't work for startups, as they operate with too much uncertainty. Also according to Ries, adopting the just-do-it mentality does not work either.[16]

Reflecting on these facts you will certainly conclude that innovation is indeed a messy business. Are you personally prepared to run a risk? A calculated risk, perhaps?

IMPROVE INNOVATION: LET'S START AT THE FRONT END

With innovation processes performing so poorly, we are well aware that there is still much to learn. A recent global innovation study by Strategy& among 500 innovation leaders shows that only 27 percent feel they have mastered the elements they will need for innovation success over the next 10 years.[17] Another study on innovation from McKinsey, interviewing 2,500 global executives in 2012 identifies areas where even innovation leaders can improve. McKinsey identified eight essentials for innovation. The most room for improvement is in creating new business models that provide defensible and scalable profit sources. With only 27 percent of the world innovation leaders saying they do this right, there are tremendous opportunities for us to improve the innovation success ratio.[18]

The front end of the innovation process includes all activities starting from the generation of an idea in the search for new opportunities up through the development of a concept. An innovation excellence study by A.D. Little reveals that idea management has the strongest impact on the increase in sales by new products. Effective idea management results in an extra 7.2% of sales from new products. A major benchmarking study by Robert G. Cooper shows however that only 19 % of businesses have a proficient ideation front-end process in place and only 31% of firms have an effective method for selecting ideas to invest in.[19] That is probably one reason innovators refer to the start of innovation as "the fuzzy front end." My ambition is to *unfuzzy* the start of innovation by offering a practical process. As Scott D. Anthony says in his book *The First Mile*, "The further you go from your core business, the less you know and the more you assume. While people generally agree with that statement, human biases mean they underestimate how much less they know and how much more they assume."[20]

You always start with 100% uncertainty. Your main role as innovator is to reduce the uncertainty to an acceptable level for yourself and your organization. This book will map the way to start innovation effectively by reducing this uncertainty to acceptable levels, and thereby leading to well-founded decisions to develop your innovations.

KEY MESSAGES FROM THIS CHAPTER

1. **Organizations approach innovation in two different ways: those who want to innovate and those who need to innovate. Who do you want to be?**
2. **Be aware that our dislike for risks means incremental innovations dominate.**
3. **Both startups and corporate innovators alike fail most of the time.**
4. **Only one in five businesses have a proficient ideation front-end process in place.**
5. **Innovation starts with 100% uncertainty. Your role as innovator is to reduce the uncertainty to an acceptable level for you and your organization.**

Notes

1 Steve Johnson, *Where Good Ideas Come From*, Penguin Books, p. 13.
2 Steve Johnson, *Where Good Ideas Come From*, Penguin Books, p. 16.
3 Source: Larry Keeley, Ryan Pikkel,Brian Quinn, Helen waters, *Ten Types of Innovation*, Wiley, Hoboken, New Jersey, 2013, p. 190.
4 Source: Eric F Shaver, PhD. http://www.ericshaver.com/the-many-definitions-of-innovation/#sthash.cv51Y1Rb.dpuf
5 Dave Richards, *The Sevens Sins of Innovation*, Palgrave Macmillan, London, 2014, p.14.
6 Max McKeown, *The Innovation Book*, Pearson, Harlow, United Kingdom, 2014, p. xxix.
7 Source: www.innovationexcellence.com/blog/2014/10/28/the-2014-global-innovation-1000-study-from-strategy/.
8 Dutch car magazine, Autoweek, 41-2013.
9 Tony Davila & Marc J. Epstein, *The Innovation Paradox*, Berret-Koehler Inc., San Francisco, 2014, p xi.
10 Tony Davila & Marc J. Epstein, *The Innovation Paradox*, Berret-Koehler Inc., San Francisco, 2014, p. 3.
11 Source: http://www.nielsen.com/content/dam/nielsenglobal/eu/nielseninsights/pdfs/Breakthrough_Innovation_Report_EU_FINAL.pdf

12 Fast company, April 4, 2012.
13 K.J. Klein & A.P. Knight, *Innovation Implementation*, American Psychological Society, Volume 14 – Number 5, pp. 244-245.
14 Robert G. Cooper, *Winning at New Products*, Basic Books, New York, 2011, p. 18.
15 The Wall Street Journal, http://www.wsj.com/articles/SB10000872396390443720 2045780049804764291910)
16 Eric Ries, *The Lean Startup*, Penguin, 2011, p. 9.
17 Innovationecellence.com, www.innovationexcellence.com/blog/2014/10/28/the-2014-global-innovation-1000-study-from-strategy/
18 McKinsey Analysis, *The Eight Essentials of Innovation*, Marc de Jong, Nathan Marston and Erik Roth, McKinsey Quarterly, April 2015.
19 Robert G. Cooper and Angelika Dreher, "Voice-of-Customer Methods: What is the Best Source of New Product Ideas." Marketing Management Magazine, Winter, 2010, p. 40.
20 Scott D. Anthony, *The First Mile*, Harvard Business Review Press, Boston, Massachusetts, 2014.

In the last few decades, so many definitions of innovation have been created. Eric F Shaver has collected over 50 of them. I have compiled a list of ten, each highlighting a different perspective that resonates with me and added my own practical definition of an innovation as number 11.

Innovation is executing new ideas to create value.
(Tim Kastelle@timkastelle)

...innovation is the process that turns an idea into value for the customer and results in sustainable profit for the enterprise.
(Carlson & Wilmot, 2006, p. 4)

11 DEFINITIONS

...innovation is the conversion of a new idea into revenues and profits.
(Lafley & Charan, 2008, p. 21)

Innovation is change that creates a new dimension of performance.
(Peter Drucker)

Something different that has impact.
(Scott D. Anthony@ ScottDAnthony)

Discontinuous improvement.
(submitted by John W. Lewis@
JohnWLewis)

Source
Eric F Shaver, PhD. http://www.ericshaver.com/the-many-definitions-of-
innovation/#sthash.cv51Y1Rb.dpuf

*...the creation
of a viable new offering.*
(Larry Keeley, Ten Types of
Innovation)

*...is the adoption of a new
practice in a community.*
(Peter J. Denning & Robert
Dunham, The Innovator's Way,
2010, p. 6)

OF INNOVATION

*...a process
of finding novel solutions
to important problems.*
(Greg Satell@Digitaltonto)

**An innovation is a relevant offering
such as a product, service, process
or experience with a viable business
model that is perceived as new and
is adopted by customers.**
(Gijs van Wulfen, 2015)

*...an idea,
practice, or object that
is perceived as new by an
individual or another unit
of adoption.*
(Rogers, 2003)

SEVEN TOP FUTURISTS MAKE SOME PRETTY SURPRISING PREDICTIONS FOR 2025

A RAPIDLY CHANGING

Dr. Michio Kaku,
professor of theoretical physics at the City University of New York and author of *The Future of the Mind*:

"In the next 10 years, we will see the gradual transition from an Internet to a brain-net, in which thoughts, emotions, feelings, and memories might be transmitted instantly across the planet."

Dr. Ray Kurzweil,
inventor, pioneering computer scientist, and director of engineering at Google:

"By 2025, 3D printers will print clothing at very low cost. There will be many free open source designs, but people will still spend money to download clothing files from the latest hot designer just as people spend money today for eBooks, music and movies despite all of the free material available."

Dr. Anne Lise Kjaer,
founder of London-based trend forecasting agency Kjaer Global:

"The World Health Organization predicts that chronic diseases will account for almost three-quarters of all deaths worldwide by 2020, so the evolution of M-Health (mobile diagnostics, bio-feedback and personal monitoring) is set to revolutionize treatment of conditions such as diabetes and high blood pressure."

Source
The Huffington Post, Jacqueline Howard, 05-12-2015.
http://www.huffingtonpost.com/2015/05/12/futurists-next-10-years_n_7241210.html

WORLD

Dr. James Canton,
CEO of the San Francisco-based
Institute for Global Futures and author
of *Future Smart: Managing the Game-
Changing Trends that will Transform
Your World*:

"Wearable mobile devices will blanket
the world. Artificial intelligence becomes
both as smart as and smarter than
humans. AI will be embedded in autos,
robots, homes and hospitals will create
the AI economy."

Jason Silva,
host of National Geographic Channel's
Brain Games:

"The on-demand revolution will become
the on-demand world, where biological
software upgrades, personalized medicine,
artificially intelligent assistants will
increasingly transform healthcare and
well-being."

Dr. Amy Zalman,
CEO & president of the World Future
Society:

"A more accurate understanding of how
we humans function -- how we trust,
cooperate and learn but also fight and
hate -- is a tool that public policy-makers
and we citizens can use to build better
governance and better futures."

Mark Stevenson,
author of *An Optimist's Tour
of the Future*:

"The technologies aren't the most
important bit -- although they are super
cool. It's what society does with them, and
right now it's institutional change that's the
sticking point.... What you really want to
look at, in my opinion, is new ways of
organizing ourselves."

TWO INNOVATION SWEET SPOTS

| INTRODUCTION | GROWTH | MATURITY | DECLINE |

ACTIVE INNOVATORS

REACTIVE INNOVATORS

Revenues

at the company, business unit, or product level

MOMENT YOU WANT TO INNOVATE

MOMENT YOU NEED TO INNOVATE

Time

A SHORTAGE OF BREAKTHROUGH NEW PRODUCT IDEAS

NEW PRODUCT DEVELOPMENT PORTFOLIOS OF COMPANIES

DEVELOPMENT PROJECT TYPE	MID-1990s	2010
NEW TO THE WORLD, NEW TO THE MARKET INNOVATIONS	20.4%	11.5%
NEW PRODUCT LINES TO THE COMPANY	38.8%	27.1%
ADDITIONS TO EXISTING PRODUCT LINES IN THE COMPANY	20.4%	24.7%
MODIFICATIONS TO EXISTING COMPANY PRODUCTS	20.4%	36.7%
	100%	100%

Source
Robert G. Cooper and Angelika Dreher, "Voice-of-Customer Methods:
What is the Best Source of New Product Ideas", Marketing Management Magazine,
Winter, 2010, p. 39.

3000

100

10

RAW
IDEAS

EXPLORATORY
PROJECTS

WELL-DEVELOPED
PROJECTS

Source
Stevens, G.A. and Burley, J., "3000 Raw Ideas = 1 Commercial Success!",
(May/June 1997) Research Technology Management, Vol. 40, #3, pp. 16-27.

**FULL-FLEDGED
PRODUCT LAUNCHES**

**SUCCESSFUL
PRODUCT**

Managers say yes to radical innovation, only if doing nothing is a bigger risk.

Gijs van Wulfen

THE INNOVATION MAZE

THE START OF INNOVATION IS INFORMAL AND EXTREMELY IMPORTANT

McKinsey identified eight essentials of innovation in a multi-year study comprising surveys of more than 2,500 executives in over 300 companies, in a broad set of industries and countries. Now, first take a look at chart 6 to check if you really innovate at your organization.

The start of innovation is described by Wikipedia as the messy getting started period of a new product development process. It is in the front end where the organization formulates a concept of the product or service to be developed and decides whether or not to invest resources in the further development of an idea. It is the phase between first consideration of an opportunity and when it is judged ready to enter the structured development process. It includes all activities from the search for new opportunities through the formation of a gem of an idea to the development of a precise concept. The Fuzzy Front End phase ends when an organization approves and begins formal development of the concept.[1] The 'front end' is the informal start of innovation and defined as "fuzzy" by many due to its lack of process and structure. Prof. Dr. Cornelius Herstatt and Birgit Verworn state on this: "Within the innovation process, we believe, the early phases ("fuzzy front end") to have the highest impact on the whole process and the result, since it will influence the design and total costs of the innovation extremely. However, the "Fuzzy Front End" is unfortunately the least well-structured part of the innovation process, both in theory and in practice." They point out further that, "Cooper and Kleinschmidt analyzed that pre development activities in the front end received the least amount of attention (only 6% of dollars and 16% of man-days of the total) compared to product development and commercialization stages. On successful product innovation successes about twice as much money and time was spent on the front end stages compared with non-performing projects. That's why the high failure rates have often been related to insufficiencies, low management attention and poor financial support during the fuzzy front end."[2]

PROFESSIONALS ON ALL LEVELS STRUGGLE WITH THE START OF INNOVATION

People struggle with the start of innovation on all levels of an organization and in different roles. In the next section, eight persons, each wearing a different innovation 'hat', explain anecdotally their view on the start of innovation in practice. I am curious as to which hat fits you.

The persistent startup founder: "I always wanted to be an entrepreneur, as I am not really fit to work in a big company with all the politics. I like to do things my own way. Together with two friends I founded a startup based on a great business idea we had together in our final year at University. We had worked out on paper the whole process beautifully in, what we thought, a foolproof plan. Six months after our start, we found out however that our expectations were way too optimistic. Unfortunately, we did not have a real backup plan in place. At this moment we are trying to raise some extra money from informal investors. One of our friends stepped back recently. My remaining partner and I stay focused and we have full faith that our new venture will eventually succeed."

The frustrated innovation consultant: "Often it's the company CEO inviting me to help start innovation. The lack of urgency and resistance to change are the biggest hurdles to overcome when I start leading an innovation project fora company. Although it requires a lot of energy, most times I succeed in having an innovation team come up with great new ideas to innovate their business. I don't mind at all how energy consuming innovation projects like this can be. What does frustrate me though is that without my presence and guidance nothing materializes after the decision-making into tangible services and products."

The despondent product manager: "Every problem in my organization related to my product group ends up on my desk. I feel like a rag with a thousand-and-one uses. I hardly have time to pay attention to innovation. I am happy if I can plan time to accompany the account manager on a visit to a client. I get ideas for new services while jogging during the weekend. In the beginning, I found the idea of innovation difficult as I had no experience and there was no practical training available. So, how do I discover a 'hole' in the market and decide what would be a good proposition? I am learning more about innovation in practice through trial and error. What really gets me down is the counterproductive way in which my bosses approach me. On the one hand they motivate me to develop new services quickly. While on the other hand, every manager

above me – right up to the CEO – must have his or her say about the new concept I present. This causes the new service to be adapted endlessly whereby the process takes forever. Enough to make me 100% despondent."

The stoic R&D specialist: "I find real innovation great as I can completely emerge myself in it. I have many ideas, but at the moment projects keep piling up on my desk in our Innovation Lab. I am involved with four projects for small modifications to products and six projects regarding cutting back the production process for the production managers and engineers. Not to mention the paperwork. I now have the fourth marketer in eight years who first wants to do market research to discover what the customer wants. But, customers do not know what they want, we have to create it for them! As I said, I have many brilliant ideas, however most marketers don't want to experiment as they are afraid a failure might ruin their careers."

The down-to-earth sales manager: "Basically, I focus on today's business and that keeps me very busy. Furthermore, I expect Marketing and R&D to come up with new products on time, so that my account managers can go to the customers with a great new story. For the moment, I have my hands full with trying to reach this term's revenue targets. Should a marketer come to me with a beautiful new introduction story and research results, then I always ask for some time to think. At home I then test the idea on my wife to see if she understands exactly what it is useful for. If she doesn't immediately understand it then neither will the customers and I do not pursue the idea. It's as simple as that."

The level-headed production director: "Everybody is talking about innovation. However, looking back over the past ten years, I dare say that of the fifty new product introductions we have had, maybe only five were successful. When looking at the production volume, these products make up only 10% of the volume, but nobody looks back to calculate what these introductions cost. A real fortune! Nobody even asks how much extra revenue we would have earned if this money went towards supporting the current products more, especially through advertising. I believe marketing and innovation is a playground for young, inexperienced academics who want to dictate to me which ridiculous new ideas I have to consider in my factory."

The procedural R&D director: "Many departments, such as Engineering, Production, Purchasing and also Marketing rely on the capacity of the R&D. Every marketer wants you to concentrate 100% on their product. If you allow them to, they will constantly drive everyone crazy with their new ideas. That's the reason why we have implemented a very strict stage-gated process for innovation. This way, we can choose which project idea will become an official R&D project and which ones will not. Furthermore, we follow exactly which project idea is in which phase of development. Preceding each of the seven stages there is a go/no-go moment for the management team, and if it is not a project, then my people aren't permitted to work on it. This is how we maintain control."

The divided CEO: "With regards to innovation I have what the Germans so aptly describe as "zwei Seelen in meiner Brust" or two souls dwelling in my breast. On the one hand we have a clear focus on the market, a professional innovation process and great people working in R&D and Marketing, but on the other hand I am not yet satisfied with its effectiveness. There are too few breakthrough products flowing forth from the innovation pipeline. One moment there is a lack of good ideas at the front end and the next moment I receive all kinds of introduction plans for 'not yet finished products' which nobody is really waiting for."

I'll admit that I may have portrayed these managers in an exaggerated way, but I hope it has brought a smile to your face as well as a flicker of recognition of their struggles. I don't want to be too negative though. That's why I would love to inspire you in chart 7 with the 9 innovation principles of Google, one of the world's most innovative companies. Let this bring you some inspiration as well!

15 OBSTACLES HINDERING INNOVATION AT ITS START

The high failure rates of new concepts and the frustrations shared by many managers and innovation professionals, some of which you might even recognize yourself, all lead to the conclusion that the start of innovation is not just informal; there are also many pitfalls to avoid.

As author, speaker and facilitator on innovation I have been traveling around the world meeting all kinds of innovators, managers and CEOs in very different cultures: from Canada to Cape Town. And from Turkey to Tokyo. I start my workshops asking them the direct question, "What are your main struggles at the start of innovation?" Almost all of them experience the start of innovation as a journey of unknown territory where you can so easily lose your way. That's why I have chosen the maze metaphor in the title of my book: *The Innovation Maze*. A recognized authority on mazes, Martin van der Gaag, introduces its origin, characteristics and development in chart 8.

From all these workshops I was able to identify fifteen factors which block you during the fuzzy front end of innovation somewhere along the path towards a successful new business case. I call them innovation obstacles.

Noam Wasserman from Harvard Business School states in *The Founder's Dilemmas* that people problems are the leading cause of failure in startups.[3] This is not really any different for big companies. The same probably holds true for large corporations as well. Personally, I hated the workplace politics, competing for scarce budgets, scarce people and scarce promotion opportunities. All the power play, games, gossip and rumors create a corporate culture full of aggression, distrust and fear which drives out creativity and innovation. Now, people problems may cover a lot of the obstacles but they don't cover all of them. Among the 15 innovation obstacles you also find technological and process issues. Let's take a look at them.

1. UNCLEAR STRATEGY

"How can we start innovation when we have no clue where to go?" is a common problem for a lot of companies. Their business strategy will mention the word innovation a lot of times, but unfortunately will neglect to mention a clear focus. "We lack focus." and "There is no vision where we want to go in the future as a company." are other quotes referring to the same issue: an unclear strategy. When you want your people to move beyond their comfort zone they will have all kinds of fears. It's difficult to make the first step, especially if you don't have a clue where you want to go yourself.

2. NO PRIORITY FOR INNOVATION

A lot of management thinkers say you must innovate continuously.[4] In practice, this is hardly the case. Of course, in big companies especially there is some basic research, a well-equipped innovation lab and a huge amount of innovation projects filling the innovation funnel. But are these projects really innovative, seen through the eyes of potential customers? In practice, the company board decides to turn right or left only when continuing straight is no longer an option. As one manager commented in a workshop, "The board is very unlikely to say 'yes' to any radical renewal program as they are the ones who have brought the company to the top." Although everybody disagrees, there's often no priority for innovation. Why run a risk when business is going up?

3. NO MARKET NEED

A lot of technology-pushed innovations hit the market and never get adopted. They might just be too early. Or too late. Whatever the case, a lot of innovation initiatives from a Research & Development (R&D) point of view come up with a new technology for which there is no market need. The biggest problem starting innovation from this perspective is that they provide solutions without a problem. I have heard engineers make complaints like: "Our stupid customers don't want it, they don't know what they are missing." Well, actually they just don't care what they're missing because they don't consider your innovation to be relevant for them.

4. NO INSIGHTS OR INSPIRATION

"We have no inspiration for new ideas." is a commonly mentioned argument at the start of innovation. It's often connected with exploring customer behavior. I learned that you only get new ideas when you have new insights. Especially when you're operating in a long value chain in a business-to-business setting it's a real challenge to identify (end) market needs, as the end user is not your direct customer. This raises issues like, "We struggle to get inside the head of the purchaser of the product or service." and "How to uncover the true customer need?"

5. NO TIME

In the top three of innovation struggles you will always hear, "I'm too busy; I can't make time for innovation." In practice, innovation is viewed as something you do 'on the side' of your normal work. One manager said to me, "Our short-term mindset overrules the long-term mindset and vision to innovate." And unfortunately there's always a short-term issue in your organization, isn't there? Now everybody knows Google's 20% time. Yahoo CEO Marissa Mayer who used to work at Google said, "I've got to tell you the dirty little secret of Google's 20% time. It's really 120% time." She said that 20% time projects aren't projects you can do instead of doing your regular job for a whole day every week. It's "stuff that you've got to do beyond your regular job."[5]

6. LACK OF RESOURCES

"There's no budget to start innovation." is one of the issues most often mentioned. And mind you, this is not only a reality for startups. Even at a company with a yearly R&D budget of over € 2 billion, managers struggle to free money to start innovation. The problem is not the absence of money. No, it's that all the money has been earmarked for existing projects. "I have to work around current budgets to get really new things financed." as one innovation project leader confided to me.

7. NO INTERNAL SUPPORT

A lack of internal support hinders almost all corporate innovators.

The reasons why, might differ though. In this category I grouped together answers like: "We do not know how to change our existing habits." "Those in our company who don't understand the idea or new product will attack and ridicule it." Or negative answers like, "We tried it in the past and it did not work in our environment – is the biggest stumbling block in our company." Lack of internal support is a showstopper for innovation because in an organization you can invent alone, but you can't innovate alone.

8. POLITICS

Workplace politics can stop anything, including innovation. This is not only an issue at big corporations, but also at startups: "The tech-team and the biz-team didn't agree on the vision and stopped communicating." "We were led by too many opinions." "Our founders fought until at last one of them left and we could get to work again."

9. INSUFFICIENT SKILLS

There is a perception that doing new things for an organization often requires new skills for its people. This becomes evident from these quotes on mindset and skills: "We don't have the right people in the room." "We can't set up a dream team for the opportunity." "A lot of people are lazy, just copying others' work." "There is a substantial lack of curiosity among people in our company." "Ideas are stopped because we do not have resources related to the needed talent."

10. FEAR OF FAILURE

A quite common obstacle is caused by the high failure rate of innovation. "There are too few ideas because people don't dare to think in an innovative way anymore." "Our past innovations were not successful and have cost us a lot of money. This blocks sparking new initiatives." "The company management is unwilling to experiment anymore." Fear of failure makes it so that only a few people are prepared to stick out their necks. I am prepared to do so as I've shown by my efforts to develop new innovation methods for the front-end. How about you?

11. NO FIT

Do you recognize this seemingly contradictory exchange? Often you are briefed, "Bring me something really new." And the common response you get when you have found it and bring it back 'home' to your business is that, "This is too far out of our business". Similar to your customers, managers often times don't know what they want even when you show it to them. A lot of ideas get shot down now because managers don't think they fit with the company. This can refer to anything from the company's technology, processes, skills, markets or brands.

12. TOO SLOW

Speed is more important than ever these days. Both for startups and incumbents. These days while you are talking among yourselves endlessly, others have started experimenting with it out on the market. I like to quote here, "Everyone in our company talks about innovation, but few know what to do differently to make it happen." Another one is, "New software is always 85% done. It takes an effort of will to push this through and get something released to users."

13. NOT FEASIBLE

"It's not do-able; we can't make it." "Your ideas are too ambitious; we can't imagine how they ever will be feasible." "We have no freedom to operate due to intellectual property rights." There are a lot of 'noes' at the start of innovation related to feasibility. It's unfortunately so true that, even before the official development process has yet to start, people reject ideas because they just can't imagine something becoming a reality.

14. NO BUSINESS MODEL

For both startups and existing companies innovation is a means to grow business. As it must generate revenues and profits, the absence of a clear vision on how to acquire customers or having a viable business model is a show-stopper at the front end: "We were way too optimistic on the cost to acquire a customer", "We have chosen a market niche which was marginal" and "It's way too expensive."

15. NOT ORIGINAL

Lack of originality blocks innovation in several ways. In fact, some organizations don't even believe they can be original: "We are uncertain if we can be creative and come up with original ideas." Others think they are original: "We thought we worked on a great unique idea, until we researched the market." And again others are only original at the start: "We don't stick to the original idea. Instead, we often take the easier way, ending up with another 100% me-too product."

INNOVATION STARTS WITH AN IDEA, A TECHNOLOGY, A PROBLEM OR A BUSINESS ISSUE

Now that we have nailed all the problems at the fuzzy front end, let's work on the solution to unfuzzy it. The way innovation starts is diverse. I identified four common patterns how people start innovation.

1. You start innovation with a new idea or opportunity, like Brian Chesky and Joe Gebbia of Airbnb. When a major design conference came to town in 2007, they saw an opportunity to earn some extra cash by renting out their spare floor space. In no time they had put together a website advertising lodging for overnight guests which they called "Airbed and Breakfast".
2. You start innovation triggered by new technology, like Google X research lab, which explores new technologies beyond Google's core business, with for example their Google Glass experiment.
3. You start innovation to solve a problem, like two students in Sweden, Anna Haupt and Terese Alstin. The prospect of being forced by law to wear a bicycle helmet caused them great concern, as they wouldn't "be caught dead wearing a polystyrene helmet." They started developing a bicycle helmet that people would be happy to wear.
4. You start innovation because your business needs to innovate, like toy-producer LEGO when in 1998 they generated their first loss in the company's history. In response to this crisis, the company announced the lay-offs of 1,000 employees and put innovation on their agenda.

I have been experimenting with a method to start innovation triggered by a business challenge, called: the FORTH innovation method (www.forth-innovation.com). Since the origin of the method in 2006 it has been applied around the world by companies and organizations who needed to innovate. Scientific research shows that the methodology doubles the rate of effectiveness of the innovation process, on average out of the 100 ideas generated, 78 are taken into development and 51 are introduced, compared to 21 in an average stage-gated innovation process. This method is very effective when you start with a business challenge, but it's structure was not made - and is not suitable for starting with an idea or a technology or to solve a problem. That's why I took a broader scope in this book and I will provide several routes to navigate you through the innovation maze depending on how you start innovation.

THE FRONT END OF INNOVATION ENDS WITH A WELL-FOUNDED NEW BUSINESS CASE

From applying the FORTH method around the world for more than ten years, I have learned that to convince the management of an organization or (in)formal investors to let your innovative idea enter the formal development process and give you the resources needed, you must bring to the table a well-founded convincing new business case. Now the crucial word in the last sentence is 'convincing'. This means you really must know your stuff. In the boardroom your idea will be evaluated from at least four perspectives:

▸ The customer: will they buy it?
▸ The technology: can we deliver it?
▸ The business model: will it pay off?
▸ The risk: What if it's a failure? What if it's a huge success?

The board will demand tangible proof before making a decision. That makes the front end of innovation so challenging and intensive. I learned in practice it will take at least ten activities to take you to this desired outcome in a structured way. I will describe them concisely here. Later in this book, you will find a whole chapter on each of these activities.

10 ESSENTIAL ACTIVITIES TO UNFUZZY YOUR FRONT END

- **Ideate:** Generating and choosing original relevant ideas for a product, service, process or experience.
- **Focus:** Defining your innovation center-of-interest including all the boundary conditions.
- **Check Fit:** Checking if your idea, technology, customer issue or business challenge fits your personal and corporate priorities.
- **Create Conditions:** Organizing the right moment, the right team, the right pace and the right funding for your innovation initiative.
- **Discover:** Discovering trends, markets, technologies and customer insights.
- **Create Business Model:** Creating a viable business model.
- **Select Technology:** Identifying and selecting the right technology to deliver your new product, service, process or experience.
- **Check Freedom to Operate:** Checking if you do not infringe intellectual property rights of others.
- **Experiment:** Carrying out a systematic research or test which validates the adoption and attractiveness of your new product, service, process or experience.
- **Create New Business Case:** Creating a well-founded convincing business case for your new product, service, process or experience.

In chart 9, I present 'The Innovation Maze'. Here, you find both the 15 obstacles and the 10 activities essential for the start of innovation. The maze has four entry points: the Idea Route, the Technology Route, the Customer Issue Route and the Business Challenge Route. In the next chapter I will present the 4 routes and how to navigate the innovation maze successfully to create new business cases for products, services and business models in a structured way.

KEY MESSAGES FROM THIS CHAPTER

1. The front end of the innovation process is the messy getting-started period of new product development processes.
2. Innovation starts with an idea, a technology, a problem or a business issue.
3. The high failure rates of innovation are related to insufficiencies, low management attention and poor financial support during the fuzzy front end.
4. Professionals on all levels struggle with the start of innovation.
5. Fifteen factors might block you somewhere during the front end of innovation on your way to a new business case.
6. To convince your management or (in)formal investors you must bring a well-founded convincing new business case to the table.
7. To unfuzzy your front end you need to undertake 10 essential activities in a structured way.

Notes
1   https://en.wikipedia.org/wiki/New_product_development#Fuzzy_Front_End
2   Prof. Dr. Cornelius Herstatt, Dipl.-Ing. Birgit Verworn, August 2001, https://www.tuhh.de/tim/downloads/arbeitspapiere/Arbeitspapier_4.pdf
3   Noam Wasserman, *The Founder's Dilemmas*, Princeton University Press, Princeton, New Jersey, 2012 p. 3.
4   Forbes, Steve Denning, Is Continuous Innovation Too Risky?, February 10, 2012
5   Business Insider UK, The 'Dirty Little Secret' About Google's 20% Time, According To Marissa Mayer, http://uk.businessinsider.com/mayer-google-20-time-does-not-exist-2015-1?r=US&IR=T#ixzz3j3sn2xIP

DO YOU REALLY INNOVATE?

ASPIRE
Do you regard innovation-led growth as critical; and do you have cascaded targets that reflect this?

CHOOSE
Do you invest in a coherent, time and risk-balanced portfolio of initiatives with sufficient resources to win?

DISCOVER
Do you have differentiated business, market and technology insights that translate into winning value propositions?

EVOLVE
Do you create new business models that provide defensible and scalable profit sources?

Source
McKinsey Analysis, "The Eight Essentials of Innovation",
Marc de Jong, Nathan Marston and Erik Roth,
McKinsey Quarterly, April 2015.

ACCELERATE
Do you beat the competition by developing and launching innovations quickly and effectively?

SCALE
Do you launch innovations at the right scale in the relevant markets and segments?

EXTEND
Do you win by creating and capitalizing on external networks?

MOBILIZE
Are your people motivated, rewarded, and organized to innovate repeatedly?

Google's 9 CORE PRINCIPLES

1.
INNOVATION COMES FROM ANYWHERE
It can come from the top down as well as bottom up, and in the places you least expect.

3.
AIM TO BE TEN TIMES BETTER
If you want radical and revolutionary innovation, think 10 times improvement, and that will force you to think outside the box.

2.
FOCUS ON THE USER
Worry about the money later, when you focus on the user, all else will follow.

4.
BET ON TECHNICAL INSIGHTS
Every organization has unique insights, and if you bet on it, it leads to major innovation.

Source
Google reveals it's 9 Principles of Innovation, Kathy Chin Leong, Fast Company, November 20, 2013

OF INNOVATION

5.
SHIP AND ITERATE
Ship your products often and early, and do not wait for perfection. Let users help you to "iterate" it.

7.
DEFAULT TO OPEN PROCESSES
Make your processes open to all users. Tap into the collective energy of the user base to obtain great ideas.

9.
HAVE A MISSION THAT MATTERS
We believe the work we do has impact on millions of people in a positive way.

6.
GIVE EMPLOYEES 20 PERCENT TIME.
Give employees 20 percent of their work time to pursue projects they are passionate about, even if it is outside the core job or core mission of the company.

8.
FAIL WELL
There should be no stigma attached to failure. If you do not fail often, you are not trying hard enough.

E.

Labyrinths in gardens of the well-to-do start being mentioned in the late 12th century. Yet the earliest surviving pictures are only found in early printed books about 'ideal gardens': Serlio's *Libri cinque d'architettura* (1537), Thomas Hyll's *The profitable arte of gardening* (1579) and Hans Vredeman de Vries' *Hortorum viridariumque (etc.)* (1583). These show 'garden labyrinths' as executed in low shrubs and flower borders, which eventually come into vogue in French and Italian estate gardens, such as at Villa d' Este (Tivoli, Italy, 1560s). D. Loris's *Le Thesor Des Parterres De L'Univers* (1579) is an early volume that also shows first maze patterns, including junctions. Late 16th century Dutch and Italian paintings show depictions of 'labyrinths of love'; simple mazes with now waist-high hedges, in which couples playfully pursue courtly love. Raising the height of hedges between paths even more, the visitor can no longer see where he is going, and combined with junctions and dead ends, around the end of the 16th century the classical 'garden maze' is born: tall, slowly growing, neatly clipped hedges, often evergreen, and deliberately designed to provide puzzling, amusing disorientation, only to relieve the visitor when he reaches the central goal.

THE MESSAGE FROM THE MAZE

B.

Art historians have shown people to produce visually challenging patterns since prehistoric times. Some of these patterns are tightly packed, meandering or spiral paths forming beautiful ornamentation. A very specific class of such path-based drawings shows an irregularly winding and turning path that is not only pleasing to the eye, but also evokes a playfully whimsical response from the spectator - an urge to follow the course of its windings, curious as to how they are connected. At first glance, they appear to be a puzzle. A closer look at these drawings - the oldest carved in stone possibly 4,000 years ago - reveals they always consist of just one single path, leading from the periphery to a center, commonly following seven concentric circles. Obviously, these 'mazes' were not meant to be solved, but were likely intended to have a symbolic meaning. Experts classify such single-pathed structures as 'classical labyrinths' - distinct from other labyrinths that may have more or fewer than seven windings - and also different from 'mazes', which also consist of winding paths towards a specific goal, yet including junctions and - optionally - dead ends, forcing the visitor to make choices along his or her journey. While labyrinths have figured in many cultures since ancient times, maze structures have only been around since the advent of the renaissance era in Western Europe.

D.

From the early 12th century onwards, these Christian labyrinths start being prominently featured on floors of gothic cathedrals in Northern France. Although the exact intentions of their builders were not clearly recorded, such 'church labyrinths' were, until the end of 13th century, used individually as an alternative for a pilgrimage to Jerusalem, and later as a layout for the ballgame *pilota*, included in dancing ceremonies of clergy around Easter celebrations. The labyrinth of Chartres Cathedral (Chartres, France, ca. 1202) is considered the archetype of this form - its pattern still popular today with labyrinth walkers. To our modern eyes, walking a life-sized labyrinth may not immediately appear as an interesting proposition. Yet, following its predestined, winding journey surprisingly does something to almost any walker's state of mind, bringing him either in confusion, repentance, consolation, or resignation. Walking the labyrinth is therefore both pursued as a healing ritual, or a pleasing spiritual experience in itself.

A.

In today's world, complexity is often an unwelcome message. We are increasingly getting used to the idea that any information needed is instantly available through the wireless internet, and that any problem can - and should - be instantly solvable. It is just a matter of getting the right app. Take traveling for instance. As contemporary motorists, all we need to do is enter our destination into our sat nav, follow the directions, and go. Arriving at our destination, we often don't have a clue how we got there. Gone are the days when we spread out our maps on the car hood, searched for road signs from behind the steering wheel, or hastily pulled over to re-check the map. Also gone are the surprises - the dead ends, the uncertainty of which road you are on, or the discovery you have actually been driving in circles. Traveling requires less and less creativity, improvisation, and planning. If you wanted to, you could eliminate the map all together and simply accept the process. Yet, allowing yourself to be challenged by disorientation is precisely what the maze is all about.

C.

Because of its iconic qualities, it is tempting to establish one single meaning of the labyrinth in ancient culture, but in fact the labyrinth appears in many different connotations. In antiquity, the classical labyrinth is associated with the legends of the conquered cities of Troy and Jericho, but most often with the myth of Theseus, the Athens prince who was able to escape from King Minos' labyrinth of the Minotaur - half man, half bull - with the help of Ariadne's thread (a plot, paradoxically enough, clearly involving a maze!). Throughout the first centuries CE, this story typically features in the square, four-sectored Roman floor mosaic labyrinths, such as the one in the Roman Villa Loig Bath Complex (Salzburg, Austria, ca. 275). From the 8th century onwards, labyrinths are featured in manuscripts produced in Christian monasteries. Besides illustrating Theseus' story, they now also serve as symbolic representations of planetary movements, as calendars, and general metaphors for complex argumentation. Manuscripts also feature new developments in labyrinth design, starting with the eleven-ring 'Otfrid' type, and eventually evolve into elaborately winding, beautifully symmetric designs, typically dictated by four axes.

F.

During the 17th and early 18th century, garden mazes become highly fashionable, especially in Italy, the Netherlands and Britain: for several decades, the estate of a man of wealth should not be without one. The most famous example of this period - and still in existence - is the maze at Hampton Court Palace (London, United Kingdom, ca. 1680). Late 17th century, changing fashions in garden design lead to the new designs of the 'block maze'. Instead of tightly packing hedges and paths together, in this style wider lanes are cut through large, densely grown woodland areas, featuring sculptures and waterworks at each junction. Here, the challenge is not so much finding a single goal, but choosing one's route such as to visit all exhibits. The most luscious block maze could be found in the royal palace gardens of King Louis XIV (Versailles, France, ca. 1669), where the visitor was challenged to visit all fountains depicting each of Aesop's fables without crossing his own path - a very complex exercise.

H.

Although premiered in early 17th century Amsterdam, puzzle mazes open to the general public also start being introduced in the 19th century - either as attractions alongside pubs and cafés, as guest facilities in hotel gardens, and as diversifying landscape elements in public parks. Post World War II, mazes become staple elements of new family theme parks, and are increasingly seen as fun for children only. However, since the early 1970s there is a true revival in puzzle maze and spiritual labyrinth interest around the world, also aimed at adult enthusiasts. Notable innovations are mathematician Greg Bright's complex mazes, such as the one at Longleat House (England, 1975) and, among his many innovations, British maze designer Adrian Fisher's use of emblematic elements into maze structures, such as at Drielandenpunt maze (Vaals, the Netherlands, 1992).

I.

The design of the Innovation Maze, central to this book, combines many maze innovations from the past. Like the classical labyrinth, it is a symbol for the reader's complex quest - to develop a new business case. Like Earl Stanhope's designs, there are no dead ends, and it is very well possible to keep going round in circles without reaching the goal. Like the maze at Versailles, it challenges the reader to contemplate all included stations along the quest. For me, designing this maze according to Gijs van Wulfen's specifications was a challenge in itself. Since, paradoxically, it is not meant to puzzle you, but provide you with the road map sometimes so desperately needed.

Martin van der Gaag
Maze designer
martinvandergaag.nl

G.

With the introduction of the romantic landscape style, the interest in garden mazes gradually disappears around the end of the 18th century, and many are cleared or neglected. From the 1840s onwards however, a renewed interest in gothic art sees first scholarly investigations into the origins of the labyrinth, and the (re) construction of many church labyrinths. A retrospective fashion in garden design also leads to the classical hedge maze coming into vogue again. Many examples are newly built in country estate gardens in the United Kingdom and The Netherlands, and now also in the United States and Australia. Some of these use only slightly modified older designs, but innovative, more difficult puzzles are invented by mathematician Earl Stanhope. While eliminating dead ends, he introduces the use of discrete sections of hedges, disabling the simple 'hand-on-the-wall' method to solve a maze - such as the one at Chevening House (England, 1820s).

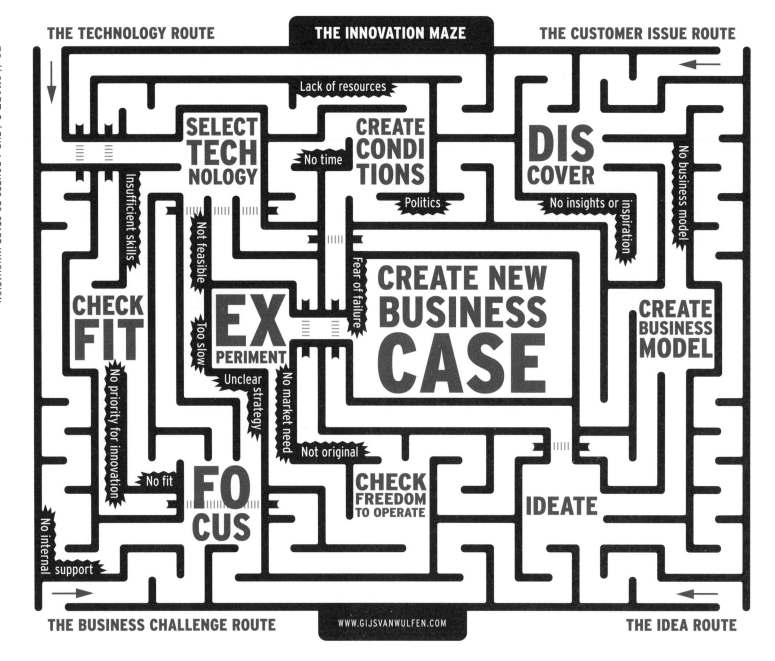

THE TECHNOLOGY ROUTE

THE INNOVATION MAZE

THE CUSTOMER ISSUE ROUTE

Lack of resources

SELECT TECH NOLOGY

CREATE CONDI TIONS

No time

DIS COVER

No business model

Politics

No insights or inspiration

Insufficient skills

Not feasible

Fear of failure

CHECK FIT

EX PERIMENT

CREATE NEW BUSINESS CASE

CREATE BUSINESS MODEL

Too slow

No priority for innovation

Unclear strategy

No market need

Not original

No fit

FO CUS

CHECK FREEDOM TO OPERATE

IDEATE

No internal support

THE BUSINESS CHALLENGE ROUTE

WWW.GIJSVANWULFEN.COM

THE IDEA ROUTE

THE 4 ROUTES TO START INNOVATION

The Fuzzy Front End of innovation ends when an organization approves and begins the formal development of a concept.[1] It's the end of the beginning. This informal start of innovation is considered as a warming-up for the real work, but is unfortunately packed with at least fifteen obstacles that should be avoided. To raise the effectiveness of your innovation efforts, this chapter gives you four structured routes through the innovation maze to well-founded convincing business cases. I believe, just like Thomas Edison, that preparation leads to success.

"Unfortunately, there seems to be far more opportunity out there than ability.... We should remember that good fortune often happens when opportunity meets with preparation." [Thomas Edison].

Innovation can start as a slow hunch, taking years before becoming a real opportunity or it may start right now as a result of an urgent business challenge. As said in Chapter 2, innovation may start in lots of ways. To me, it's not a question of how innovative you are. It's a question of how you are innovative! Whether you start with a business challenge, with a (startup) idea, with a technology or with a problem of one of your clients; you just have to pick the right route through the maze.

A 2011 study by the American Productivity and Quality Center among more than 200 companies proved that having a clearly defined new product development process in the form of a game plan, playbook or stage-gated system that guides innovation projects is an important condition for success. Nearly all the best performers (90 percent) had some kind of formal process in place, compared to only 44 percent of the worst performers.[2] The four routes presented in this chapter won't eliminate the risk of failure completely of course. The structured routes though will reduce this risk of failure because they will guide you along 15 pitfalls and obstacles identified in the previous chapter. The four routes through the innovation maze give you better chances to create a well-founded convincing new business case and eventually a great new product, service, process or experience.

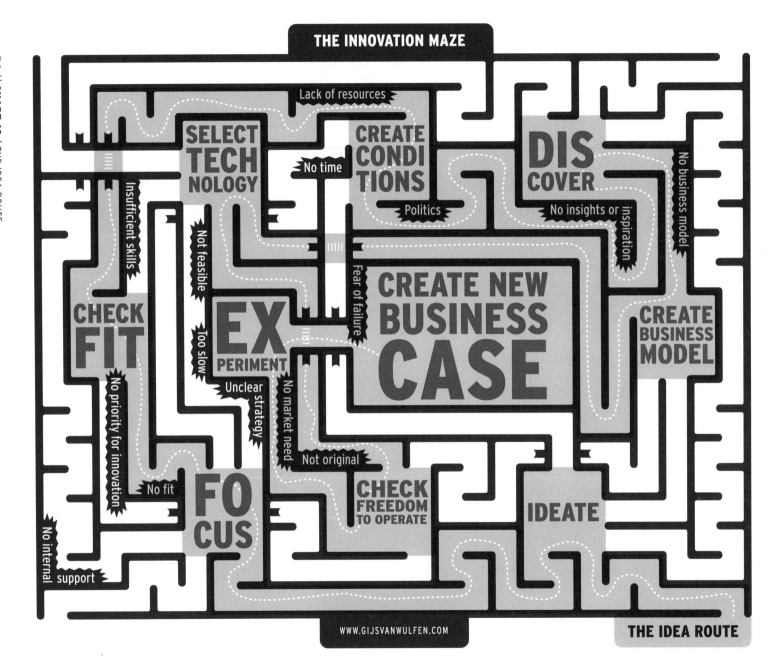

THE INNOVATION MAZE

THE IDEA ROUTE

WWW.GIJSVANWULFEN.COM

THE IDEA ROUTE

Steven Johnson, author of *Where Good Ideas Come From*, describes ideas as slow hunches. Some of them may take years to hatch. Others might hit you overnight. Now, how do you develop your idea or opportunity into a well-founded convincing new business case, as a startup or as a corporate innovator? Just follow the blue Idea Route through the innovation maze in chart 10.

In this case you have already ideated a rough business idea – or spotted a great opportunity for a new product, service, process or experience. So, ideate is your starting point at the bottom right of the maze. Your next step is Focus, where you will make your idea or opportunity concrete in an innovation assignment. You make all your expectations and boundary conditions explicit, like: why do you want to innovate? What is it? For whom? Where: regions and countries? When: year of introduction? And which criteria should your new idea or opportunity meet? As the third activity you check if your idea or opportunity fits your personal and corporate priorities. If not, here's your first exit moment. Be realistic. If it fits, you create the right conditions for success; picking the right moment, getting the right team together, determining the right pace for your idea and raising the funds you need for the front end. As the next activity you go out to Discover. You and your team will orientate yourselves getting new insights by discovering relevant trends, visiting and analyzing relevant markets, investigating new technologies and discovering new insights from customers by observing, listening and talking to them. Obviously, your idea or opportunity will change along the way during your discovery process. Armed with what is happening out there you will be creating a viable business model around your pivoted idea as the next step. Now that you have defined your new offering, you can focus on the 'how' by identifying and selecting the right technology to deliver your new product, service, process or experience. Right after selecting your technology it's wise to Check the Freedom to Operate (FTO) to research if you do not infringe intellectual property rights of others, thereby avoiding problems later in your formal development process. Once you have defined the what, how and for whom; you're ready to learn if you're on the right track. You will start to Experiment, carrying out a systematic research or test which validates the adoption and attractiveness of your new product, service, process or experience. Once your experiments have been successful you have all the ingredients to create a New Business Case: a well-founded convincing business case for your new product, service, process or experience.

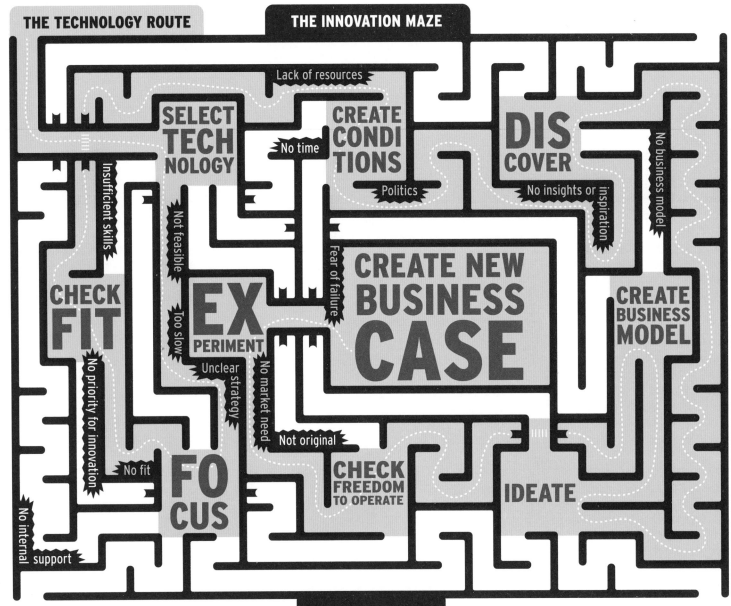

THE TECHNOLOGY ROUTE

THE INNOVATION MAZE

THE TECHNOLOGY ROUTE

New technologies spark innovation. For example, the development of new game consoles, the internet of things or 3D printing give huge opportunities for the development of new products and services. How do you transform a new technology into a well-founded convincing new business case for new products and services? Just follow the yellow Technology Route through the innovation maze in chart 11.

As you have picked a new technology as an opportunity you start at Select Technology. Following the yellow route, your next step is Focus, where you will make the goals of your technological opportunity explicit in an innovation assignment. You make all your expectations and boundary conditions explicit, like: why do you want to innovate with this technology? What is it? Who's our target group? Where: regions and countries? When do we want to introduce new products of services? And based on this new technology, which criteria should your products/services meet? As the third activity you check if this new technology fits your personal and corporate priorities. Be aware if the answer is no, then this is a warning to stop. If it does fit, you create the right conditions for success: picking the right moment, getting the right team together, determining the right pace for your technological opportunity and raising the funds you need for the front end. As the next activity you go out to Discover. You and your team will orientate yourselves getting new insights by discovering the new technology intensively. You might visit leading universities and research institutes. Analyze markets, where the new technology is already available. Check out

lead-users of the new technology. And you try to catch new insights from your target market by observing, listening and talking to them. Then you Ideate. You generate and select concrete new product or service ideas based on the new technology, which match relevant needs from your target audience. As a next step you will create a viable business model around your new product or service ideas. After you have generated new business models, it's wise to check the Freedom to Operate to research if you do not infringe intellectual property rights of others. As you have defined the what, how and for whom, you're ready to learn if you're on the right track. Similar to the other routes you will start to Experiment, carrying out a systematic research or test which validates the adoption and attractiveness of your new product, service, process or experience. Once your experiments have been successful you have all the ingredients to create a New Business Case: a well-founded convincing business case for your new product, service, process or experience based on your new technology.

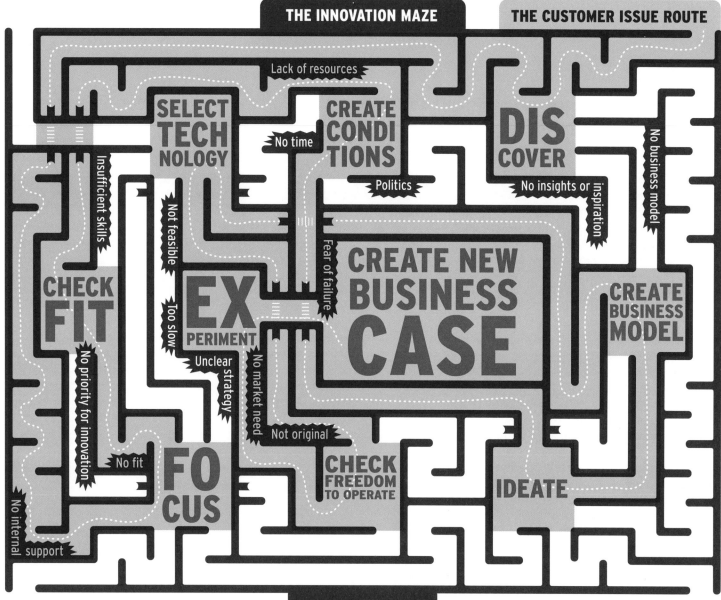

THE INNOVATION MAZE

THE CUSTOMER ISSUE ROUTE

Lack of resources

SELECT TECH NOLOGY

CREATE CONDI TIONS

No time

DIS COVER

Politics

No insights or inspiration

No business model

Insufficient skills

Not feasible

CHECK FIT

EX PERIMENT

Too slow

Fear of failure

CREATE NEW BUSINESS CASE

CREATE BUSINESS MODEL

No priority for innovation

Unclear strategy

No market need

No fit

Not original

No internal support

FO CUS

CHECK FREEDOM TO OPERATE

IDEATE

THE CUSTOMER ISSUE ROUTE

A lot of innovations are born out of frustration. Virgin Group founder and serial innovator Richard Branson has often said, many of his best business ideas were born out of frustration. As a frequent air traveler in America, he was constantly frustrated by the terrible service offered on almost all of the domestic US carriers. His solution was to launch Virgin America, which now consistently tops customer service rankings.[3]

In this case your innovation journey through the maze starts on the upper right side and you follow the green route in chart 12. As you start with a customer issue or frustration the first step is to explore and discover if this is a relevant issue for a broader group by observing, listening and talking to them. Furthermore, you discover relevant trends, visiting and analyzing relevant markets and investigating new technologies. Following the green route, your next step is Focus, where you will make the goals of your innovation initiative explicit in an innovation assignment. You make all your expectations and boundary conditions explicit, like: why do you want to solve this customer issue? Who's your target group? Where: regions and countries? When do you want to introduce new products of services? And which criteria should your products/services meet? As the third activity you check if solving this customer issue in an innovative way fits your personal and corporate priorities. Be aware if the answer is no, then this is a warning to stop. If it does fit, you create the right conditions for success: picking the right moment, getting the right team together, determining the right pace for your innovation project and raising the funds you need for the front end.

Then you Ideate. You generate and select the best concrete new product or service ideas to solve the customer issue from your target audience. As the next step you will create a viable business model around your new product or service ideas. Once you have generated and chosen a business model, you have defined your new offering and you can focus on the 'how' and by identifying and selecting the right technology to deliver your new product, service, process or experience. After this step you obviously Check the Freedom to Operate to research if you do not infringe intellectual property rights of others. As you have defined the what, how and for whom, you're ready to learn if you're on the right track. Similar to the other routes you will start to Experiment, carrying out a systematic research or test which validates the adoption and attractiveness of your new product, service, process or experience. Once your experiments solving the customer issue have been successful, you have all the ingredients to create a New Business Case: a well-founded convincing business case for your new product, service, process or experience in which you solve a relevant customer issue in a brilliant way.

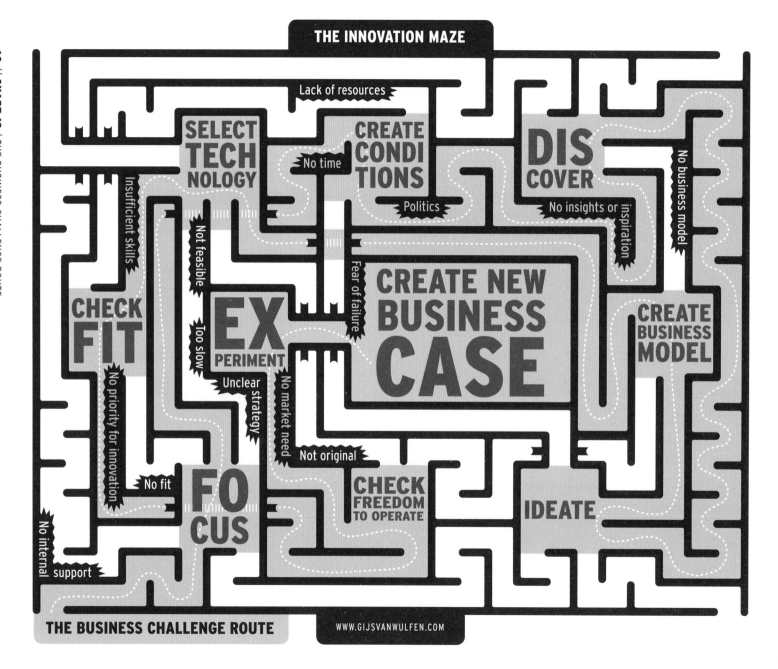

THE INNOVATION MAZE

Lack of resources

SELECT TECHNOLOGY

CREATE CONDITIONS

No time

Politics

DIS COVER

No insights or inspiration

No business model

Insufficient skills

Not feasible

Fear of failure

CHECK FIT

EX PERIMENT

Too slow

CREATE NEW BUSINESS CASE

CREATE BUSINESS MODEL

No priority for innovation

Unclear strategy

No market need

Not original

No fit

FO CUS

CHECK FREEDOM TO OPERATE

IDEATE

No internal support

THE BUSINESS CHALLENGE ROUTE

WWW.GIJSVANWULFEN.COM

THE BUSINESS CHALLENGE ROUTE

Now suppose your organization is an active innovator, which wants to innovate giving innovation priority at the end of the growth stage of its revenue stream. This is the case for ESKA in the Netherlands, the world market leader in solid board, selling its board business-to-business to manufacturers of office binders, publishers of hardbound books and board games producers. While Eska's total revenue is still growing as their market share increases, the end-user markets are declining due to the digitalization of offices, literature and games. Their business challenge is to find new markets for solid board.

The Business Challenge Route starts on the lower left side of the Innovation Maze. Just follow the pink route in chart 13. Your first step is Focus, where you will draft your innovation assignment. You make all your expectations and boundary conditions explicit, like: why do you want to innovate? What are we looking for? For which target markets? Where: for which parts of the world? When: year of introduction? And which criteria should your new products or services meet? As the second activity you create the right conditions for your innovation project to succeed: picking the right moment, getting the right team together, determining the right pace for your challenge and raising the funds you need for the front end. As the next activity you go out to Discover. You and your team will orientate yourselves getting new insights by discovering relevant trends, visiting and analyzing relevant markets, investigating new technologies and discovering new insights from (potential) customers by observing, listening and talking to them. Inspired by

what is happening out there you will then Ideate new concepts which fit your innovation assignment. You generate and select the best concrete new product or service ideas to solve the customer issues from your target audiences. As the next step you will create a viable business model around your new product or service ideas. Once you have generated and chosen a business model, you have defined your new offering and you can focus on the 'how' by identifying and selecting the right technology to deliver your new product, service, process or experience. After identifying the new concepts and technology used, you check the fit of the new innovations with your personal and corporate priorities. If there's a good fit you Check the Freedom to Operate to research if you do not infringe intellectual property rights of others. As you have defined the what, how and for whom, you're ready to learn if you're on the right track. Similar to the other routes you will start to Experiment, carrying out a systematic research or test which validates the adoption and attractiveness of your new product, service, process or experience. You test the new concepts and adapt them of course based on the customer feedback and results, until your experiments with the new concepts have been successful. You now have all the ingredients to create a New Business Case: a well-founded convincing business case for your new product, service, process or experience with which to help you with your challenge.

PICK THE RIGHT ROUTE AND STAY FLEXIBLE

Each of the four innovation routes contains all ten activities. The great news is that whether you start with an idea, a technology, a customer issue or a business challenge you can use the same activities and the same tools. I will explain each of the activities in more depth in chapters 8 - 17. The order in which the ten activities are undertaken depends on how you start innovation. Be aware that doing things in the right order has a huge impact on the effectiveness.

TEAMWORK DOES PAY OFF, IF YOU DO IT RIGHT

A 2015 study unearthed key factors that differentiate high-performance product teams from their less successful counterparts. It identified twenty-three statistically significant contributors to the effectiveness of successful product teams, which you will find in chart 22 in chapter 11.[4] Be sure to pick a diverse, well-balanced team with an emphasis on group tolerance.

In the next four chapters I will discuss each of the Routes in greater detail with a practical example. I suggest that you pick the ones which are the most relevant for you at the moment.

KEY MESSAGES FROM THIS CHAPTER

1. Having a clear, defined process that guides innovation projects is an important condition for successful innovation.
2. Four routes guide you through the Innovation Maze: the Idea Route, the Technology Route, the Customer Issue Route and the Business Challenge Route.
3. All routes contain ten important activities. The order in which the ten activities are undertaken depends on how you start innovation.
4. Ten activities at the Front End are: Ideate, Focus, Check Fit, Create Conditions, Discover, Create Business Model, Select Technology, Check Freedom to Operate, Experiment and Create New Business Case.

Notes

[1] https://en.wikipedia.org/wiki/New_product_development#Fuzzy_Front_End

[2] Robert G. Cooper and Scott J. Edgett, "Best practices in the Idea-to-Launch Process and Its Governance", Research Technology Management, March-April 2012, p. 47.

[3] Forbes, Alison Coleman, "How Entrepreneurs Like Branson Hatch Their Best Business Ideas, July 7, 2015.

[4] THE STUDY OF PRODUCT TEAM PERFORMANCE 2015, ACTUATION CONSULTING, http://www.actuationconsulting.com/wp-content/uploads/Study_Product_Team_Performance_2015w.pdf

THE IDEA ROUTE:
I HAVE AN IDEA; NOW WHAT?

Google, currently a company with a market capitalization of $ 500 billion on the US Stock Exchange, started as an idea. In 1995, the idea for "downloading the entire web onto computers" came to Google inventor Larry Page in a dream when he was 23 years old. He claimed, "I spent the middle of that night scribbling out the details and convincing myself it would work."[1] And it did, as we all know. And he is not the only one who took an idea to market as a startup and made it big. The Wall Street Journal and Dow Jones VentureSource are tracking venture-backed private companies valued at $1 billion or more. The top 10 highest valued startups contains a lot of well-known names like Uber ($ 50.0 billion), Xiaomi ($ 46.0 billion), Airbnb ($ 25.5 billion), Palantir ($ 20.0 billion), Snapchat ($ 16.0 billion), Flipkart ($ 15.0 billion), Didi Kuaidi ($ 15.0 billion), SpaceX ($ 12.0 billion), Pinterest ($ 11.0 billion) and Dropbox ($ 10.0 billion).[2] You've probably used the services of a couple of these yourself.

The start of corporate innovation often doesn't differ much from a startup, as most corporate innovators similarly start with an idea or opportunity. It all starts with a conscious spark triggered by new observations and associations, making new connections in the human brain. A big idea might come to you as a slow hunch or it may strike you like lightning. However, unless you take action it will simply drop dead on the floor. Quoting Ijuri and Kuhn: "Innovation is the process of taking those ideas to market or to usefulness."[3] Now, think about how often you have said, "That's a great idea, I must make it a reality." But what ends up happening most of the time? Nothing. Be aware that most of the time nothing materializes because you don't have the courage, resources, time and/or money to take action. Yes, transforming an idea into a reality (regardless of the required investment of time and money) is extremely difficult. That's why I want to help you along.

The main question is: "How do you develop your idea or opportunity into a well-founded convincing new business case?" The Idea Route through the innovation maze helps you with that.

I would like to guide you through the innovation maze in chart 10 on the basis of a practical example. Let's take the origin of Airbnb. It's a website where you can list, find and rent lodging all over the world. It has over 1.5 million listings in 34,000 cities and 190 countries. It started in 2007 when Brian Chesky and Joe Gebbia of Airbnb, based in the US, saw an opportunity to earn some extra cash by renting out their spare floor space when a major design conference came to town. In no time, they had put together a website advertising lodging for overnight guests, which they called "Airbed and Breakfast". After pivoting their concept to regular tourists and getting backed by venture capital, the company grew in five years to 25 million guests bookings in 2014. Airbnb will generate more than $900 million in revenue in 2015, half of which is generated in Europe. There's a huge chance that you are one of their customers. I certainly am one. It took the founders of Airbnb more than 2 years to cruise the innovation maze with their idea. Most of it was not very well-planned, except at the end of their front-end when they participated in a 12-week structured program of the Y-Combinator. That set them off. Read their story in chart 14. I will illustrate how you can start innovation with an idea following the structured Idea Route, using the Airbnb idea as a source of inspiration.

THE IDEA ROUTE

1. IDEATE:
GENERATING AND CHOOSING ORIGINAL RELEVANT IDEAS

The basic idea of Brian Chesky and Joe Gebbia of Airbnb is quite simple: the opportunity to earn some extra cash by renting out spare floor space when big events come to town. That's our starting point.

2. FOCUS:
DEFINING YOUR INNOVATION CENTER-OF-INTEREST
INCLUDING ALL THE BOUNDARY CONDITIONS

Instead of directly rushing into action, let's take a step back to prepare and bring some focus to your initiative. Draft your innovation assignment, to make all the expectations and boundary conditions explicit, with the help of six simple Wh-questions:

Why? Do you want to get rich with this lodging idea? Do you sincerely want to help people? Or, do you want to kill the hotel business? What do you want out of this?

What? Do you want to develop a kind of standard product, controlling all the space you rent out? Or do you want to be a 'man-in-the-middle' service? Or do you want to create a unique experience? Do you want it to be revolutionary or not? Or are you completely blank and are all options open?

Who? Do you want to target event and conference visitors? Or regular tourists who are looking for a cheap place to bunk?

Where? Do you want start in your town? Or your region? Or country-wide from the start?

When? Do you want your new service 'live' within 3 weeks? 3 months? Or three years?

Which? Which criteria will you use to assess your business case? How much revenue are you aiming for? What margins? How much can you invest yourself? How much money are you aiming for from venture capitalists or informal investors?

The deliverable is a concrete innovation assignment for your Airbnb idea. (see chapter 9).

3. CHECK FIT:
CHECKING IF YOUR IDEA FITS YOUR PERSONAL (AND CORPORATE PRIORITIES)

As you are a startup, ask yourself the question: Is my Airbnb opportunity really my priority in life at this moment? Do I really want to do this? Why? In this way you check your personal commitment to your idea. If you have any doubts. Don't do it, as the road to reality will be hard and bumpy. So, let's assume of course that you say 'YES!'☺

4. CREATE CONDITIONS:
ORGANIZING THE RIGHT MOMENT, THE RIGHT TEAM, THE RIGHT PACE AND THE RIGHT FUNDING FOR YOUR INNOVATION INITIATIVE

Create a fruitful environment for you to realize your Airbnb idea. Pick the right moment for you personally to start your venture. Do you want to do this alone? Or is it wiser to do it in a team? If so, make inventory of what skills and competences you need in your team to be successful. And gather the right team around you. At the start, Brian and Joe of Airbnb asked Nathan Blecharczyk, a previous roommate of Joe's to work on the technical backend of the "Airbed and Breakfast" website, as a side project in his spare time. Organize enough money to get you started with your initiative until the moment where you have a convincing new business case for investors.

5. DISCOVER:
DISCOVERING TRENDS, MARKETS, TECHNOLOGIES AND CUSTOMER INSIGHTS

First of all, let's go out first and explore your Airbnb opportunity with an open mind to learn and to make our basic idea better. Let's first of all map the market for lodging in the US, our potential home market. How big is it anyway? What types of lodging is offered? Who are the dominant players? Which customer groups do they target? What are the dominant trends? What's happening elsewhere around the world 'in lodging'? Have initiatives like ours been introduced elsewhere? Were they successful? Why? Why not? What can you learn from them? Can you copy or franchise them?

What are other successful initiatives in the new 'sharing economy'? What are new 'sharing' platforms? What 'sharing' business models are prevalent in other sectors like, for example, car-sharing initiatives? What can you learn from them?

Connect to your potential lodging customers in real life. Who are heavy users of lodging? And why? Who are light or even non-users of lodging? And why? What's the typical buying process of selecting and booking lodging? What are the dislikes and pain points of both the tenants and their temporary landlords and B&B owners? Organize focus groups or just go out and visit people at B&Bs and ask them. You might even film them to use their quotes later as a source of inspiration for yourself and to convince others.

As a user of his own service Brian Chesky rented one of the apartments listed on their very first website. As it happened though, he carelessly forgot to pay his hosts in cash for two days straight and this oversight quickly cooled the hosts' warm hospitality. This learning inspired Chesky to modify the services of Airbnb. They prioritized the development of a payment in advance booking system. The benefits were two-fold. Guests were now able to pre-pay for their stay with a credit card and hosts could avoid the hassle of late payments.

As you will understand Discovery is a crucial step. You learn tremendously. At the end of discovery, decide whether to persevere with your present Airbnb idea, or to abandon your idea and pivot it into something new and better than the original.

6. CREATE BUSINESS MODEL:
CREATING A VIABLE BUSINESS MODEL

So, how are you going to earn any money with your Airbnb service? Do you charge the guests for your services? Do you charge the hosts? Or do you charge them both? Work out several models and be inspired also by business models in sectors other than the accommodation sector. Airbnb chose to charge both the guests and the hosts. In their business model they charge the guest a service fee for a reservation and the host a commission fee as percentage of the booking.

7. SELECT TECHNOLOGY:
IDENTIFYING AND SELECTING THE RIGHT TECHNOLOGY TO DELIVER YOUR NEW PRODUCT, SERVICE, PROCESS OR EXPERIENCE

You will have to understand web technology. In this case it is crucial to make the right choices for your Airbnb idea. You will also have to design a great user experience as well for orientation and booking. Furthermore, orienting and selecting a proper booking and payment system will also require some efforts. What are the insource opportunities?

8. CHECK FREEDOM TO OPERATE:
CHECKING IF YOU DO NOT INFRINGE INTELLECTUAL PROPERTY RIGHTS OF OTHERS

Patents are probably not an issue in our Airbnb case, as it is a service, although we must not forget to check. Our freedom to operate could however also be limited due to trademark infringements. So do keep in mind to check your Airbnb trademark at the United States Patent and Trademark Office, even at this early stage.

9. EXPERIMENT:
CARRYING OUT A SYSTEMATIC RESEARCH OR TEST WHICH VALIDATES THE ADOPTION AND ATTRACTIVENESS OF YOUR NEW PRODUCT, SERVICE, PROCESS OR EXPERIENCE

As a startup, like Airbnb, you are creating a new product or service under conditions of extreme uncertainty. That's why experimenting is crucial when you start with 'just an idea'. Similarly to Airbnb, you should experiment both with your offering, your target groups, your business model and ways to attract customers. And in reality they did. Small scale 'live' tests have proven to be of great value for Airbnb, as they started learning by doing. At the start they targeted visitors of events and conferences, marketing Airbnb towards business travelers as a more affordable alternative to hotels. In 2008 they undertook several trials in Denver during the week of the Democratic National Convention and at the presidential inauguration in the Washington D.C. area. Without any special events, their weekly revenue amounted to roughly $200 in the fourth quarter of 2008 and they were on the brink of shutting down their initiative.

10. CREATE NEW BUSINESS CASE:
CREATING A WELL-FOUNDED CONVINCING BUSINESS CASE FOR YOUR NEW PRODUCT, SERVICE, PROCESS OR EXPERIENCE

With all the learnings in the first nine activities you will draft a new business case: a well-founded concise plan which proves your idea is attractive, feasible and viable. The three founders of Airbnb pivoted their idea to the Airbnb concept we now all know, when they joined Y-Combinator in 2009. This is a start-up incubator program located in Mountain View, California. Paul Graham, the leader of the program decided to accept them and financed them with $20,000. At the so-called Demo Day in April 2009, Airbnb pitched their business case in a convincing way with Sequoia Capital taking notice. They raised $600,000 of capital.

The Journey of Airbnb is an amazing one. I hope it inspires you to transform your idea into reality. Now when you're looking where to locate your startup, you might check chart 16 which lists the top 20 startup cities in the world. In the next chapter we will take another route through the innovation maze: the Technology Route, inspired by Google Glass.

KEY MESSAGES FROM THIS CHAPTER

1. You are not the only one who will take an idea to market as a startup, and make it big. Apple, Google, Facebook, Twitter, Uber, Airbnb, Snapchat, Pinterest and Dropbox have already shown you the way.
2. Startups are creating a new product or service under conditions of extreme uncertainty. That's why both Discovery and Experiment are crucial when you start with 'just an idea'.
3. Use all your learnings to decide whether to persevere with your idea or to abandon your idea and pivot it into something new and better than the original.

Notes

[1] Duncan D. Bruce & Dr Geoff Crook, *The Dream Café*, Wiley, 2015, p. 31.
[2] Valuation by The Wall Street Journal and Dow Jones VentureSource, August 2015, http://graphics.wsj.com/billion-dollar-club/
[3] Dave Richards, *The Sevens Sins of Innovation*, Palgrave Macmillan, London, 2014, p. 25.

AIRBNB: FLAGSHIP PLATFORM FOR THE NEW SHARING ECONOMY

Two years after graduating from the Rhode Island School of Design in 2005, Brian Chesky and Joe Gebbia moved to San Francisco where they shared a three-bedroom apartment. When a major design conference came to town in 2007, they saw an opportunity to earn some extra cash by renting out their spare floor space. In no time they had put together a website advertising lodging for overnight guests. Later on, Chesky and Gebbia approached Joe's former roommate, Nathan Blecharczyk, about handling the technical side of the "Airbed and Breakfast" website, as

something of a side gig. As they explain, their concept had quite a casual character from the start, "We were offering full bed and breakfast service, but we didn't have any beds, so we called it Airbed and Breakfast."

The idea to turn this service into a real business came to them when they realized there was an unmet demand for no-frills lodging at a stranger's home for one or two nights. Originally, Chesky and Gebbia were simply offering basic accommodation and expected that the concept would only appeal to recent graduates like themselves with little money to spend on hotels. However, as Gebbia recalls, "We had a 38-year-old female who worked at Razorfish. And then we had an industrial designer from Salt Lake City who was even older. They slept on air mattresses on our kitchen floor. They broke every assumption we ever made about who would stay on an airbed at a stranger's house."

The Airbnb founders' next step was to seek out an event as a pilot for their new business venture. They chose the South by Southwest (SXSW) music and film festival in Austin, Texas which hosts over 150,000 visitors. The event organizers, however, were not enthusiastic about the "Airbed and Breakfast" concept and rejected a partnership. This did not deter the three entrepreneurs and they responded by launching the second version of the Airbed and Breakfast website two weeks prior to

the festival. They used local blogs and social media to advertise their lodging services. They had lodging addresses to accommodate up to 80 guests. By way of an informal market test, Brian Chesky rented one of the apartments listed on their own website. As it happened though, he carelessly forgot to pay his hosts in cash for two days straight and this oversight quickly cooled the hosts' warm hospitality. It also inspired Chesky to modify their services. Their company prioritized the development of a payment in advance booking system. The benefits were two-fold. Guests were now able to pre-pay for their stay with a credit card and hosts could avoid the hassle of late payments. Service was further improved by introducing two other features: an online booking system similar to the one used for hotel reservations enabling users to book space in someone's home online and a "Reviews" box where guests could post their comments about the accommodation, host(s) and overall experience as a reference for other guests.

In August 2008 an improved Airbed and Breakfast website was introduced and was marketed towards business travelers as a more affordable alternative to hotels. Airbed and Breakfast got a lot of media coverage and even caught the attention of The Wall Street Journal. In their business model they charged the guest a service fee of 6 to 12 percent for a reservation, and the host a 3 percent commission fee.

The next trial run took place in Denver during the week of the Democratic National Convention. Convention delegates had access to 900 lodging options via the Airbed and Breakfast website. The start-up site ultimately booked 50 accepted reservations during the convention. Without any additional special events, Airbed and Breakfast's weekly revenue amounted to roughly $200 in the fourth quarter of 2008. Discouraged, the founders questioned whether it was time to just throw in the towel. However, it was anticipated that the upcoming presidential inauguration would draw millions of visitors to the Washington D.C. area. This was the next real opportunity for Airbed and Breakfast. They were able to generate free publicity on the site and successfully generated 150 bookings. Nevertheless, once the event ended, the company's prospects remained bleak. As the number of bookings staggered, the Airbed and Breakfast website was on the brink of being shut down. Instead, the pivotal decision was made in 2009 to join Y-Combinator, a start-up incubator program located in Mountain View, California.

The Y-Combinator incubator provided much needed seed funding, access to investors, and mentoring. Its motto "Make something people want" sums up the spirit of the program and is printed on the T-shirts handed out to all the participants on their first day. The impact of this program was immense according to Chesky, "They were the most important three months in the company's history." During the 12-week program, Blecharczyk, Chesky and Gebbia changed the name of their site to Airbnb and shifted to expand beyond event accommodations. They focused on New York as a popular tourist destination and had meetings with their New York-based users, both hosts and guests. These interactions were very important, as Gebbia said, "We'd go to the city, talk to people who had listings, take professional pictures of their space. And in many cases write their listings for them. After making several trips, we had a really solid offering of good-looking spaces in New York City. It got us critical mass; we were able to set a lot of community standards, and we used the listing base we built in those weeks as a base off which to grow." The $20,000 of funding from angel investor and co-founder of Y-Combinator, Paul Graham, led to an additional $600,000 from venture capitalists on Demo Day at the end of the program.

The Airbnb concept has proven to be hugely successful. Primarily, Airbnb provides a digital tool that connects people in need of an affordable place to stay with people who can supply afford-able lodging. Secondly, there is the appeal of the Airbnb concept. Guests can live like a local and connect with hosts, form friendships and partake in local experi-ences they wouldn't have found otherwise.

Over time, the initial concept and experi-ence for both the guests and the hosts has had to evolve to maintain successful. Some major modifications introduced by Airbnb include a 24/7 customer support service as well as providing $1 million insurance for the host. Most recently, Airbnb launched a new product called instabook. With the click of a button you can make your reser-vations just like you do for a hotel. Commenting on the potential of instabook, Chesky says, "One thing that we're doing is trying to shift every host to mobile. We'll eventually get to a place where every booking is instabook."

Demonstrating a very visible emphasis on community and connectedness, as part of Airbnb's company strategy in 2014, its new brand logo, the Bélo, was introduced and dubbed the universal symbol of belonging. In November 2014, the Airbnb Open, a host convention, was organized to inspire hosts as well as teach them practical tips when they rent out their homes and rooms to travelers. About 1,500 hosts from 40 countries came to the Fort Mason Center in San Francisco for the weekend event. In addition, Airbnb facilitates host groups for knowledge sharing, integrated into a host application that also embeds hospitality standards and guidelines, as well as stand-alone meet-ups for hosts to exchange information. As it expands, Airbnb continues to invest significantly in creating a global community and sense of partner-ship.

From 2009 onwards, Airbnb's financial conquest of the world really takes off. In November 2010, Airbnb was able to raise an additional $7.2 million from a venture capitalist. Following this, the company received a further $112 million in venture funding in July 2011 and was reportedly valued behind the scenes at $1.3 billion.

Five years after the start, Airbnb was valued a $2.5 billion company with revenues of $250 million, with a presence in over 34,000 cities around the globe.

While Airbnb is still financing its expansion and burning cash with a forecasted operating loss of about $150 million in 2015, The Wall Street Journal reports that Airbnb's value is currently estimated around $25.5 billion.

The company continues to grow quickly with 25 million guests bookings via Airbnb in 2014. In 2015, it's expected that Airbnb will generate more than $900 million in revenue, half of which is generated in Europe.

As of 2015, the website has around 1.4 million listings which include modest apartments, exotic beach homes and quirky properties. Paris, the French capital, is now Airbnb's largest market, with 40,000 listings. More than 517,000 people stayed in Paris in summer 2014, which is a 20-fold increase compared with 2011.

As Airbnb grows in these markets, it also encounters new challenges especially concerning local city regulations and tax laws. In some countries, legislation is being reviewed to check the legality of Airbnb-type rentals.

What began as a simple idea to earn some extra income and help out travelers from out-of-town eventually took off globally. The Airbnb story has since attracted a lot of attention and is being perceived as a flagship platform for the new sharing economy.

www.airbnb.com

Sources
Danielle Sacks, "The Sharing Economy," Fast Company, April 18, 2011, http://www.fastcompany.com/1747551/sharing-economy (February 20, 2013). "Airbnb: A Spare Room for Debate", Larry Downes, Harvard Business Review, June 26, 2013.
Harvard Business School, Joseph B. Lassiter III & Evan Richardson, "Airbnb", March 28, 2014. Stanford Business, Airbnb, CASE: E470, April 13, 2013. "Airbnb: The story behind the $1.3bn room-letting website", Jessica Salter, The Telegraph, September 7, 2012. https://gigaom.com/2013/06/18/Airbnb-is-20-to-50-cheaper-than-a-hotel-unless-youre-in-vegas-or-houston. "What Airbnb Gets About Culture that Uber Doesn't", Arun Sundararajan, Harvard Business Review, November 27, 2014. "CEO Brian Chesky on Building a Company and Starting a 'Sharing' Revolution" Thompson, The Atlantic, August 13, 2013. "INSIDE Airbnb'S GRAND HOTEL PLANS", Fast Company, Austin Carr, March 17, 2014. "Airbnb Tops Challenges of Spark Implementation", Wall Street Journal, Clint Boulton, July 1, 2015. "Paris Confronts Airbnb's Rapid Growth", The Wall Street Journal, Sam Schechner and Matthias Verbergt, June 25, 2015. "Airbnb is an old idea with a new tech twist", Chip Conley, August 29, 2014 http://www.hotelnewsnow.com/Article/14343/Airbnb-is-an-old-idea-with-a-new-tech-twist. http://www.justmeans.com/blogs/Airbnb-a-successful-business-model-where-everyone-wins

THE WORLD'S TOP 20

WHERE SHOULD YOU LOOK TO START YOUR NEW COMPANY FOR YOUR BIG IDEA? CHECK OUT THIS LIST OF THE TOP 20 STARTUP CITIES IN THE WORLD

CITIES FOR STARTUPS

1. **Silicon Valley**
2. **New York City**
3. **Los Angeles**
4. **Boston**
5. **Tel Aviv**
6. **London**
7. **Chicago**
8. **Seattle**
9. **Berlin**
10. **Singapore**
11. Paris
12. Sao Paulo
13. Moscow
14. Austin
15. Bangalore
16. Sydney
17. Toronto
18. Vancouver
19. Amsterdam
20. Montreal

Source
Compass, a provider of automated software for 34,000 startups around the globe. The Global Startup Ecosystem Ranking 2015 is based on insights from over 200 interviews with entrepreneurs and local experts from 25 countries, and data from 11,000 surveys completed by startups, investors and other stakeholders. Download the full study at: http://blog.startupcompass.co/the-2015-global-startup-ecosystem-ranking-is-live

Note: Unfortunately, this graph does not yet include data from startup cities in China, Taiwan, Japan, or South Korea.

THE TECHNOLOGY ROUTE:

I DISCOVERED A NEW TECHNOLOGY, NOW WHAT?

New emerging technology is an important driver and enabler of innovation. Edible food packaging. Microbes that can make energy. Lab-grown meat. Fabric that generates electricity from body heat. Augmented reality contact lenses. These are all new technologies that might change our world in the coming decades.

One technology driving innovation which has a huge impact on industries at the moment for example is 3D printing. The earliest 3D printing technologies first became visible as early as the late 1980s. At that time, it was called rapid prototyping technology, as the process was originally conceived as a fast and more cost-effective method for creating prototypes for product development

reasons. Throughout the 1990s and early 2000s a host of new 3D technologies continued to be introduced, still focused wholly on industrial applications. During the mid-nineties, the sector started to diversify in high and low-end applications. The high-end applications of 3D printing were still very expensive systems and focused on the production of high value complex parts. A new lower end of the market emerged with incremental improvements in printing accuracy, speed and materials. But it wasn't until January 2009 that the first commercially available 3D printer was offered for sale: the BfB RapMan 3D printer.[1] In 2012, many different mainstream media channels picked up 3D printing as a new technology. A 2014 study by PwC of more than 100 manufacturing companies, revealed that 11% had already switched to volume production of 3D printed parts or products.[2] A great example, mentioned in the Harvard Business review is GE Aviation, which started to 3D print the fuel nozzles of certain jet engines offering them a 75% manufacturing cost cut because the original nozzle used to be assembled from 20 separate parts into one piece. The number of inventions with 3D is growing exponentially as well. In 2005, only 80 patents relating to additive manufacturing materials, software, and equipment were granted. By 2013 that number had risen to 600 new patents. It is expected that 3D printing is about to go mainstream in a big way.[3]

It is considered a classic innovation 'mistake': a technology oriented entrepreneur who first discovers a new technology (like 3D printing), and later tries to figure out how people can use it. Without a need there will of course be no market. And without a market there's no viable business model. A great recent example of this issue is the Google Glass introduction in 2012. A Glass user stated that it was an experience that was far less helpful than expected: "I found that it was not very useful for very much, and it tended to disturb people around me that I have this thing."[4] In January 2015, Google shut down their Google Glass Explorer program as you can read in chart 16. Now, I don't consider starting with technology a mistake provided you incorporate a front end activity to match your new technology with relevant market needs, as the yellow Technology Route through the innovation maze will show you. I will illustrate how you can start innovation with a technology following the structured Technology Route in chart 11, using Google Glass as a source of inspiration.

THE TECHNOLOGY ROUTE

1. SELECT TECHNOLOGY:
IDENTIFYING AND SELECTING THE RIGHT TECHNOLOGY TO DELIVER YOUR NEW PRODUCT, SERVICE, PROCESS OR EXPERIENCE

On April 4, 2012, Google creates a Project Glass account on Google+ and the team at Google X shares its first public post that begins with this mission statement: "We think technology should work for you – to be there when you need it and get out of your way when you don't. A group of us from Google[x] started Project Glass to build this kind of technology, one that helps you explore and share your world, putting you back in the moment."[5]

2. FOCUS:
DEFINING YOUR INNOVATION CENTER-OF-INTEREST INCLUDING ALL THE BOUNDARY CONDITIONS

The mission is rather vague though. Where should you start? A statement of Serge Brin, one of Google's founders, helps you to get more focused. He questioned whether we should be "walking around looking down" at our smartphones. He asked, "Is this how you want to connect to other people in your life, how you want to connect to information?... Is this what you were meant to do with your body?" Instead, Google designers wanted to make something "that frees your hands...frees your eyes."

So what's your focus? I suggest we narrow it down to "the next wearable communication technology." As a wearable device, Google has chosen glasses. In this phase I suggest though that you keep your scope wider.

3. CHECK FIT:
CHECKING IF YOUR IDEA, TECHNOLOGY, CUSTOMER ISSUE OR BUSINESS CHALLENGE FITS YOUR PERSONAL AND CORPORATE PRIORITIES

As a Google employee, you ask yourself "does this really fit my company and me?" Well, creating this revolutionary new technology fits perfectly with the ambition of Google and of Google X, whose aim it is to develop so-called 'moonshots' and improve technologies by a factor of 10, developing science fiction-sounding solutions, like the self-driving car.

4. CREATE CONDITIONS:
ORGANIZING THE RIGHT MOMENT, THE RIGHT TEAM, THE RIGHT PACE AND THE RIGHT FUNDING FOR YOUR INNOVATION INITIATIVE

Where better could you develop a new wearable device than at Google X? Probably nowhere, or perhaps at Apple. Google's X lab is a great creative environment, as Jon Gertner of Fast Company describes: "Mostly, X seeks out people who want to build stuff, and who won't get easily daunted. Inside the lab, now more than 250 employees strong, I met an idiosyncratic troupe of former park rangers, sculptors, philosophers, and machinists; one X scientist has won two Academy Awards for special effects."[6]

5. DISCOVER: DISCOVERING TRENDS, MARKETS, TECHNOLOGIES AND CUSTOMER INSIGHTS

First of all, let's go out first with an open mind and explore your new "technology to explore and share our world." What technologies are already out there? What is already feasible? What patents are filed in this domain and are interesting for you? What are the latest technological trends? What are other successful initiatives new communication technology? What can you learn from it?

What kind of wearable devices are out there on the market and in development? Let's buy them, use them and take them apart. What can you learn? Who are the dominant players in wearable devices? Are they successful? Why? Why not? What's on their R&D agenda? What can you learn from them?

Connect to potential users. Reach out and connect to users of smartphones and other communication technology: your potential customers in real-life. Who are heavy smartphone & tablet users? And why? Who are light or even non-users of smartphones & tablets? And why? What are the dislikes and pain points of both smartphone & tablet users, as well as non-users? And what are their big dreams in communication? Organize focus groups and do ethnographic research of following people 24/7 mapping their communication behavior, pain points and likes and dislikes. Especially in this case, film them to see what's happening and use their quotes later as a source of inspiration for yourself and to convince others.

Be sure to balance your discovery efforts on both sides of the equation: on the technology side and on the potential needs side.

6. IDEATE:
GENERATING AND CHOOSING ORIGINAL RELEVANT IDEAS FOR A PRODUCT, SERVICE, PROCESS OR EXPERIENCE

Inspired by the trends, technologies and customer insights, you together with your team at Google X start ideating new ideas for wearable devices to connect to other people in your life and connect to information in a new, free way. First, by generating real outside-the-box ideas and postponing your judgement. Later, by assessing those ideas with questions like "can it be made?"

In reality, the Glass Google came up with is a so-called optical head-mounted display. It is a wearable device that has the capability of reflecting projected images as well as allowing the user to see *through it.*[7] *The Google Glass prototype came in five colors, were worn like eyeglasses and weighed about the same. Though, instead of lenses, there was a display that was activated by a 30-degree tilt of the head or by a tap of the touchpad. Just above the right eye, a semi-transparent prism reflected an image or 10-word max text from a LED projector directly onto the retina. Navigation was conducted through simple voice commands or by swiping and tapping the touchpad. The touchpad, battery, and other electronic components were housed in the right-side arm. The plastic casing with a processor, camera, and display were also on the right side. Google Glass could be connected to Wi-Fi and Bluetooth.*

7. CREATE BUSINESS MODEL:
CREATING A VIABLE BUSINESS MODEL

Google Glass is a completely new to the world product. The question is, what do you do with the business model? Google kept it quite simple by selling them at a fixed price, like you would do with any other communication device these days. For the experiment in the next phase, the sale price was set at $1,500.

8. CHECK FREEDOM TO OPERATE:
CHECKING IF YOU DO NOT INFRINGE INTELLECTUAL
PROPERTY RIGHTS OF OTHERS

Especially when you develop new technology, there is a huge risk that you might infringe someone's patents. That's why you should check in which space you have the right to operate early on in the new product development process. In reality, Google X registered a huge amount of patents while developing Google Glass. I guess that generating intellectual property rights might be a secondary objective of Google X. And at the same time Google has acquired patents within the scope of the project such as a patent from former Indy 500 driver Dominic Dobson's Motion Research Technologies, Inc.: multi-use eyeglasses with human Input/Output interface embedded.

9. EXPERIMENT:
CARRYING OUT A SYSTEMATIC RESEARCH OR TEST
WHICH VALIDATES THE ADOPTION AND ATTRACTIVENESS
OF YOUR NEW PRODUCT, SERVICE, PROCESS
OR EXPERIENCE

This is the moment to test your prototype to check if it's attractive, if it really works and if you can make a business out of it. In reality at Google X, it was decided to test in public on a large scale. 8,000 consumers were selected by Google as early adopters or 'Explorers' of Glass on the basis of paying the fee of $ 1,500 and by creatively responding on their Twitter or Google+ account to the hashtag prompt #ifihadglass. As you can read in the Google Glass case in chart 17, the launch of the Google Glass test was world news. The 'public character' of the test was a deliberate decision: "We debated this decision extensively. Major new consumer tech products are rarely brought out of the lab at this stage of development. But we knew that by putting prototypes into the wild, we'd start to learn how this radical new technology—something that sits on your face, so close to your senses—might be used. We knew that Glass would be unfamiliar and would raise questions about social acceptance, so we wanted to start a public discourse early. In doing so, we hoped to better shape the way the product's story would be told over time."

The experiment brought Google great new insights both on how Google Glass was perceived by the public, as well as a lot of malfunctions in the product itself: "The product changed so much from when I first started working on the project until I left." Another source says, "We were having people pay $ 1,500 to tell us how to fix this thing." The early Google Glass Explorers gave tons of feedback on what needed fixing. In turn, Google responded swiftly; acting on customer complaints as quickly as they could.

10. CREATE NEW BUSINESS CASE:
CREATING A WELL-FOUNDED CONVINCING BUSINESS CASE FOR YOUR NEW PRODUCT, SERVICE, PROCESS OR EXPERIENCE

When it was launched, the Google Glass Explorer's Program quickly caught the attention and enthusiasm of the business sector. Early on, Deloitte Consulting predicted that "smart glasses" would sell four million units in 2014 at an average price of $500, with demand surpassing 100 million units by 2020. This did not become reality, as Google Glass could not meet internal expectations at Google. A source at Google stated, "We kept missing the benchmarks we had set. All the grand plans that we had at the beginning just did not materialize." In 2014, Google stopped the experiment. Google X can draw heavily upon the massive lessons learned from their Google Glass public experiment, which they used to pivot the original idea. A new version of Google Glass is expected soon.

In the next chapter we will take another route through the innovation maze: the Customer Issue Route, inspired by Hövding –the invisible helmet for cyclists.

KEY MESSAGES FROM THIS CHAPTER

1. **It is considered a classic innovation 'mistake': a technology oriented entrepreneur who first discovers a new technology, and later tries to figure out how people can use it.**
2. **Incorporate, at the start of innovation, an activity to match your new technology with relevant market needs.**
3. **When you start with new technology, doing experiments with tangible prototypes among potential customers is the best way to learn.**
4. **An experiment can never fail, because even when the prototype does, you have massive learnings, which you can use to pivot your original idea.**

Notes

[1] History of 3D Printing, http://3dprintingindustry.com/3d-printing-basics-free-beginners-guide/history/
[2] The 3D printing revolution, Harvard Business Review, May 2015, https://hbr.org/2015/05/the-3-d-printing-revolution
[3] The 3D printing revolution, Harvard Business Review, May 2015, https://hbr.org/2015/05/the-3-d-printing-revolution
[4] The Top Technology Failures of 2014, Antonio Regalado on December 31, 2014, http://www.technologyreview.com/news/533546/the-top-technology-failures-of-2014/
[5] http://glassalmanac.com/history-google-glass/#sthash.kdcsONvA.dpuf
[6] FastCompany, May 2014, http://www.fastcompany.com/3028156/united-states-of-innovation/the-google-x-factor
[7] Wikipedia, https://en.wikipedia.org/wiki/Optical_head-mounted_display

THE GOOGLE GLASS EXPERIMENT

Development of Google Glass began in 2010. It was developed by Google's secret Google X research lab, the facility exploring new technologies beyond Google's core business. In April 2012, Google co-founder Sergey Brin chose a fundraising event for the Foundation Fighting Blindness for the first public appearance of the Google Glass prototype. In an interview, Brin elaborated on the motivations that led to the new concept of Google Glass. It came down to a series of questions. He questioned whether we should be "walking around looking down" at our smartphones. He asked, "Is this how you want to connect to other people in your life, how you want to connect to information?...Is this what you were meant to do with your body?" Instead, Google designers wanted to make something "that frees your hands...frees your eyes".

The Google Glass prototype comes in five colors, is worn like eyeglasses and weighs about the same. Though, instead of lenses, there is a display that is activated by a 30-degree tilt of the head or by a tap of the touchpad. Just above the right eye, a semi-transparent prism reflects an image or 10-word max text from a LED projector directly onto the retina. Navigation is conducted through simple voice commands or by swiping and tapping the touchpad. The touchpad, battery, and other electronic components are housed in the right-side arm. The plastic casing with a processor, camera, and display are also on the right side. Google Glass can be connected to Wi-Fi and Bluetooth.

When Google went to market with Google Glass, it was still an early prototype. Glass product manager Steve Lee explained the decision to start public beta testing so early:

"We debated this decision extensively. Major new consumer tech products are rarely brought out of the lab at this stage of development. But we knew that by putting prototypes into the wild, we'd start to learn how this radical new technology— something that sits on your face, so close to your senses—might be used. Some of the most compelling use cases for Glass are outdoors, so it would have been hard to test the product only through Google employees in our own offices. And unlike a new phone, which you can slip into your pocket, you can't hide Glass. Most importantly, we knew that Glass would be unfamiliar and would raise questions about social acceptance, so we wanted to start a public discourse early. In doing so, we hoped to better shape the way the product's story would be told over time."

There was massive hype in the pre-launch period of Google Glass. In spring 2013 Google invited third-party developers to create the so-called Glassware. Among them were Twitter, Facebook, CNN, The New York Times and Evernote. At the same time, some 8,000 consumers were selected as early Adopters or 'Explorers' of Glass on the basis of paying the $1,500 fee and creatively responding on their Twitter or Google+ to the hashtag prompt #ifihadglass. These Explorers were enrolled in Google's "Explorers Program" and invited to visit Google's Basecamps in San Francisco, Los Angeles and New York City in the US. Explorers were treated in true VIP fashion during their visit to the Google Glass Basecamps, where they received a Glass fitting, a personal demo and training how to use Google Glasses.

Glass product manager Steve Lee explained the need for this large-scale approach to testing the Glass prototype. "We could have beta tested with fewer users if our only goal was getting feedback on the product and insight on use cases. But we also understood that Glass would entail radical behavioral change, and this would require education and demonstration. We have thousands of Explorers, together forming a diverse set of people who each show Glass to hundreds of others, including policy makers, the media, and other influencers."

The secrecy surrounding Glass meant that many of the new hires at the Google Glass Basecamps did not know what their jobs would be at first. It was thrilling work though with all the buzz around Google Glass. After the launch, the Basecamp teams were giving dozens of demos a week to the selected Explorers. Aside from the prototype's obvious bugs, the Explorers were generally positive about Glass: "This is like having the Internet in your eye socket, but it's less intrusive than I thought it would be. I can totally see how this would still let you be in the moment with people around you." Some voiced concerns though about its acceptance. Expert-user and Gizmag's Mobile Tech Editor, Will Shanklin, commented, "My first impressions of Glass are that it's the boldest product I've ever used ... and maybe also the most terrifying. Its potential reaches far beyond typical consumer lust, but gaining that mainstream acceptance might also be its biggest challenge."

The initial excitement about Google Glass started to wane as problems became increasingly apparent. Google relied heavily on customer feedback to improve Google Glass. A Google source reported, "The product changed so much from when I first started working on the project until I left." Another source says, "We were having people pay $ 1,500 to tell us how to fix this thing." The early Google Glass

Explorers gave tons of feedback on what needed fixing. In turn, Google responded swiftly; acting on customer complaints as quickly as they could.

At the same time, the more the public was confronted with Google Glass the more consumers and policy makers raised their concerns about privacy issues. There was a general public backlash. One Explorer commented, "From my perspective, I was wearing a computer, a tool that gave me constant, easy ability to access information quickly. To everyone else, I was just a guy with a camera on his head." Soon the term "glasshole" was coined to describe obnoxious Google Glass users. When it was launched, the Google Glass Explorer's Program quickly caught the attention and enthusiasm of the business sector. Early on, Deloitte Consulting predicted that "smart glasses" would sell four million units in 2014 at an average price of $500, with demand surpassing 100 million units by 2020. Ultimately, results soon fell short of the high expectations.

Google Glass could not meet internal expectations. A source at Google stated, "We kept missing the benchmarks we had set. All the grand plans that we had at the beginning just did not materialize." As the number of appointments at the

Basecamps declined, employees had to be let go and morale dropped overall. In 2014, Google announced it would be closing Glass showrooms and discontinuing appointments at the Basecamps.

Google can draw heavily upon the massive lessons learned from their Google Glass public experiment. Reflecting on this, Glass product manager Steve Lee shared his thoughts on the wide range of challenges and expectations that need addressing.

"At the outset, we saw several potential barriers to adoption. First, would the device obstruct your field of view and prove distracting? Early on, we learned that with the right design, this is not a problem at all; new users adapt to the device very quickly. A second potential barrier was engineering the product for comfort, fit, and ease of use. We've made great progress on that front; many Explorers comfortably wear the device for 16 hours at a stretch. And in terms of ease of use, we can still do more to improve software setup, which is okay now but not yet great. A third concern has been creating a product perceived as fashionable, stylish eyewear. Fourth, does Glass deliver enough utility? Finally, will social acceptance be forthcoming? After three years, we've learned a lot about styling, utility, and social reactions, but we still have lots of work to do. Bringing Glass to market will be a marathon, not a sprint! I'm happy we launched early and accelerated our learning. But the early launch also created tons of issues for our team. Major Google product launches always get a lot of attention, but the volume and intensity of reactions to Glass have been remarkable. That's been fun for our team, but also distracting. And it's created challenges for us with managing people's expectations about what the product could and couldn't do, and when new versions might be ready."

In January 2015, Google announced that it was shutting down the Explorer program. They have put Nest CEO and former Apple executive Tony Fadell in charge of the next generation of Glass. To be continued...

Sources
An insider's look at the tumultuous Launch of Google Glass, Jilian D'Onfro, February 28, 2015. http://uk. businessinsider.com/google-glass-launch-2015-27r=US. Harvard Business School, Thomas Eisenmann, Lauren Barley & Liz Kind, Case description Google Glass, June 4, 2014. Daniel J. Simons and Christopher F. Chabris, "Is Google Glass Dangerous?" New York Times Blogs, May 24, 2013, http://www.nytimes. com/2013/05/24/opinion/sunday/google-glass-may-be-hands-free-but-not-brain-free.html. Daily Mail, Good camera, great internet but poor speaker: What real people - and not just the geeks - think of Google Glass, http://www.dailymail.co.uk/news/article-2402934/ Google-Glass-users-experience-having-Internet-eyesocket.html. Glass to exit Google X, report to Nest's Tony Fadellhttp://fortune.com/2015/01/15/glass-to-exit-google-x-report-to-nests-tony-fadell/. Google Glass: Early impressions, Will Shanklin - December 14, 2013, http://www.gizmag.com/initial-google-glass-review/30129/.

THE CUSTOMER ISSUE ROUTE:

I IDENTIFIED A CUSTOMER PAIN POINT; NOW WHAT?

Another great driver and starting point for innovation is when customers experience relevant pain points making them dissatisfied or even frustrated with the status quo. It creates the willingness to change and be open to any new solutions that you might develop for them. Let me give you three brief examples.

Richard Branson, serial innovator and the founder of the Virgin Group has often said that many of his best business ideas were born out of frustration as a customer. As a frequent air traveler in America, he was constantly frustrated by the terrible service generally offered by most of the domestic US carriers. The solution, he says, was to launch Virgin America, which now consistently tops customer service rankings.[1] There are many more other similar examples where customer frustration sparked creativity. In 1978, James Dyson became frustrated with his vacuum cleaner's diminishing performance. Taking it apart, he discovered that its bag was clogging with dust, causing suction to drop. He'd just recently built an industrial cyclone tower for his factory that separated paint particles from the air using centrifugal force. Could the same principle work in a vacuum cleaner? He set off to work. Five years and 5,127 prototypes later he had invented the world's first bagless vacuum cleaner.[2] Gary Symons, the current CEO of Vericorder in Canada, recalls how it was when he was a journalist, "I spent years as a journalist dragging around heavy, cumbersome, expensive, and often unreliable gear for reporting from the field." Through research and his inside knowledge of the industry, he knew that he could solve his frustrations and move the industry into the 21st century by allowing journalists to file the story and broadcast without returning to the office. "I could see that traditional media was dying, dragged down by high production costs and new competition from Internet-based companies," says Gary. He decided to build 'mobile journalism kits' enabling companies to make the smooth transition to online media and mobile journalism.[3]

There's a common saying that necessity is the mother of invention. From stories like Gary's and others I have learned that in many cases, customer frustration is in fact the mother of invention.

The key is to pin down the problem. Once you've got that; you've got half of the solution. Albert Einstein once said, "If I had an hour to solve a problem I'd spend 55 minutes thinking about the problem and 5 minutes thinking about the solution." Einstein is so right. That's why the Discovery phase is so important in the Customer Issue Route through the innovation maze.
Let's now turn to Sweden for a great example of what can develop from 'thinking extensively about a problem'. The year is 2005 when a new law is introduced in Sweden requiring children up to 15 years old to wear bicycle helmets. This sparked a heated debate on whether mandatory helmet use should be extended to include adults as well. In the same year, design students Anna Haupt and Terese Alstin were working together on a joint master's thesis in industrial design to complete their studies at the Faculty of Engineering at Lund University in Sweden. The prospect of being forced by law to wear a bicycle helmet was cause for concern. This was particularly true for people like Anna and Terese who said, they "wouldn't be caught dead wearing a polystyrene helmet." As they explained, "Producing a bicycle helmet that people would be happy to wear looked like a much better way to go than legislation forcing people to wear one or else." They realized that their industrial design master's thesis would be the perfect platform to study how

to improve the traditional bicycle helmet. It was the start of a revolutionary new product and the start of their company called Hövding. You will find their case in chart 17.

Using Hövding as a source of inspiration, I will illustrate how you can start innovation with a customer pain point following the structured Customer Issue Route in chart 12.

1. DISCOVER:
DISCOVERING TRENDS, MARKETS, TECHNOLOGIES AND CUSTOMER INSIGHTS

You are now joining two design students Anna Haupt and Terese Alstin, who are working together on a joint master's thesis in industrial design to complete their studies at the Faculty of Engineering at Lund University in Sweden. The prospect of being forced by law to wear a bicycle helmet is cause for concern for people like Anna and Terese who say they wouldn't "be caught dead wearing a polystyrene helmet." You share their standpoint that producing a bicycle helmet that people would be happy to wear is a much better way to go than legislation forcing people to wear one or else. So, your starting point is a customer issue: I don't like wearing polystyrene bicycle helmets.

First of all, let's check if this is also a relevant pain point for more people than just Anna and Terese. Connect to cyclists in real life. Who are heavy users of cyclist helmets? And why? Who are non-users of bicycle helmets? And why? What's the typical buying process of selecting and buying a helmet? Who is retailing bicycle helmets? What are the dislikes and pain points of the users of cyclist helmets? And of the retailers? Organize focus groups or just go out and interview cyclists and ask them. You might even film them so you can use their quotes later on for inspiration and convincing others. Do store checks as well.

Secondly, you'll map the market for bicycle helmets in Sweden, our potential home market. How big is it anyway? What types of helmets are offered? Who are the dominant manufacturers? Which customer groups do they target? What are the dominant trends? What's happening elsewhere in 'the world of cycling'? Have initiatives for helmet alternatives like ours been introduced elsewhere? Were they successful? Why? Why not? What can you learn from them?

You might want to check as a third activity what's going on in other helmet markets, for instance: racing helmets for professional cyclists, motorcycle helmets or even military helmets? Are there any new solutions there? What can you learn from them?

As a fourth activity, you can check out new, soft materials and new technology used for protection which are available on the market or are being developed.

In reality, Discovery was Anna and Terese's first step. They started surveying people on the streets in Sweden asking why so few people wore bicycle helmets. The long list of reasons they were given included the following: 'They're a pain to carry about', 'They all look hideous', 'They ruin your hair', 'Nobody else wears them', and 'You can't put your hat on underneath'. Some objections sounded reasonable enough, while others were simply flimsy excuses. The message was clear; bicycle helmets were controversial.

2. FOCUS:
DEFINING YOUR INNOVATION-CENTER-OF-INTEREST INCLUDING ALL THE BOUNDARY CONDITIONS

Instead of rushing directly into action, let's take a step back to prepare and bring some focus to your initiative. Draft your innovation assignment making all the expectations and boundary conditions explicit, with the help of six simple Wh-questions: Why? What do you want out of this? What? Do you want to develop an improved or completely new revolutionary product? Who? Do you want to target

bicycle helmet wearers or the non-wearers like Anna and Terese? Where? Do you want start country-wide from the start? Or take a worldwide perspective? When? Do you want your new helmet solution in 3 months? Or three years? Which? Which criteria will you use to assess your business case? How much revenue are you aiming for? What margins? How much can you invest yourself? The deliverable is a concrete innovation assignment for your bicycle helmet issue. (see Chapter 9).

3. CHECK FIT:
CHECKING IF YOUR IDEA, TECHNOLOGY, CUSTOMER ISSUE OR BUSINESS CHALLENGE FITS YOUR PERSONAL AND CORPORATE PRIORITIES

Does pursuing a solution to this issue fit your personal priorities? As it is often a long journey be honest with yourself. If it's not, abandon it. In reality, Anna Haupt and Terese Alstin, were working together on a joint master's thesis in industrial design to complete their studies at the Faculty of Engineering. They realized that their industrial design master's thesis would be the perfect platform to study how to improve the traditional bicycle helmet.

4. CREATE CONDITIONS:
ORGANIZING THE RIGHT MOMENT, THE RIGHT TEAM, THE RIGHT PACE AND THE RIGHT FUNDING FOR YOUR INNOVATION INITIATIVE

In this case, all the conditions were set as their industrial design master's thesis provided an ideal opportunity and strict deadline.

5. IDEATE:
GENERATING AND CHOOSING ORIGINAL RELEVANT IDEAS FOR A PRODUCT, SERVICE, PROCESS OR EXPERIENCE

In practice, being out there in the discovery phase among non-users of the traditional bicycle helmet hearing all their frustrations brings out great ideas. The spark that created the basic idea for Hövding, was a remark by one cyclist, saying she wanted something "invisible". This was what the world was waiting for: "An invisible bicycle helmet. That wouldn't ruin your hair."

The solution Anna and Terese came up with was a collar that cyclists could wear discreetly around their necks. An airbag is folded into the collar and is not visible until the event of a collision. It's manufactured in collaboration with the airbag manufacturer Alva Sweden and includes clever high-tech devices also found in automobile airbags. The collar contains motion sensors that are tuned specifically to changes in momentum that are characteristic of a cycling accident. When the Hövding detects an impending crash, helium from a cartridge inflates the hood before the head makes contact with the windshield or asphalt. It stays inflated for a few seconds in case of multiple impacts during the same accident.

6. CREATE BUSINESS MODEL:
CREATING A VIABLE BUSINESS MODEL

The founders chose selling their product via their website and the retail channel. The recommended retail price of the invisible bicycle helmet is SEK 3,998 including VAT (about $475), making Hövding a premium priced solution. Traditional bicycle helmets are sold in a price range of $ 30 - $ 250. Hövding was first available at the DesignTorget's stores in Sweden and Norway and via the Hövding website.

7. SELECT TECHNOLOGY:
IDENTIFYING AND SELECTING THE RIGHT TECHNOLOGY TO DELIVER YOUR NEW PRODUCT, SERVICE, PROCESS OR EXPERIENCE

Choosing airbag technology to make an invisible helmet was an outside-the-box idea, resulting in a new-to-the-world innovation. Anna and Terese went far beyond making an improved traditional bicycle helmet. As a consequence, the development of the Hövding required seven years from idea to market launch. When you select technologies to create completely new solutions be sure that you select the right R&D partners, as their role is crucial. Also be sure that your project is among their priorities as well.

8. CHECK FREEDOM TO OPERATE:
CHECKING THAT YOU ARE NOT INFRINGING INTELLECTUAL PROPERTY RIGHTS OF OTHERS

Implementing a technology in a new application creates opportunities for filing patents to protect your invention. At an early stage, though, be sure that you first check your freedom to operate in your domain.

Hövding's unique application is patent protected. The founders filed a US Patent in October 2006 titled "a system and method for protecting a body part" (US 8402568 B2): A system and a method for protecting the head of a user in case of an abnormal movement, such as a fall or a collision. The system comprises an apparel (1), an airbag (2), an inflator (3), and a trigger. The airbag includes a first part (7) for surrounding the neck and back head portion of the user after inflation, and a second part (8) for forming a hood surrounding the skull of the user after inflation. The first part (7) and second part (8) are folded and arranged in the apparel (1) before inflation. The apparel is arranged around the neck of the user, like for example a collar or a scarf.[4]

9. EXPERIMENT:
CARRYING OUT A SYSTEMATIC RESEARCH OR TEST WHICH VALIDATES THE ADOPTION, ATTRACTIVENESS AND FEASIBILITY OF YOUR NEW PRODUCT, SERVICE, PROCESS OR EXPERIENCE

After the company was set up, the development of the Hövding required seven years from idea to market launch. How is it then possible to experiment in the idea phase at the start of innovation? Try to produce and confront potential customers with visuals of your new product (or service) idea or better yet: pretotypes or prototypes. Use their feedback for checking the attractiveness of your ideas and for improving it. Do this for as many times as is necessary. You can read more on pretotyping and prototyping in chapter 16.

10. CREATE NEW BUSINESS CASE: CREATING A WELL-FOUNDED CONVINCING BUSINESS CASE FOR YOUR NEW PRODUCT, SERVICE, PROCESS OR EXPERIENCE

The new concept was presented by Anna and Terese in a convincing way. They were awarded the Innovationbron's Ideas Grant, which kick started the process of developing Hövding into a real product. Hövding won the Venture Cup the following year in 2006, after which Hövding Sweden AB was founded. The development of the Hövding required seven years from idea to market launch. The company has 20 employees in Malmö. Since June 16, 2015, Hövding has had a listing on Nasdaq First North in Stockholm.

The story of Hövding is an amazing one. I hope it inspires you to transform a customer issue into a relevant new solution. In the next chapter, we will take the fourth and final route through the innovation maze: the Business Challenge Route, inspired by LEGO.

KEY MESSAGES FROM THIS CHAPTER

1. **A customer's pain point creates a willingness to change and to be open for new solutions that you might develop for them.**
2. **Once you pin down your customer's problem, you will be halfway to the solution. Keep digging deeper.**

Notes
1   Alison Coleman, "How Entrepreneurs Like Branson Hatch Their Best Business Ideas", Forbes, July 7, 2015.
2   Dyson website. http://www.dyson.co.uk/community/aboutdyson.aspx
3   https://news.gov.bc.ca/stories/frustration-the-mother-of-invention-for-entrepreneur
4   https://www.google.com/patents/US8402568

HÖVDING:
THE INVISIBLE BICYCLE HELMET

Statistics show that in Sweden cycling accidents cause about 40 deaths and about 30,000 injuries each year. One-third of cyclists involved in an accident sustain injuries to the head. A law requiring children under 15 years old to wear bicycle helmets was introduced by Sweden in 2005. The new law sparked a heated debate on whether mandatory helmet use should be extended to include adults as well.

In 2005, two students at Lund University in Sweden, Anna Haupt and Terese Alstin, were working together on a joint master's thesis in industrial design to complete their studies at the Faculty of Engineering. The prospect of being forced by law to wear a bicycle helmet was cause for concern. This was particularly true for people like Anna and Terese who say they wouldn't "be caught dead wearing a polystyrene helmet." As they explained it, "Producing a bicycle helmet that people would be happy to wear looked like a much better way to go than legislation forcing people to wear one or else." They realized that their industrial design master's thesis would be the perfect platform to study how to improve the traditional bicycle helmet.

Their first step was to survey people on the street asking why so few people wore bicycle helmets. The long list of reasons they were given included the following: 'They're a pain to carry about', 'They all look hideous', 'They ruin your hair', 'Nobody else wears them', and 'You can't get your hat on underneath'. Some sounded reasonable enough, while others were simply flimsy excuses. The message was clear; bicycle helmets were controversial. One way or another, everyone had a strong opinion about wearing a helmet. Many people who cycle say that they experience a sense of freedom on the road. Although most people know the traffic risks, they still aren't persuaded to wear a helmet. Basically, people want to protect their heads from injury in an accident, but draw a line about what is acceptable to wear. Based on these findings, Anna and Terese concluded that it wasn't the cyclists who needed to change; it was the product that needed to change.

Secondly, the survey asked people to describe the ideal bicycle helmet of the future. Some of the responses given were:

▸ 'Like a cool hat with a built-in helmet'
▸ 'Something small that you can fold up and put in your pocket'
▸ 'Something that lets you change what it looks like, like you can with mobile phone skins or wigs'
▸ 'Invisible'

Anna and Terese realized they were on to something the moment they saw the word "invisible". This was what the world was waiting for: "An invisible bicycle helmet. That wouldn't ruin your hair."

What started out as a graduation project resulted in a new-to-the-world concept. They named their airbag helmet Hövding, which is Swedish for chieftain. Their new concept was awarded the Innovationsbron's Ideas Grant, which kick-started the process of developing Hövding into a real product. Hövding won the Venture Cup the following year in 2006, after which Hövding Sweden AB was founded.

Hövding is a collar that cyclists can wear discreetly around their necks. An airbag is folded into the collar and is not visible until the event of a crash. It's manufactured in collaboration with the airbag manufacturer Alva Sweden, and includes clever high-tech devices also found in automobile airbags. The collar contains motion sensors that are tuned specifically to changes in momentum that are characteristic of a cycling accident. The sensors are charged via a USB cable and last for approximately 18 hours. The airbag can only be activated when the collar is put on, zipped up and the On-Off button fastened. When Hövding detects an impending crash, helium from a cartridge inflates the hood before the head makes contact with the windshield or asphalt. It stays inflated for a few seconds in case of multiple impacts during the same accident.

Anna and Terese pointed to tests that demonstrated that traditional plastic and foam bicycle helmets allow for high G-forces leading to an alarmingly high percentage of fatalities in accidents. Their breakthrough design – a motion-triggered inflatable helmet – shields a much greater portion of the head and neck, and provides a softer landing.

In 2012 the Swedish insurance company Folksam tested 13 bicycle helmets on the market. They carried out an impact test on the same principles for CE marking but with a higher impact speed, 25 km/h instead of 20 km/h. All the traditional helmets reached G-force values ranging from 196 to 294G. The lower the value, the better the helmet's ability to protect the cyclist's head. Hövding achieved 65G, providing at least three times better shock absorption than the other helmets.

The development of the Hövding required seven years from idea to market launch. After seven years and € 13 million in funding, sales of Hövding started in November 2011 at a recommended retail price of SEK 3,998 including VAT (about $475). Hövding was first available at the DesignTorget's stores in Sweden and Norway and via the Hövding website. In November 2011, Hövding held a fashion show to celebrate the sales launch and world premiere.

On June 8, 2015 Hövding signed a strategic development and production agreement with the Japanese company Nihon Plast, one of the leading airbag manufacturers. Nihon Plast will support their product development while providing production capacity to meet the increasing demand. Since being launched internationally it is now available in 15 markets in Europe and Japan. Hövding's products are sold in over 400 stores. In Sweden alone, Hövding's products can be found in more than 70 stores. The company has 20 employees in Malmö. Since June 16, 2015, Hövding has a listing on Nasdaq First North in Stockholm.

Anna Haupt left the company in December 2014 and Terese Alstin left in February 2015.

Source
http://www.hovding.com/pdf/hovding_once_upon_a_time_en.pdf. http://www.bbc.com/autos/story/20140626-no-helmet-no-problem. Business Week, An "Invisible" Bike Helmet From Sweden, Venessa Wong, April 26, 2012. Wikipedia. The Guardian, The Hövding collar: the cycle helmet that's more airbag than skid lid, May 18, 2014. De Zeen Magazine, February 1, 2011.

THE BUSINESS CHALLENGE ROUTE:

I FACE A BUSINESS CHALLENGE: NOW WHAT?

Market conditions can change spectacularly fast. You will be confronted with opportunities and threats like:

▸ Changing customer behavior due to newly available digital technology, which you do not yet provide and which in the long term will reduce your sales.
▸ Startups entering your market with quite a new offering, attracting a small innovative segment of your customers.
▸ A competitor coming up with a completely new business model, which you envy.

▸ The government changing the 'market rules' by liberalizing your market or changes their policy on subsidization of certain activities.
▸ Changing demographics, like a fast-growing elderly population.

Facing these business challenges, you have the choice of either being an active – or a reactive innovator. Active innovators, who want to innovate, give priority to innovation while company revenues are still growing. Before they reach maturity, they want to innovate to keep their revenue stream growing and stimulate an innovative mindset. One good example of this is Schattdecor, a € 600 million privately owned company in southern Germany. Schattdecor is the global market leader in printed decor paper. Their products find use in the kitchen, furniture and laminate flooring industry. The company operates 13 production facilities in Germany, Poland, Switzerland, Italy, Russia, China, Brazil, Turkey and the U.S.A. Total revenues of Schattdecor are still growing year by year as their market share increases. Still, they are well aware of new digital technologies, which might have a strategic impact on their markets. They innovate successfully with new products to grow the company further.

Reactive innovators, on the contrary, wait. Wary of all the innovation obstacles, they put blinders on when it comes to the early warning signals affecting their business environment and continue 'business as usual'. They often wait too long or until they get hit by a financial crisis. By that time, their markets may be saturated or have been disrupted by new technologies and/or business models. Once they have reached the decline stage; they not only need to prioritize innovation, but also reorganize and lay-off people. An excellent example of this is a toy company that we are all familiar with: LEGO, the producer of the colorful interlocking plastic blocks. Founded in 1916, LEGO had become really trendy by the 1980s with sales surging and profits doubling every five years. LEGO's growth was followed by a long period of stagnation lasting over a decade. The 1990s marked the end of a natural growth cycle. Between 1993 and 1998, LEGO had hoped to keep growing by tripling the number of new products to its line. Unfortunately, rather than increasing sales, this strategy only increased costs. Thus, resulting in 1998 in the first loss in LEGO's company history. In response to this crisis, the company announced the lay-off of 1,000 employees. Kjeld Kristiansen, the third generation of the Kristiansen family stepped down after heading the company for 20 years. He brought in a turnaround manager to do something major to change LEGO's course. LEGO needed to innovate.

In the Business-Challenge Route, I will illustrate how you can start innovation yourself when faced with a business challenge. Simply follow the 10 activities through the Innovation Maze in chart 13, using LEGO as a source of inspiration.

1. FOCUS:
DEFINING YOUR INNOVATION-CENTER-OF-INTEREST INCLUDING ALL THE BOUNDARY CONDITIONS

LEGO has just undergone a re-organization and you're on the LEGO innovation team now. Where do you start? First of all, by giving your innovation efforts some focus. In their first attempt, LEGO innovated in a variety of directions which only led to increasing risks and costs; proving that focus is essential.

Draft your innovation assignment. Make all the expectations and boundary conditions explicit with the help of six simple Wh-questions: Why? What do you want out of this as LEGO? What? Do you want to focus on products, or can LEGO expand to services too? Do you want to develop improved or completely new revolutionary products? Do you still want to focus on the toy market or do you want to broaden the scope? Who do you want to focus on as the target group for your innovation efforts? Children? For what age groups? Their families, as toy buyers? Where? Do you want to start to innovate in one country? Europe? Or take a worldwide perspective? When? Do you want your new products or services in 3 months? Or three years? Which? Which criteria will you, as LEGO, use to assess your new business cases? How much revenues are you aiming for? What margins? How much can LEGO still invest after its crisis? The deliverable is a concrete innovation assignment for LEGO, which will guide your innovation efforts (see chapter 9).

In reality, in their first innovation attempt LEGO headed off in lots of different directions. LEGO created its own children's clothing line and put a division of the LEGO Group in charge of pitching new ideas for books, movies and TV shows; all of these represented a completely new territory for LEGO. They introduced lots of different toys, some of which were big hits like LEGO Star Wars, LEGO Harry Potter and Bionicle. It soon became apparent that the company's growing complexity was becoming a huge problem. Innovating LEGO in a variety of directions only led to increasing risks and costs. After another reorganization, LEGO focused and decided to innovate much closer to the company's core.

2. CREATE CONDITIONS:
ORGANIZING THE RIGHT MOMENT, THE RIGHT TEAM, THE RIGHT PACE AND THE RIGHT FUNDING FOR YOUR INNOVATION INITIATIVE

Is this the right moment for LEGO? Well, LEGO waited until a financial crisis hit them, which means that the urgency was there. After the lay-off of 1,000 of your colleagues, it's your challenge to get the right team together at the start. Be sure to include top management in your project team. With a worldwide scope, be sure to include team members from all around the world. The more diverse in terms of cultures, roles and sexes a team is, the more creative it gets, provided the team atmosphere is good. Especially in a crisis be sure to address the pace and funding of the innovation initiative. In my experience, innovating after a crisis makes speed essential. If you can identify an innovative quick win in your project, be sure to prioritize it for the short term as it will build trust within the company that you indeed can innovate.

3. DISCOVER:
DISCOVERING TRENDS, MARKETS, TECHNOLOGIES AND CUSTOMER INSIGHTS

First of all, you need to get the blinders off at LEGO, which have been there for decades. Scrutinize trends that are happening in the way kids in several age categories on several continents spend their time. You might zoom in on markets where LEGO sales are going down sharply, to find out why this is happening.

Discover other product or service categories which focus on kids and are doing very well. Ask yourself the question: what can we learn from the successes of other products in 'kids entertainment'?

Be sure you also check out 'new technologies' used in toys. What is already out there? What is already feasible? What patents are filed in this domain and are interesting for you? What are the latest technological trends? What are successful initiatives of technology used in kids toys? What can you learn from these?

Connect to your users. Reach out and connect to both the buyers and users of LEGO. Who are heavy users? And why? Who are light or even non-users of LEGO? And why? What are the dislikes and pain points of both LEGO users and non-users? And what are their big dreams during playtime? Organize focus groups and do ethnographic research following users, mapping their playing behavior, pain points, likes and dislikes.

4. IDEATE:
GENERATING AND CHOOSING ORIGINAL RELEVANT IDEAS FOR A PRODUCT, SERVICE, PROCESS OR EXPERIENCE

Inspired by the trends, technologies and customer insights, It's now time for you together with your team at LEGO to start ideating new ideas for your LEGO innovation assignment. First, by generating real outside-the-box ideas and by postponing your judgment. Later by assessing those ideas on the criteria you set out in your innovation assignment.

In reality, in their second more focused attempt, LEGO went back to the original LEGO brick. They focused more on the police stations, the fire trucks and all the other things related; not only because that's what their fans wanted most, but also because it was the most profitable.

LEGO Friends is one example of LEGO's innovation success. In 2011, boys made up 90% of LEGO consumers. LEGO Friends, the new line developed for girls, consists of five distinct little dolls with names like Andrea, Mia, Olivia, Stephanie and Emma. Their LEGO sets encourage girls to build karate studios, beauty parlors and veterinary offices. The line doubled sales expectations in 2012, the year it was launched. In that year alone, LEGO tripled its sales to girls.

5. CREATE BUSINESS MODEL:
CREATING A VIABLE BUSINESS MODEL

After ideating, you try to come up with the right business model. Lego did not innovate their business model until recently when it launched LEGO's Ideas platform, where LEGO fans create proposals for new LEGO sets. It's up to the fans who make the proposals to look online for supporters for their new concepts. When a proposal attains 10,000 supporters, the project qualifies for review by LEGO's set designers and marketing representatives. The concept creator is featured in the set materials, receives a 1% royalty on sales of the total net sales of the product, and is recognized as the product creator.

6. SELECT TECHNOLOGY:
IDENTIFYING AND SELECTING THE RIGHT TECHNOLOGY TO DELIVER YOUR NEW PRODUCT, SERVICE, PROCESS OR EXPERIENCE

Once you've selected the best ideas, you identify and select the best technology to deliver it. As LEGO stayed 'so close to home', it used their common technologies, meaning not much excitement in this activity.

7. CHECK FIT:
CHECKING IF YOUR IDEA, TECHNOLOGY, CUSTOMER ISSUE OR BUSINESS CHALLENGE FITS YOUR PERSONAL AND CORPORATE PRIORITIES

An essential question for you is whether the new ideas fit the corporate priorities. Be sure to select the ones which will fit best, as they have the greatest chance to be successfully implemented in the back-end of the innovation process.

8. CHECK FREEDOM TO OPERATE:
CHECKING IF YOU DO NOT INFRINGE INTELLECTUAL PROPERTY RIGHTS OF OTHERS

When you're implementing a new technology it creates opportunities to file patents to protect your invention. Be sure before implementing it, though, that you first check if you do not infringe intellectual property rights of others.

9. EXPERIMENT:
CARRYING OUT A SYSTEMATIC RESEARCH OR TEST WHICH VALIDATES THE ADOPTION, ATTRACTIVENESS AND FEASIBILITY OF YOUR NEW PRODUCT, SERVICE, PROCESS OR EXPERIENCE

By experimenting of confronting your target audience with your new offering, you reduce risks and learn 'a hell of a lot'. Reducing risks is especially important when you start with a business challenge after a company has been reorganized. The next step must be a success, because you can't afford anymore failures. It took LEGO four years of research and experiments to figure out how to address the girls' market. As mentioned before, LEGO Friends, the new line developed for girls, turned out to be one of the biggest successes in LEGO's history.

10. CREATE NEW BUSINESS CASE:
CREATING A WELL-FOUNDED CONVINCING BUSINESS CASE FOR
YOUR NEW PRODUCT, SERVICE, PROCESS OR EXPERIENCE

With all the learnings in the first nine activities you draft a new business case: a well-founded concise plan which proves your idea is attractive, feasible and viable.

The innovation journey of LEGO, with one failed attempt and a very successful second one, has turned out to be a famous innovation case (chart 18). It provides great insights for vested incumbents in old markets; even if you haven't been innovative for decades you can still achieve innovative successes.

This marks the fourth and final Innovation Route through the innovation maze. In the next chapters, I will take you more in depth through each of the ten activities, starting in chapter 8 with Ideate.

KEY MESSAGES FROM THIS CHAPTER

1. Active innovators, who want to innovate, give innovation priority at the end of the growth stage. Reactive innovators, on the contrary, wait. They give innovation priority when the decline has set in.
2. When you're innovating after a crisis be sure to prioritize any innovative quick wins you have identified, as this will gain you trust within the company that you indeed can innovate.
3. By experimenting or confronting your target audience with your new offering you reduce risks, which is vital when your next move on the market must be a success because you can't afford anymore failures.

LEGO: INNOVATING CLOSE TO THE CORE

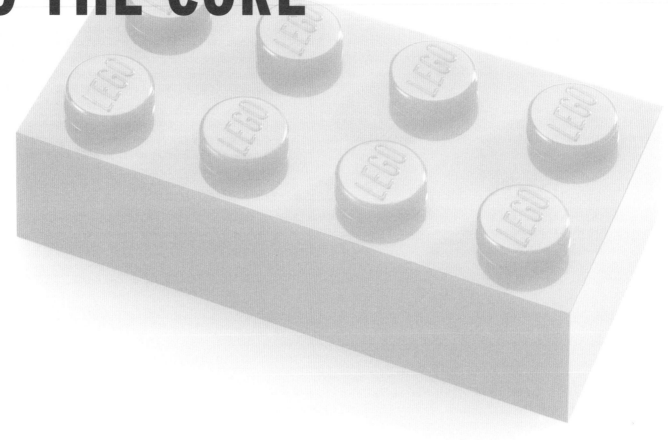

The origin of LEGO began in a carpenter's workshop in the town of Billund, Denmark in 1916. Ole Kirk Kristiansen switched from building houses and furniture to crafting wooden toys, which he named "lego" from the Danish "leg godt," meaning "play well." In 1947, Ole Kirk Christiansen expanded his product line with the purchase of the first plastic injection molding machine and started manufacturing plastic toy building-block bricks. His son, Godtfred Kirk Kristian-sen, worked at his side from the age of 12. By 1949, LEGO had developed the now-familiar plastic building blocks with circular interlocking studs. This was considered a great improvement over traditional wooden blocks. Now, children could create a greater variety of shapes held together with LEGO's unique interlocking blocks. By 1951, plastic blocks represented half of LEGO's output. The company continued to grow steadily throughout the sixties and seventies. By the 1980s, LEGO had become really trendy with sales surging and profits doubling every five years.

LEGO's growth was followed by a long period of stagnation lasting over a decade. The 1990s marked the end of a natural growth cycle. Birth rates declined in the Western world, children had less time to play and LEGO toys didn't offer the same instant gratification as video games. Another factor was that the Chinese were now able to copy the LEGO concept and manufacture the toy bricks at a fraction of the cost.

Between 1993 and 1998, LEGO had hoped to keep growing by tripling the number of new products to its line. Unfortunately, rather than increasing sales, this strategy only increased costs. Thus, resulting in 1998 in the first loss in the company history of LEGO. In response to this crisis, the company announced the lay-offs of 1,000 employees. Kjeld Kristiansen, the third generation of the Kristiansen family stepped down after heading the company for 20 years. He brought in turnaround manager Poul Plougmann to succeed him. Plougmann understood that the children's toy market was rapidly changing, with big retailers like Toys R Us and Walmart dominating the market and pushing prices down. Meanwhile, LEGO was still being produced in Denmark; making it unable to compete with the much cheaper toys produced in China. Plougmann knew LEGO had to do something major to change its course.

LEGO needed to innovate. And off they went; heading in lots of different directions. LEGO created its own children's clothing line and put a division of the LEGO Group in charge of pitching new ideas for books, movies and TV shows; all of these represented completely new territory for LEGO. They introduced lots of different toys, some of which were big hits like LEGO *Star Wars*, LEGO *Harry Potter* and Bionicle. In addition, LEGO building sets became increasingly complex with intricate components. Adding more bricks

meant products were harder to assemble, forecasts harder to determine, and inventory harder to manage.

It soon became apparent that the company's growing complexity was becoming a huge problem. Innovating LEGO in a variety of directions only led to increasing risks and costs. LEGO lost control of its innovative initiatives. In his book *Brick by Brick*, Professor David Robertson describes how the failed launching of LEGO's new product, Galidor, exemplifies just how vulnerable LEGO had become during this period of misguided innovation.

"This was one of the company's attempts to develop a full spectrum of innovation a family of complementary new products that reinforce and support each other. It featured a Power Rangers-like line of action figures that came with its own ecosystem of branded accompaniments. The toys themselves were intended to take LEGO into new aisles of the toy store; a risky journey, as only one in five action figures ends up a success. But the toys were only the beginning of Galidor's intended cross-pollination. There would also be Galidor Happy Meals at McDon-ald's, Galidor video games and Galidor DVDs. To cap it all, there would be that ultimate in toy marketing: a TV show serving as an extended commercial for the Galidor line. But when trying to fill an entire spectrum, it doesn't help if there's a gaping hole in the middle. The TV show that was supposed to be the foundation of the line's appeal turned out to be so bad that, in the words of Niels Milan Pedersen, one of Galidor's designers, top executives were 'gobsmacked with disgust'. Lacking an effective vehicle to publicize the toys, LEGO watched as sales essentially went nowhere. Less than a year after it was launched, Galidor was gone."

Similarly, sales of the successful LEGO sets from *Star Wars* and *Harry Potter* turned out to be very dependent on the release of new movies, leaving LEGO in 2003 and the first half of 2004 with only one profitable product, Bionicle. By 2003, LEGO was virtually out of cash and had lost $300 million.

The original turnaround needed to be reconsidered. Jørgen Knudstorp, the 35-year-old director of strategic development, was appointed CEO in 2004. Acting swiftly in order to survive, LEGO sold a majority stake in its successful Legoland theme parks for $460 million, moved management out of their Danish headquarters building into a nearby factory and outsourced the majority of its plastic brick production to cheaper plants in Mexico and the Czech Republic.

Knudstrop realized that more innovation was still needed. In a toy market with intense global competition and rapidly changing trends, you have to renew your product line every one or two years. And so, LEGO was left with no other choice than to innovate; but this time it needed to be effective and well thought out. The consensus at the LEGO headquarters was that the same outside-the-box-thinking that had driven them from 1999 to 2003 was also responsible for nearly driving them into the ground. LEGO's management gave everyone within the company room to ideate and create new growth initiatives. This time though, all the ideas contributed went through rigorous testing beforehand and needed to comply with the LEGO company mission to be universally recognized as the best company for family products. LEGO then developed a design process model around this and named it "Design for Business" (D4B) to ensure the continual linkage between innovation and its business plan. D4B marked a shift in strategy for innovation from being product-focused to being company-focused.

In essence, everything LEGO did from 2003 onwards evolved from the choice to go back in the box and innovate closer to the company's core. They went back to the original LEGO brick. They focused more on the police stations, the fire trucks and all the other things related; not only because that's what their fans wanted most, but also because it was the most profitable. When they went back in the box, they not only found that there was a lot of money in that box; they also found that LEGO fans were returning to the brand.

LEGO brought the creative team out of its silo and connected it to the company's business goals, allowing it to create under the umbrella of a company-wide strategy. The move brought LEGO's strategy back to life, with products that met both creativity and business needs. In his book *Brick by Brick*, Professor David Robertson credits LEGO for their approach, "They are wonderful at achieving that balance between giving their people the space to be creative, but the direction and focus to deliver profitable innovation."

Now if you work for LEGO in an innovation project, it's very likely you will be told: "Work on a great police station. Work on a great fire truck. Give us a great LEGO racecar. And by the way, don't use just any kind of piece or shape that you want or color that you want. Use this very limited palette of pieces. Because we can use these pieces in lots of different sets and make them in very high volume and make a lot of profit from every set that you make."

LEGO Friends is one example of LEGO's innovation success. In 2011, boys made up 90% of LEGO consumers. It took LEGO four years of research to figure out how to address the girls' market. LEGO Friends, the new line developed for girls, turned out to be one of the biggest successes in LEGO's history. LEGO Friends consists of five distinct little dolls with names like Andrea, Mia, Olivia, Stephanie and Emma.

Their LEGO sets encourage girls to build karate studios, beauty parlors and veterinary offices. The line doubled sales expectations in 2012, the year it was launched. In that year alone, LEGO tripled its sales to girls.

LEGO made good money from their inside-the-box-innovation approach by integrating small ideas and small innovations into their operation and by listening to their customers. In a 2013 interview, LEGO researcher Professor David Robertson summed up LEGO's recent results, "LEGO has been growing sales at 24% per year every year for the past five years and growing profits at 40% per year every year for the last five years. So they're doing something right."

Nowadays, LEGO has fully embraced the principles of open innovation and is recognized as one of the best practices in this field. On the LEGO Ideas platform (http://ideas.lego.com) LEGO fans create proposals for new LEGO sets. It's the fans who make the proposals who have to look online for supporters for their new concepts. When a proposal attains 10,000 supporters, the project qualifies for review by LEGO's set designers and marketing representatives. Once LEGO's criteria are met, the new LEGO set proposal can go into production, where the concept creator continues to provide input to the LEGO designers, whose job it is to create the final set. Once complete, it goes to the factory for manufacturing before being shipped around the world and released for sale. The concept creator is featured in set materials, receives a royalty on sales of 1% of the total net sales of the product, and is recognized as the product creator. Since the start in 2011, there have been 13 new LEGO sets introduced through this platform.

With a 15% increase in profit in 2014 to 7.03 billion Danish kroner ($1.05 billion) and a 24.6% operating profit margin, LEGO is still doing great. Its strategy of innovating close-to-the-core has really paid off.

Sources

1. Brickipedia, http://lego.wikia.com/wiki/LEGO_Ideas. 2. "Learning More About Creativity And Innovation From LEGO", Smashing Magazine, Rafiq Elmansy, August 8, 2014.
3. HBS CASES: "LEGO", Maggie Starvish, March 18th 2013, http://hbswk.hbs.edu/item/7170.html.
4. "How LEGO Stopped Thinking Outside the Box and Innovated Inside the Brick" http://knowledge.wharton.upenn.edu/article/how-lego-stopped-thinking-outside-the-box-and-innovated-inside-the-brick/.
5. "Innovation Almost Bankrupted LEGO – Until It Rebuilt with a Better Blueprint ", Knowledge@Wharton, July 18, 2012. http://knowledge.wharton.upenn.edu/article/innovation-almost-bankrupted-lego-until-it-rebuilt-with-a-better-blueprint/
6. *Brick by Brick: How LEGO Rewrote the Rules of Innovation and Conquered the Global Toy Industry*, David Robertson and Bill Breen, Crown Business, 2014.
7. "Lego Tries to Build a Better Brick", Wall Street Journal, July 12, 2015.
8. "Building success: how thinking 'inside the brick' saved Lego", Wired, October 9, 2013, David Robertson.
9. "Girls' Legos Are A Hit, But Why Do Girls Need Special Legos?", Neda Ulaby, June 29, 2013 http://www.npr.org/sections/monkeysee/2013/06/28/196605763/girls-legos-are-a-hit-but-why-do-girls-need-special-legos.

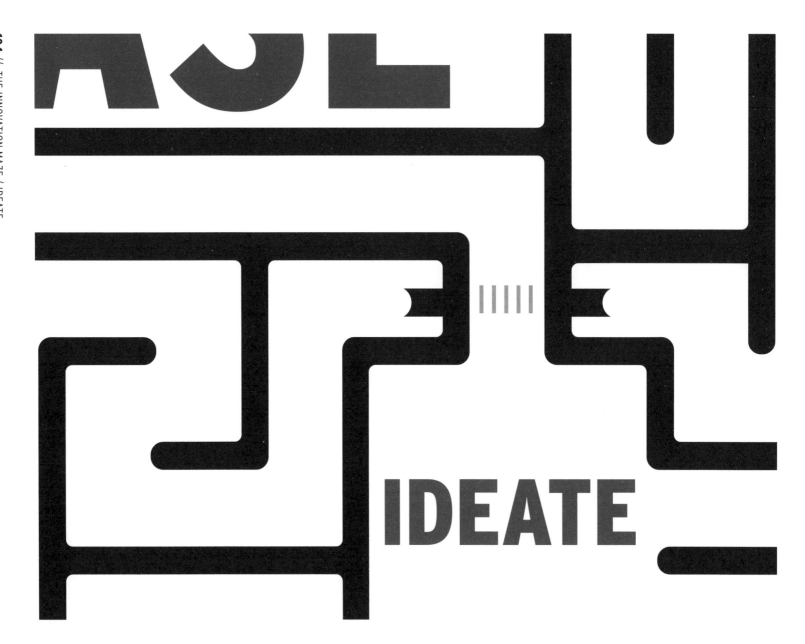

IDEATE

IDEATE

No matter how you start innovation, without any ideas there is no innovation. Ideation is an essential activity, incorporated in every route to a new offering. I would like to start this chapter discussing the moment ideas pop into your mind. Then, I will discuss the features of great ideas. In innovation your ideas will be about original new products, services, business models, experiences or processes. I will give you a great framework to come up with original ideas, called 'the 10 types of innovation', which I have used myself with great success. In a lot of cases you will ideate in a team and that's why I would like to help you with some practical tips on how to hold a great ideation workshop. Finally, I would like to share with you my five favorite idea generating techniques. In chapter 21, you'll find a full range of 21 ideation techniques for both generating and selecting ideas.

IDEAS ARE MOSTLY SLOW HUNCHES

Steven Johnson, author of *Where Good Ideas Come From*, describes ideas as slow hunches. He tells the wonderful story of how Tim Berners-Lee, invented the World Wide Web. "From a child's exploration of a hundred-year-old encyclopedia, to a freelancer's idle side project designed to help him keep track of his colleagues, to a deliberate attempt to build a new information platform that could connect computers across the planet, Berners-Lee's idea needed time – at least a decade's worth – to mature: Journalists have always asked me what the crucial idea was, or what the singular event was, that allowed the Web to exist one day when it hadn't the day before. They are frustrated when I tell them there was no

"Eureka" moment... Inventing the World Wide Web involved my growing realization that there was a power in arranging ideas in an unconstrained, web-like way. And that awareness came to me through precisely that kind of process. The Web arose as the answer to an open challenge, through the swirling together of influences, ideas and realizations from many sides, until, by the wondrous offices of the human mind, a new concept gelled. It was a process of accretion, not the linear solving of one problem after another."

An innovator like Richard Branson recognizes this 'slow hunch concept' in his daily work. He says: "Light bulb moments make for great stories, but we can't all be fortunate enough to come to realizations in the same manner as Sir Isaac Newton. For many, it's a gradual awakening rather than a sudden flash of genius."

Breakthrough innovations just don't happen overnight. Take a look at Nespresso for example, which very successfully commercialized the coffee-per-cup concept. The technology Nespresso uses dates back to the 1960s. Nestlé's R&D department had worked for about ten years tweaking the technology until it made a great cup of coffee. And after that it took another ten years in which Nestle worked out their innovative business model and marketing approach.[1]

YOUR BEST IDEAS POP UP IN YOUR MIND DURING SLACK TIME

It's scientifically proven that slack time sparks creativity. Let me ask you the question: At which moments of the day do you get your best ideas? Probably outside of work, right? You get them for example when you're just out of bed, under the shower, in the car or on a jog. Research on this subject among business professionals from all over the world on LinkedIn confirms this, as you can read in the following quotes.

My best ideas come to me....

▸ "in my dreams, either sleeping or day dreaming, while walking in the woods or outdoors in nature, but rarely when I am in the office."
▸ "lying in my bed just before sleeping; I often get up then to write down the idea in order not to forget it; when showering; when doing a walk in nature."
▸ "whilst driving, many times I have had to call my own phone leaving a voice mail with the idea before I forget it!"
▸ "walking the dog, I almost see things more clearly than sitting at a desk. Quieting the conscious mind giving the unconscious mind room to breathe."
▸ "late at night about 10 min after I go to bed. When my brain has slowed down and I am free to think whatever I want."

Now, there is a second reason explaining how innovation benefits from slack time. A recent study by professor Ajay Agrawal, Christian Catalini and Avi Goldfarb highlights a new aspect.[2] Slack time also makes you more innovative the more active you become. They analyzed activity on Kickstarter, the crowdfunding website, in nearly 6,000 American cities. They found out that "mundane, execution-oriented tasks, such as those associated with launching a crowdfunding campaign (e.g., administration, planning, promotion), are an important input to innovation that may benefit significantly from slack time." Slack time offers you the opportunity to DO something with your creative ideas. To get your idea launched requires a huge amount of work. So a time-off from your regular duties is a great enabler for getting all the operational and organizational red tape done. Both corporate innovators and startup founders know this so well from practice. Paul Graham, Founder of the renowned Y-Combinator, says in *How to Get Startup Ideas*: "It's

no coincidence that Microsoft and Facebook both got started in January. At Harvard that is (or was) Reading Period, when students have no classes to attend because they're supposed to be studying for finals."[3]

A lot of companies that struggle with becoming more innovative put extra pressure on their people, making them work harder to innovate in overtime. From practice I know that when pressure gets too high, no original ideas materialize. That's why renowned companies like Google, 3M and Wella have special slack time policies to spark innovative ideas and activities among their employees. So, if you want to be innovative, do yourself and your employees a favor; give yourself some slack! In this way you create an inspiring environment where people can get 'slow hunches' and work on them, which is essential to spark innovation.

GREAT IDEAS ARE RELEVANT, FEASIBLE AND VIABLE

Have you ever shared new big ideas at work? What happened...? Did they give you a standing ovation? Did someone bake you a cake to celebrate? Did you get promoted? Or am I being a little too optimistic? Well you're in good company as you can see in chart 20, where I list 10 great ideas that were originally rejected, like: the telephone, the copier, overnight delivery service like Federal Express and the Nautilus fitness machines.

Of course, there are companies with a great culture for innovation where new big ideas are embraced by everyone. However, most of you were probably victims of the more common 'Not-Invented-Here' phenomenon. Your colleagues rejected your new idea because of an unwillingness to value the work of others or fear from a lack of understanding. Although many people say they are entrepreneurial, in practice most people are adverse to risk. You probably got shot down with some idea-killer remarks like these:

▸ Yes, but...
▸ Our customers won't like that!

- We don't have time...
- NO!
- It's not possible...
- It's too expensive!
- Let's be realistic...
- That's not logical...
- GET REAL...

Innovation is a paradox for most of us. On the one hand you are well aware that you have to turn off somewhere before you reach the end of the dead end street you're heading down. On the other hand, it is risky. It takes a lot of time. And it takes a lot of resources. As an innovator you can fight this risk-adverse culture, as a kind of modern Don Quixote fighting windmills. Or you can accept it. It is only when you have accepted it, that you can deal with it.

I have learned that to convince the management of an organization or (in)formal investors to let your innovative idea enter the formal development process and give you the resources needed, you must bring a well-founded convincing new business case to the table. Now the crucial word in the last sentence is 'convincing'. This means you really must know your stuff. In the boardroom your idea will be evaluated from at least four perspectives:
- The customer: will they buy it?
- The technology: can we deliver it?
- The business model: will it pay off?
- The risk: will it be a failure? Will it be a huge success?

Now if you want to bring back a new business case fulfilling these criteria, it means your great new idea must be relevant, feasible and viable.

I have five tips that might get you more support for your great ideas.
1. Dogs bark at what they don't know. So beware of this. Make clear in advance what kind of innovative ideas they can expect (a small improvement or revolutionary new to the world idea).

Include them when you make an innovation assignment for your project.
2. Make clear "what's in it for us". So present your innovative idea with a concrete case for new business showing estimates of sales and profit potential, as I will show you in chapter 17.
3. Make the feasibility clear. Can we make it? What will it cost?
4. Make clear there's a market out there from your experiments. Lead users and co-creation partners are perfect advocates to prove there's a potential market.
5. Invite top managers or financers to join your innovation journey from the start.

IDEATE ON 10 TYPES OF INNOVATION

When you innovate, most people automatically focus on the product. It's an obvious starting point. A product has a lot of aspects though and a lot of other types of innovation to integrate into your new offering. Larry Keeley and his colleagues did a wonderful job in structuring innovation in 10 types, analyzing nearly 2,000 examples of the then best innovations as of 1998.[4] The framework, presented in chart 21, has been improved ever since. Based on this framework, they developed over 100 innovation tactics which are very useful to ideate breakthroughs for your sector. When coming up with new product (or service) ideas consider the following types of innovation.

1. Profit model. How you make money.
2. Network. How you connect with others to create value.
3. Structure. How you organize and align your talent and assets.
4. Process. How you use signature or superior methods to do your work.
5. Product performance. How you develop distinguishing features and functionality.
6. Product System. How you create complementary products and services.

7. Service. How you support and amplify the value of your offerings.
8. Channel. How you deliver your offerings to customers and users.
9. Brand. How you represent your offerings and business.
10. Customer engagement. How you foster compelling interactions.

First, analyze the present offerings in the industry in which you want to innovate. And then ideate with the help of the 100 innovation tactics. Use these tools to come up with original new ideas where you try to innovate among as many types as possible for each new offering. Experience has shown that with real breakthrough innovations at least 5 of the 10 types can be checked off.

GREAT IDEATION WORKSHOPS ARE LIKE A COMPLEX PUZZLE TO SOLVE: EVERY PIECE COUNTS.

The American Alex Osborn is the spiritual father of brainstorming. He is also one of the founders (and the 'O') of the renowned worldwide advertising agency BBDO. In 1948, he published a book called *Your Creative Power*. In the chapter "How to Organize a Squad to Create Ideas", he describes how members of a group working together should engage in a "brainstorm," that is; "using the brain to storm a creative problem—and doing so in commando fashion, with each stormer attacking the same objective." Two essential rules are:

▸ Defer your judgment
▸ Go for quantity

The underlying assumption of brainstorming is that people are scared of saying something wrong. In a period when employees were not encouraged to speak up, brainstorming was experienced as revolutionary. Since the fifties a lot of people have challenged the effectiveness of brainstorms. Keith Sawyer, a psychologist at Washington University, once summed up the science concluding that, "Decades of research have consistently shown that brain-storming groups think of far fewer ideas than the same number of people who work alone and later pool their ideas." Research of Bernard Nijstad and Wolfgang Stroebe confirmed that brainstorming in a group has two major shortcomings.[5]

1. Individuals often produce fewer ideas and ideas of lower quality in group settings as compared when they work alone.
2. When people have to wait for others to complete their turn before presenting their idea, ideas are often lost.

Nijstad elaborated to say that being part of a group only gives you the illusion of group productivity. His findings show that group members are more satisfied with their performance than individuals, despite having generated fewer ideas. The group setting makes you feel more productive. This feeling is attributed to the group experiencing fewer instances in which someone is unable to generate ideas.

Luckily, ideation has evolved since the fifties. Back then, it was common practice that all participants could spontaneously shout out their ideas. This led to chaotic situations whereby the individual thought process was constantly interrupted. Furthermore, in large brainstorming groups most participants had to wait too long before they could unleash their ideas, which caused some ideas to vanish before anyone even had a chance to hear them.

Being aware of the pitfalls of a brainstorm with a group, I fine-tuned the method of brainstorming. Team members first get the opportunity to start generating new ideas in complete silence. They each write their ideas on separate post-it notes: brainwriting. Afterwards, everybody quickly reads their ideas out loud to the group. This has a very stimulating effect on the participants as they are encouraged to continue listening and to elaborate on their own ideas. How the participants are positioned in the room also has a stimulating effect as they are seated in a horseshoe formation (without tables) and can see each other clearly. This way, the idea of one participant is a source of inspiration for the other. Brainstorming this way for a couple of rounds using different techniques usually leads to 750+ ideas on the idea wall.

Of course, a lot of other factors matter as well. In my practice, I have found 25 elements which are necessary in creating a perfect ideation workshop:

Highly relevant
▸ Define a relevant innovation assignment, which is a challenge for the organization and the people you invite.
▸ Make the assignment concrete and s.m.a.r.t.
▸ Create momentum for ideation. Something important must happen now!

Diverse group of participants
▸ Invite people for whom the assignment is personally relevant.
▸ Invite people for both content as well as decision-making capabilities.
▸ Include outsiders and outside-the-box thinkers.
▸ Include an even mix of men and women, young & old, et cetera.
▸ Invite the internal senior problem-owner (CEO or vice president) to participate.

Special setting
▸ Look for a special and harmonious venue, fitting your innovation assignment.
▸ Create an (emotionally) safe environment where you can be yourself.
▸ Don't allow smartphones and iPads to ring or flash.
▸ Never - and I really mean never do any brainstorming at the office.

Effectively structured process
▸ Allow at least two days for effective ideation to reach concrete new concepts.
▸ Spend twice as much time on the convergence process as on the divergence process.
▸ Plan and prepare an effective combination of idea-generating techniques.
▸ Be open to suggestions from the group to adapt the process.

▸ Make sure it is enjoyable. Fun promotes good results.
▸ Time box. Make sure everybody is aware of the time limits- and sticks to them.
▸ Hire a visualizer or cartoonist to visualize the results
▸ Keep up the pace; otherwise it becomes long-winded and boring.

Facilitated by a professional
▸ Appoint an (internal) facilitator, who stays in the background and exercises light control.
▸ The facilitator should reflect the opposite energy of the group. If the group is too active: exert calmness.
▸ The facilitator mustn't lose sight of sub groups; constantly monitoring their progress.

Concrete output
▸ Make the output very concrete and clear to anybody.
▸ Creating concepts together with your colleagues generates maximum internal support.

The experience of sharing ideas in a structured process and drafting concrete concepts from the best ideas has a great impact on group dynamics. At the end the whole group feels ownership of all the concepts. That is essential. New ideas need a lot of 'parents' to survive the product development process in a corporate culture.

MY 5 FAVORITE IDEA-GENERATING TECHNIQUES

There are a lot of Ideation techniques available. Every day new variations are being made. In chapter 20, I have shared a full range of 21 ideation techniques both for generating – and selecting ideas. Although in the creative process converging is at least as important as diverging, I would like to give you some insight into my own preferences in idea generation techniques. Why? Because there are hundreds of them you could use, many more than on the converging side.

Here are my 5 favorite idea-generating techniques, which are described more extensively in chapter 21.

1. The Braindump. The brain dump is the starting technique for any ideation workshop; to empty your mind, unleashing the first spontaneous ideas. The participants 'brain dump' whatever comes to mind first and the facilitator then harvests these ideas. Postponing your judgment is essential. Emptying your head is essential. Before any new, original ideas can pop-up, all the old ideas must first be out of your mind.

2. Customer Frictions. Customer frictions are pain points of users or non-users of a product or service category. Meeting customers in person and finding out the frictions of the customer provide a wonderful source of inspiration for innovative ideas. Select the most relevant customer frictions from the Discovery phase and ideate solutions for them with this technique to be sure you're ideating relevant new ideas.

3. "Crawl into the Skin of". This is a fun technique to do and brings out essential new ideas. You identify yourself with the "product your innovating", for example frozen yogurt. You crawl into its skin and ask yourself two questions: 1. "If I was frozen yogurt, how would I feel?" Once you really get into it, you ask the question: 2. If I was frozen yogurt, how would I innovate myself?" This generates real outside the box ideas. I promise.

4. "What Would Apple Do?" As in the last technique you crawl into the skin, but now of another organization. With this brainstorming technique ideas are generated by crawling into the skin of another company, organization or group like Apple, IKEA, McDonald's or Toyota. When the participants imagine themselves as working for this company, ideas are created in their new role. With this technique people cross the barriers of their own organization. Works perfectly. Every time.

5. The Trends Dance. This energizing brainstorming technique will take you far outside the box combining various future trends. It gets people up on their feet, moving and dancing, and is very well-suited as the final idea generation tool. You select as many future trends as there are participants and write down each one separately on a stringed card. Turn on dancing music at a high volume. When the music plays, have the participants start dancing and moving around the room. When the music stops, instruct the participants to stop dancing and team up in pairs. Their assignment is to come up with as many ideas as possible based on the trends on both cards and jot these down on the post-its. This is repeated several times. I really love this one as it generates a huge number of ideas. Tip: you might also use "the 100 innovation tactics of the ten types of innovation", instead of trends.

To finalize this section on ideating, I like to quote Scott D. Anthony.[6] He hits the nail on the head in his statement, "every great idea is partially right and partially wrong." For us, as innovators, it's of the highest priority to find out which of the elements of a new concept belongs to which category. That's why experimentation is such an important activity to get you through the maze with an idea that is right at the end of the beginning.

In the next chapter on Focus, I will describe how you can draft an excellent innovation assignment which gives clear directions.

KEY MESSAGES FROM THIS CHAPTER

1. No matter how you start innovation; when there are no ideas, there is no innovation.
2. Ideas are mostly slow hunches.
3. Your best ideas pop up in your mind during slack time.
4. Great ideas are relevant, feasible and viable.
5. Defer your judgment, most of the time, or you will kill everything.
6. Every great idea is partially right and partially wrong. [Scott D. Anthony]

Notes

[1] Tony Davila & Marc J. Epstein, *The Innovation Paradox*, Berret-Koehler Inc., San Francisco, 2014, p. 88.

[2] Social Science Research Network, Slack Time and Innovation, April 25, 2015, http://papers.ssrn.com/sol3/papers.cfm?abstract_id=2599004

[3] Social Science Research Network, Slack Time and Innovation, April 25, 2015, http://papers.ssrn.com/sol3/papers.cfm?abstract_id=2599004

[4] Larry Keeley, Ryan Pikkel, Brian Quinn, Helen waters, *Ten Types of Innovation*, Wiley, Hoboken, New Jersey, 2013, p. 16-17.

[5] Bernard Nijstad, *How the Group Affects the Mind: Effects of Communication in Idea Generating Groups*, 2000.

[6] Scott D. Anthony, *The First Mile*, Harvard Business Review Press, Boston, Massachusetts, 2014, p 184.

10 GREAT IDEAS THAT WERE

"This 'telephone' has too many shortcomings to be seriously considered as a means of communication. The device is inherently of no value to us." Western Union internal memo dated 1876.

"I do not believe the introduction of motor-cars will ever affect the riding of horses" Mr. Scott-Montague, MP, in the United Kingdom in 1903.

"The wireless music box has no imaginable commercial value. Who would pay for a message sent to nobody in particular?" David Sarnoff's Associates rejecting a proposal for investment in the radio in the 1920s.

"Who the hell wants to hear actors talk?" H.M. Warner (Warner Brothers) before rejecting a proposal for movies with sound in 1927.

"This is typical Berlin hot air. The product is worthless." Letter sent by Heinrich Dreser, head of Bayer's Pharmacological Institute, rejecting Felix Hoffmann's invention of aspirin. At that point, Bayer was standing by its 'star' painkiller diacetylmorphine. This alternative drug reportedly made factory workers feel animated and 'heroic', which is why Bayer decided to aptly name it 'heroin'. Later on, due to its 'funny' side effects it was decided to take heroin off the market. Bayer's chairman eventually intervened to overrule Dreser's decision and accept aspirin as Bayer's main painkiller. More than 10 billion tablets of aspirin are swallowed annually.

"Who the hell wants to copy a document on plain paper???!!!" Rejection letter in 1940 to Chester Carlson, inventor of the XEROX machine. In fact, over 20 companies rejected his "useless" idea between 1939 and 1944. Even the National Inventors Council dismissed it. Today, the Rank Xerox Corporation has an annual revenue in the range of one billion dollars.

"The concept is interesting and well-formed, but in order to earn better than a 'C,' the idea must be feasible." A Yale university professor in response to Fred Smith's paper proposing reliable overnight delivery service. Smith went on to found Federal Express.

ORIGINALLY REJECTED

"There is no reason anyone would want a computer in their home." Ken Olsen (President, Chairman and founder of Digital Equipment Corp) in 1977.

"You want to have consistent and uniform muscle development across all of your muscles? It can't be done. It's just a fact of life. You just have to accept inconsistent muscle development as an unalterable condition of weight training." Rejection letter to Arthur Jones, who invented the Nautilus Fitness Machine.

"So we went to Atari and said, 'Hey, we've got this amazing thing, even built with some of your parts, and what do you think about funding us? Or we'll give it to you. We just want to do it. Pay our salary, we'll come work for you.' And they said, 'No.' So then we went to Hewlett-Packard, and they said, 'Hey we don't need you. You haven't got through college yet.' Apple Computer Inc. founder Steve Jobs on attempts to get Atari and HP interested in his and Steve Wozniak's personal computer.

Source
Greekchat.com. http://www.greekchat.com/gcforums/showthread.php?t=45503

10 TYPES OF INNOVATION

PROFIT MODEL	NETWORK	STRUCTURE	PROCESS	PRODUCT PERFORMANCE
How you make money	How you connect with others to create value	How you organize and align your talent and assets	How you use signature or superior methods to do your work	How you develop distinguishing features and functionality
(e.g. premium, metered use or micro transactions)	(e.g. alliances, franchising or supply chain integration)	(e.g. asset standardization, incentive systems or organizational design)	(e.g. lean production, on-demand production or user-generated)	(e.g. ease of use, customization or styling)

CONFIGURATION
4 Types of innovation are focused on the innermost workings of an enterprise and its business system

OFFERING
2 Types of innovation are focused on an enterprise's core product or service

Source
Larry Keeley, Ryan Pikkel, Brian Quinn, Helen Waters, Ten Types of Innovation,
Wiley, Hoboken, New Jersey, 2013, pp. 16-17.

PRODUCT SYSTEM	SERVICE	CHANNEL	BRAND	CUSTOMER ENGAGEMENT
How you create complementary products and services	How you support and amplify the value of your offerings	How you deliver your offerings to customers and users	How you represent your offerings and business	How you foster compelling interactions
(e.g. complements, modular systems or product bundling)	(e.g. lease or loan, self-service, total experience management)	(e.g. experience center, go direct, pop-up presence)	(e.g. brand leverage, co-branding, private label)	(e.g. curation, experience simplification or status and recognition)

EXPERIENCE
4 Types of innovation are
focused on more customer-facing
elements of an enterprise and its
business system

QUOTE BY MICHAEL DELL

WHAT:
FOUNDER OF DELL INC.

HOW TO BE SUCCESSFUL:
1. HAVE A BIG DREAM
2. BREAK THE REGULAR VALUE CHAIN (SELL DIRECT)
3. SPEND TIME WITH CUSTOMERS

Sources
1. http://www.entrepreneur.com/article/197566#ixzz2swNJpj69
2. Dell: The secrets to his success http://www.inc.com/articles/1999/09/15567.html
3. http://www.biography.com/people/michael-dell-9542199
4. http://en.wikipedia.org/wiki/Michael_Dell

'YOU DON'T HAVE TO BE
A GENIUS OR A VISIONARY
OR EVEN A COLLEGE GRADUATE
TO BE SUCCESSFUL.
YOU JUST NEED A FRAMEWORK
AND A DREAM.'

ority for innovation

No fit

ategy

arket need

No

FO
CUS

FOCUS

How do you start innovation in practice? Often there's a senior manager experiencing an urgent need for something new, fueled by a business challenge. A new competitor may have entered the market; revenues may have decreased dramatically or a big contract has been lost. And something needs to happen: we must innovate. One essential point is often missed at the start: innovation ideas for what? That's the question! When you focus your efforts, you're much more productive. That's what this chapter is about: choosing a clear focus for innovation. I will give an example of Zumba's focus and show you how to draft a concrete innovation assignment.

CHOOSE A CLEAR FOCUS FOR INNOVATION

When you read the strategy reports of your organization, do you get a clear picture of the direction your organization is headed? Generally, strategic reports tend to be vague on innovation. Lots of times they mention that we have to innovate, but not how, where and for whom.

The innovation opportunities for your organization are infinite. There are hundreds of great ideas out there. You should guide and sometimes even restrict your activities in the front end of innovation to certain specific areas, as your resources are limited in terms of time, people and money. In practice, I have experienced that focusing increases the chance that you will find great opportunities that match your organization. The better you know what you are looking for, the easier it will be to spot it.

Apple is an example of a very successful company with a clear innovation focus. As Michael Schrage describes in his book *The Innovator's Hypothesis*: "Steve Jobs was a strategic value innovator. The numbers -not just his company's products - say so. Apple spent far less on research and development (R&D) than its competitors during its recent decade of rapid growth. Despite the competition investing more R&D dollars on both an absolute and a percentage of sale basis, Apple enjoyed significantly greater innovation returns. Did Apple have its innovation failures? Of course. But none were spectacularly expensive. Steve Job's company carved out remarkable safety margins in its innovation investment. How was that possible? Focus. Apple focused on its interface design and form factors, as well as facilitating elegantly simple and simply elegant user experiences. Lower prices matter less than higher perceived value."[1]

Zumba, the popular fitness routine is a great example in the services industry of an explicit focus which provides clear criteria for assessing potential innovations. Zumba's founders rely on two simple rules that help them quickly identify the most promising innovations from the flood of proposals they receive. First, any new product or service must help the instructors—who not only lead the classes but carry Zumba's brand, and drive sales of products—to attract clients and keep them engaged. Second, the proposal must deliver FEJ (pronounced "fedge"), which stands for "freeing, electrifying joy". Read chart 21 for more on Zumba's focus.

SHOULD YOU FOCUS ON INCREMENTAL INNOVATIONS, BREAKTHROUGH INNOVATIONS OR BOTH?

Should you focus on incremental innovations, radical innovations, or both? This depends on your role and situation. Startups mostly enter a market with a radical innovation. Facebook, and Twitter created new markets with new-to-the-world offerings. Tesla, Uber and Airbnb broke into existing markets surprising the incumbents with their new-to-the-world offerings. Existing organizations are mostly reactive innovators, which puts them in the situation where they have to quickly come up with innovations as the urgency is high. For them, incremental innovations are faster to develop with less risk. However, that won't be enough in the long term as they also have to come up with radical innovations in order for their organization to grow again in the longer term. It's essential that you find a good balance between incremental innovations, improvement of present products and services, and radical innovations focusing on big ideas which are outside the present comfort zone of your organization. With incremental innovations you prove to your customers and staff that you indeed can innovate and thereby build the confidence you will need to make bigger strides, once your radical innovations hit the market later.

HOW TO DRAFT AN INNOVATION ASSIGNMENT

To draft an innovation assignment you invite the relevant stakeholders, mostly your senior management, for an innovation focus workshop, where they will have to be explicit about their expectations on the results from the innovation process. This forms the guidelines for your innovation team when you are underway. You can formulate the innovation assignment with the help of the following six questions:

1. Why? (Why do we want to innovate?);
2. Who? (Who is the target group: BtB vs BtC; existing vs new customer groups);
3. Where? (For which distribution channels, countries, regions or continents)
4. What? (Evolutionary or revolutionary: products, services or business models)
5. When? (Intended year of introduction)
6. Which? (Which criteria should the new concepts meet?)

Often your board has not yet defined the criteria the new offerings should meet. Then it helps to ask some questions. In practice, you will go a long way with the following eight questions:

1. Revenues. How much revenue must the innovations realize during the first three years? Or, if new offerings compete with existing products, how much extra revenue must be realized?
2. Profit. What profit margin or EBIT (earnings before interest and taxes) should the new concept realize?
3. New. Should the new concept be new to the company, new to the market, new to the country or new to the world?
4. Appeal. How attractive and pioneering to the target group does the new product concept need to be?
5. Promotion. To what extent do we want the product concept to create buzz and hype among potential customers?
6. Positioning. To what extent should the new product concept fit the current brand positioning?
7. Production. Do we produce the new product ourselves (with our own manufacturing facilities) or can we co-create with partners?
8. Strategic fit. To what extent should the new product concept fit the business strategy of the organization?

Be sure to be ambitious when you quantify these criteria, as "The greatest danger for most of us is not that our aim is too high and we miss it, but that it is too low and we reach it." [Michelangelo, Italian sculptor, painter, architect, poet, and engineer]

A real-life example of an innovation assignment drafted by The City Bin Co., an Irish company and part of environmental solutions provider Averda, helps get you on the right track.

"The B2B waste collection industry is tired and stale. It has not evolved, in relative terms, resulting in a business model and approach that has gone unquestioned for decades. Hence, we firmly believe an opportunity exists to create innovations that distance The City Bin Co., in meaningful ways, from the competition.

Our mission is to disrupt the B2B waste collection industry! We will transform the status quo by unleashing a distinctive, elegant offering that creates exceptional value for customers and provides an experience which they would fear to lose. Equally, competitors will be unable or unsure how to react.

For the company, it will mean an explosion in revenue and profit. We will become 'the' leader in our chosen markets and a case study for other firms globally.

We will focus on the Dublin SME sector, or comparable organizations where decisions can be made quickly.
At the end of our assignment, we will generate at least four mini new business cases (MNBCs) which can be launched to the Irish market in 2015/2016. At least one significant MNBC will be introduced in 2015. Furthermore, at least one MNBC will unearth an unserved business need that is capable of expanding the market.

Each new MNBC must meet the following criteria:
1.   € 15M turnover by the end of the second year.
2.   An EBITDA of 25% within 6 months of launch.
3.   A CAPEX requirement at least 30% less than the current norm.
4.   A mechanism for managing customer churn to below 5%.
5.   Transferable to the UK within 12 months and to the USA within 24.
6.   Capable of creating WOWs in the form of written compliments."

Once you have a smart, clear and concise innovation assignment that has the support of your management, it will easier for you to proceed with selecting the best team members for your innovation journey. Before starting though, in the next chapter we will first Check the Fit of the assignment with your personal and or corporate goals to be sure that you are off on the right route.

KEY MESSAGES FROM THIS CHAPTER

1.   **If an innovation initiative doesn't fit the focus of your organization it will be killed sooner or later.**
2.   **It's essential that you find a good balance between incremental innovations and radical innovations.**
3.   **When you draft an innovation assignment invite your senior management to be explicit about their expectations on the results of the innovation process.**
4.   **Be sure to be ambitious when you quantify your goals.**

Note
[1]   Michael Schrage, *The Innovator's Hypothesis*, The MIT Press, Cambridge, Massachusetts, 2014, p. 53.

The Zumba fitness routine was developed when Alberto Perez, a Colombian aerobics instructor, forgot to take his exercise tape to class and used what he had at hand – a tape of salsa music. Today, Zumba is a global business that offers classes at 200,000 locations in 180 countries to over 15 million customers drawn by the ethos "Ditch the workout. Join the party."

Zumba's executives actively seek out suggestions for new products and services from its army of over 100,000 licensed instructors. Other companies routinely approach Zumba with possible partnership and licensing agreements. In fact, it is deluged by ideas for new classes (Zumba Gold for baby boomers), music (the first Zumba Fitness Dance Party CD went platinum in France), clothing, fitness concerts, and video games, such as Zumba Fitness for Nintendo Wii.

ZUMBA'S INNOVATION FOCUS

Zumba's founders rely on two simple rules that help them quickly identify the most promising innovations from the flood of proposals they receive. First, any new product or service must help the instructors—who not only lead the classes but carry Zumba's brand, and drive sales of products—to attract clients and keep them engaged. Second, the proposal must deliver FEJ (pronounced "fedge"), which stands for **"freeing, electrifying joy"** and distinguishes Zumba from the "no pain, no gain" philosophy of many fitness classes.

Zumba's rules are few in number, which makes them straightforward to remember, communicate, and use. They also make it easy for the founders to describe the kinds of innovations most likely to be chosen and to explain why specific ones weren't. Capping the number of rules forces a relentless focus on what matters most, as well.

Zumba's success depends on the passion of its instructors and the differentiation of its offering from less playful exercise options. The rules encapsulate the essence of the company's strategy.

Source
McKinsey Quaterly, May 2015, Donald Sull. http://www.mckinsey.com/insights/innovation/the_simple_rules_of_disciplined_innovation

QUOTE BY
SHIGERU MIYAMOTO

WHAT:
CREATOR OF SUPER MARIO, DONKEY KONG AND THE NINTENDO WII

HOW TO BE SUCCESSFUL:
1. **START FROM SCRATCH**
2. **BE THE FIRST ONE**
3. **LISTEN TO YOUR INNER VOICE**

Sources
1. http://www.brainyquote.com/quotes/authors/s/shigeru_miyamoto.html#WZx0qatd6whZruQ4.99
2. http://nintendoeverything.com/why-shigeru-miyamoto-makes-games/
3. http://www.newyorker.com/reporting/2010/12/20/101220fa_fact_paumgarten
4. http://www.timeforkids.com/news/get-know-shigeru-miyamoto/84311
5. http://www.mariomayhem.com/shigeru_miyamoto.php
6. http://www.entrepreneur.com/article/200524#ixzz2tZIQ0qie

'TO CREATE A NEW STANDARD, YOU HAVE TO BE UP FOR THAT CHALLENGE AND REALLY ENJOY IT.'

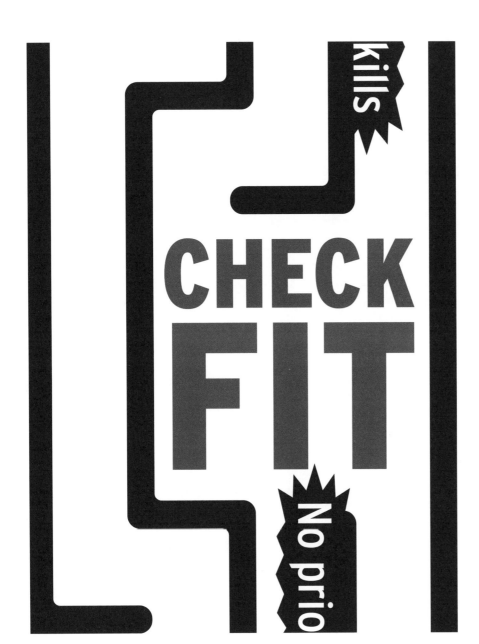

CHECK FIT

When you (and your team) have come up with great ideas the question is how to make them reality. In practice, I have learned that if they don't fit your personal goals as a start-up founder or your organizational goals as a corporate innovator, nothing will materialize in the end. It is essential to check this fit as early as possible in your journey through the innovation maze. As soon as you've got ideas and a business model worked out be sure to check if there's a good match. That's why in this chapter I will be going deeper into checking this.

IDEAS ARE STOPPED BY A LOT OF 'NOES'

The single biggest obstacle at the start of innovation is one single word: no. As your idea is new, otherwise it's not innovation, it will get a lot of opposition. As startup partners and financers will confront you with a lot of doubts. As a corporate innovator it will be your colleagues and managers giving comments like:
1. No, we have always done it this way...
2. No, our customers won't like that!
3. No, we don't have time for this...
4. No, it's not possible...
5. No, it's too expensive!
6. No, let's be realistic...
7. No, that's not logical...
8. No, we need to do more research...
9. No, there's no budget...
10. No, top management won't agree...
11. No, the market is not ready yet...
12. No, it might work in other places but not here...
13. No, that's way too risky...
14. No, it doesn't fit our strategy...
15. No, that's for the future...

Be prepared to be met by all these idea-killers along the way. It might even spin you out of your company, as there is strong evidence that many of the new ideas implemented in new ventures are generated while the employee was working for a parent firm in the same industry: 71% of all startups replicated or modified an idea encountered in previous jobs.[1]

PEOPLE AND COMPANIES ARE RISK-AVERSE

The origin of all the opposition you encounter is that in essence most people and companies avoid risks. Moving beyond what they normally do makes them uncertain. In my lectures when I ask, "Who of you wants to be an innovator?" most hands go up in the air. When I follow up with, "Who of you wants to run a personal risk?" a lot of those hands go back down. For corporate innovators it's very frustrating when you've been assigned to come up with great new ideas only to see nothing materialize because the same managers who gave you your assignment say 'no' to every idea, business case or prototype you present. First of all, it's a pity for all the work you and your team have put into it. And secondly, your organization is still lacking innovative solutions. However, your chances of surviving the innovation maze will rise if your idea meets the company's strategy and innovation criteria. Therefore, as an innovator ask yourself two questions. Does your idea match with you? And does it match with your fellow startup founders or organizational goals?

ARE YOU PREPARED TO QUIT YOUR PRESENT JOB TO MAKE YOUR IDEA BECOME REALITY?

When you come up with a new idea, does it match your passion? Are you enthusiastic about it yourself? That is a first and very important litmus test. If you're not utterly enthusiastic about your idea; why should others be? When you are the parent of a great idea which you really want to pursue, it must feel like it's one of your own children. If you don't have any kids (yet), then make sure it feels like your favorite little niece or nephew. Do you want to do tasks you don't like but are necessary to get your idea to market? A lot of startup founders spent all their time building their products and applications, being more of an inventor type. But you will have to get out there yourself half the time talking to executives who can either help you build the business or are potential customers. For corporate innovators the same principle counts.

As a startup or corporate innovator presenting your business case, will you want to run the risk of implementing it yourself? There are a lot of innovative start-up ideas you never hear about, because it was just a project a couple of guys started on the side while working at their day jobs, but gradually abandoned. Do you, as a would-be founder have the determination it takes to start a company? Or is the reason you will not invest more time in your potential startup is that you know it's a bad investment? Would you be willing to quit your day job to make your idea become reality? If so, you have a perfect match, as most founders of failed startups don't quit their day jobs, and most founders of successful ones do.

The same principle applies for corporate innovators. Are you prepared to quit your present job in the company to make your idea become reality? If deep down you have any personal doubts about your own idea then discontinue your innovation journey, because your intuition is generally right. Be brave to stop it here instead of spending more time and energy in a concept which will never see the light of day anyway.

IS YOUR ORGANIZATION PREPARED TO ADOPT YOUR IDEA AND MAKE IT REALITY?

Helmut Panke, the ex-CEO of the BMW Group, said, "My biggest challenge is saying 'no' to projects that are exciting, but don't fit BMW's strategy."[2] He hits the nail on its head. Your idea might be really exciting, but if it does not fit your company it will be killed sooner or later, most often early on at the front end. That's why it's wise to check this is as early as possible in the innovation process.

In my view there are 7 criteria you can use to check if your idea fits your organization:
1. Has your idea the potential to attain revenue and profit targets for new products? If not, rethink your business model.
2. Does your idea fit the processes of your company? If not, would your organization be open to co-create it with others?
3. Does your idea fit the people of your company? If not, would your organization be open to hiring new people with different skill sets or operate it with others?
4. Does your idea fit the strategy of your company? If not, how can we tweak it to make it inclusive?
5. Does your idea fit the investment budgets of your organization? If not, how can we lower the investments and/or find external financers to join in?
6. Does your idea fit the customers of your organization? If not, how can we get access to these new target groups? Can we co-market the idea?
7. Does your idea fit the present brand(s) of your organization? If not, can we introduce a new brand or co-brand the idea?

Well, if you have ticked six or seven boxes you've got a match. You can proceed with the next activity and work out the details later in the new business case. If you have ticked three to five boxes the match with your organization is doubtful at the very least. Try to pivot your idea and business model to come up with a great idea which matches your organization better. Or you might spin out your idea as a separate startup. If you have ticked two or even fewer boxes, there is no match at all with your organization and spinning out your idea and the intellectual property rights could be a good option, which is actually a common practice at leading technical universities around the world.

Let's suppose your innovative concept fits great with you and your organization. In the next chapter "Create Conditions", we will explore how you can create the best conditions to proceed with your idea through the innovation maze.

KEY MESSAGES FROM THIS CHAPTER

1. **The single biggest obstacle at the start of innovation is one small word: no.**
2. **Are you prepared to quit your present job to make your idea become reality?**
3. **If an innovative idea does not fit your company, it will be killed sooner or later.**
4. **When there's no match between your idea and your organization, leave your organization and approach others with a better match.**
5. **Don't spend time on ideas with no chance of becoming reality.**

Notes

1   *Developing New Ideas: Spin-outs, Spinoffs or Internal Divisions*, Radoslawa Nikolowa, May 2011, working paper, p 2.
2   "Performance Driver: Helmut Panke", Businessweek, June 7, 2004, p. 40.

QUOTE BY DESMOND TUTU

WHAT:
ARCHBISHOP, SOCIAL RIGHTS ACTIVIST (OPPONENT OF APARTHEID) AND SOCIAL INNOVATOR

HOW TO BE SUCCESSFUL:
1. **BE AUTHENTIC**
2. **BE CRITICAL AND SPEAK OUT**
3. **NEVER GIVE UP**

Sources
1. http://www.theguardian.com/social-enterprise-network/2013/feb/15/social-entrepreneurship-inspiring-change-africa
2. http://www.brainyquote.com/quotes/authors/d/desmond_tutu.html
3. http://www.forbes.com/sites/ashoka/2013/03/27/social-entrepreneurship-on-the-high-seas/
4. http://en.wikipedia.org/wiki/Desmond_Tutu
5. http://www.nobelprize.org/nobel_prizes/peace/laureates/1984/tutu-bio.html 6. http://www.bbc.co.uk/news/world-africa-10725711

'I WISH I COULD SHUT UP,
BUT I CAN'T,
AND I WON'T.'

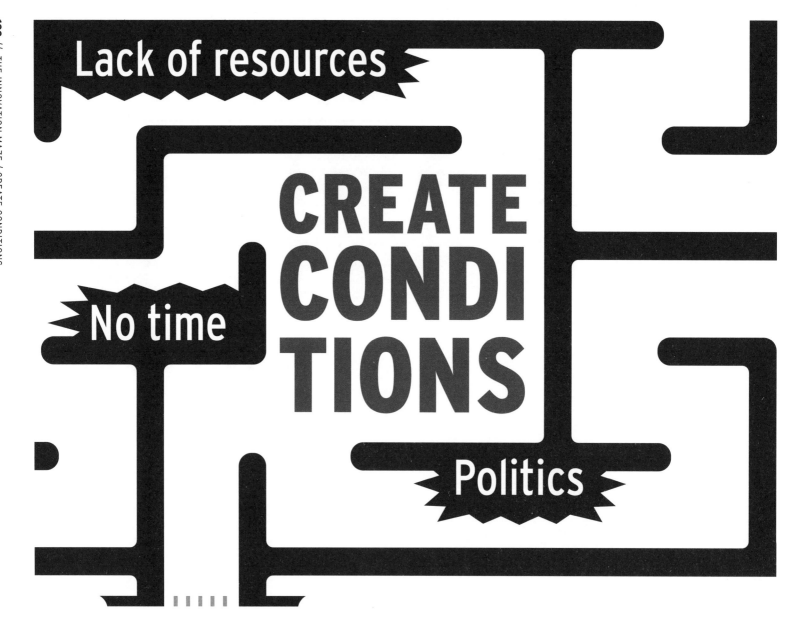

CREATE CONDITIONS

Innovation can start as a slow hunch taking years before evolving into a real opportunity or it might start straight away as a result of an urgent business challenge. As I mentioned in chapter 3, innovation can start in various ways. It's not a question of how innovative you are. It's a question of *how* you are innovative! Regardless if you start with a business challenge, a (startup) idea, a technology or with a problem of one of your clients; it is essential that you create the right conditions for a successful journey through the innovation maze. We all know the journey will be full of hazards and the failure rate is extremely high. Therefore, preparing yourself well and starting under the right conditions will reduce your failure rate.

Of course you need a sufficient budget to start innovation. Though, it's worth mentioning, that money isn't the only factor in becoming a successful innovator. Studies show there is no statistically significant correlation between the financial performance and R&D spending of a company, in terms of either total R&D spending or R&D as a percentage of revenues.[1] There are additional important factors at play. In this chapter, my advice is to do at least four things right. Be sure to choose:

1. ... the right moment.
2. ... the right team.
3. ... the right leader.
4. ... the right route.

CHOOSE THE RIGHT MOMENT TO INNOVATE; THAT'S WHEN IT'S TIME TO EXPLORE

If there are great opportunities to easily grow your business either by up-selling or cross-selling present products or services, then my advice would be to wait and not to innovate at this time. My motto is to exploit first and then explore. Why? Because when your business is profitable, there is no urgency and motivation at all to start trying different things or doing things differently. So, don't innovate if:

▸ ... in the coming years your brand and line extensions bring you lots of extra turnover and profits,
▸ ... your organization is working at full capacity to meet the current huge demand, or
▸ ... your latest innovations are very successful and still need further exploitation.

Start innovating when it's time to explore instead of exploit. In practice, people go beyond their comfort zones only when they have to. As Max McKeown so wonderfully wrote in *The Innovation Book*: "The true parents of creativity are curiosity and necessity."[2] This is so true.

In practice, you see organizations deal with innovation in two ways: there are those companies that want to innovate and those that need to innovate. I call those that want to innovate the active innovators and the ones who need to innovate the reactive innovators. As you can see in chart 3, their roles are defined by the moments they really innovate their business. Every company, business unit or product has its lifecycle of introduction, growth, maturity and decline. Active innovators who want to innovate give innovation priority at the end of the growth stage. Before they reach maturity they want to innovate, often for several reasons simultaneously:

▸ To keep their revenue stream growing;
▸ To maintain an innovative mindset;
▸ To boost internal entrepreneurship (intrapreneurship);
▸ To address changing needs and wants of customers;
▸ To lead in technology;
▸ To expand their business by new business models, distribution channels and customer groups;
▸ To anticipate on new governmental regulations or a market liberalization.

Reactive innovators, on the contrary, wait. They wait until they get hit by a crisis when their markets are saturated or get disrupted by new technologies and/or business models. They reorganize, lay-off people and prioritize innovation only at the start of their decline stage when they need to innovate. They need to innovate most often with only one goal in mind: to stop revenues and profits from falling and build a new future for their organization.
Both types of innovators have their own challenges. The good news for active innovators is that there are plenty of resources available as the company is doing well at the end of the growth stage. Their challenge is to cope with a lack of urgency at the operational level of the organization. "Why should we innovate? We're damn busy and doing great!" The good news for the reactive innovators is the fact that there is great urgency at the operational level of the organization. This is often in the form of a collective layoff resulting from the business slow-down. Their challenge is both a lack of resources and a lack of time, as they will have to move quickly. From a personal perspective you have to choose the right moment too. As a potential start-up founder or corporate innovator, ask yourself three questions:

1. Am I prepared to take the risk to fail?
2. Am I prepared to go 'the extra mile' even if this is at the expense of my private life in the coming period?
3. Am I prepared, to deliver a convincing new business case, to play a (huge) role in the execution in the next phase to get it to market?

When one or more of the answers is 'no', rethink if starting or being involved in an innovation journey is personally the right thing for you to do at this moment.

PUT TOGETHER A WELL-BALANCED DIVERSE TEAM AND WORK ON GROUP TOLERANCE

As a young manager, I learned that you may be able to invent alone, but you cannot innovate alone. You will need an awful lot of colleagues, partners and bosses to make innovation really happen. That's because after the ideation of your product, you'll need to design it, to develop it, to prototype it, to test it, to produce it, to sell it, to invoice it and to service it. That's why I advise you to start innovation in a team directly from the start. When you innovate together, sooner or later everybody will adopt an innovative mindset at the front end, as you get new insights, new ideas and make new business cases yourselves. There's an African saying, "It takes a village to raise a child." It's the same for getting a new product, service, process or experience to market.

Back in 1989, Steve Jobs had already pointed out the importance of the right team during an interview for Fortune Magazine: "Innovation has nothing to do with how many R&D dollars you have. When Apple came up with the Mac, IBM was spending at least 100 times more on R&D. It's not about money. It's about the people you have, how you're led, and how much you get it."[3]

I would like to inspire you with two recent studies on teamwork in new product development. They generate great lessons to be learned; one being about creative success and the other being about high team performance. Both are essential at the start of innovation.

New scientific research reveals insights into how some of the world's greatest video games were created from the adventures of Lara Croft in Tomb Raider to the apocalyptic drama of Fallout. Mathijs de Vaan, David Stark and Balazs Vedres focused on the question: what accounts for creative success when you're innovating in a team?[4] Their extensive research focused on the video games industry. They collected data on 12,422 video games that were produced from the inception of the industry in 1979 to 2009 and on the teams that developed them.

Here's a selection of some of their scientific findings:

▸ Game changers are likely to be developed by teams that include cognitively different groups (subgroups with varying cognitive sets) that tolerate and exploit overlapping membership across such groups.
▸ Tensions within teams allow for the development of products that stand out.
▸ A game is more distinctive if the developer team accommodates larger cohesive groups but this effect declines as the mean size of groups grows further.
▸ Teams comprising industry veterans are less likely to produce games that deviate from the norm. Including newcomers is a significant positive predictor of distinctiveness.
▸ Teams with many above-average developers are unlikely to develop distinctive games, while teams with a few absolute standouts (and some that performed poorly in the past) are more likely to produce creative outliers.
▸ Games developed and published by one firm are more likely to be distinctive than games produced by multiple firms, as less negotiation is necessary and consensus need to be reached.
▸ Teams embedded within older firms produce games that are less likely to stand out, which proves that older firms, which

have established their position within the industry, are less likely to provide the context in which distinctive games can be developed.
▸ Teams with high cohesion, but with cognitively close developers lead to a narrow focus.
▸ Creative success was facilitated when cognitively distant groups were socially folded. Yes, something must be shared. But it is not necessarily mutual understanding. It creates a workable space where some misunderstanding is tolerated.

In summary, Professor David Stark says the most successful new video games were created because the creative teams behind the most iconic video games had the ideal mix of career backgrounds and working relationships.

There are 7 important lessons for you to boost creative success in your team at the start of innovation:

1. Set up your innovation team as "a group of groups".
2. Make the 'cohesive groups' within the team larger.
3. Work on group tolerance.
4. Tension sparks creativity in a tolerant group.
5. Include newcomers.
6. 'One-firm' teams need to compromise less and make more distinctive concepts.
7. Compose a team of cognitively different innovators.

Another really interesting study researches which major factors explain high performance in new product teams. Thus far, 23 factors have been identified in this annual study by Actuation Consulting among product develop teams of start-ups, small and medium sized companies and big corporations in 40 countries.[5] You will find a full list of all the factors in chart 23. I have highlighted 8 of these factors as the most relevant for the front end of innovation:

1. Unwavering executive team support - the key word is "team".
2. Strong product team alignment with strategy.

3. Assigning core product team members based upon the skills needed.
4. Business unit leader engagement.
5. Common goal or purpose.
6. Inclusion of user experience professionals.
7. Strong project manager or scrum master.
8. Strategic decision-making aptitude.

Keep the lessons learned from both studies in mind when you are composing your team to navigate the innovation maze. I can pass on two additional tips from my own experience guiding innovation teams at the front end in corporate environments. Be wise and also include non-innovators often times your finance director in your team. Why? Because the non-innovators determine the pace of your organizations. When everyone else leans back nothing moves forward unless you include non-innovators in your innovation team who gain their own new market insights, generate innovative ideas, see how customers react and are able to build new business cases themselves. By doing so, non-believers are turned into believers. At the end of your innovation route they will convince others to say 'yes' to implementing the new concepts generated. The same applies to the directors and the board of your organization. Be sure to include some of them in your team. And I don't mean in a steering group –working group relation. That doesn't work at the front end of innovation. The steering committee will say 'no' to everything the working group proposes as they lack the new insights and don't want to run any personal risk. When the decision makers join your team they themselves will be convinced and support the outcomes in their role as 'family-member'.

CHOOSE THE RIGHT LEADER

No matter how you start innovation. You always start with 100% uncertainty. The main role an innovation leader is to reduce the uncertainty during the innovation process to an acceptable level for yourself, your team and your organization. The right leader for an innovative team will reduce the uncertainty by picking the right path and doing the right activities in the right order at the right moment.

Tom & David Kelley state that 'creative confidence' is the heart of innovation. "It is about believing in your ability to create change in the world around you. It is the conviction that you can achieve what you set out to do. Creative confidence is like a muscle – it can be strengthened and nurtured through effort and experience." The Kelleys tell the story of Geshe Thupten Jinpa, who has been the Dalai Lama's chief English translator for more than twenty years, sharing an insight with them on the nature of creativity. Jinpa pointed out that there's no word in the Tibetan language for "creativity" or "being creative". The closest translation is "natural". Basically, if you want to be creative, you just have to be natural." [6] In my opinion, creating creative confidence in the team is one of the most important roles for the leader. Create a way of working and a team atmosphere in which everyone can be themselves. This does not mean that you should always strive for consensus. On the contrary. Tension sparks creativity in a tolerant group. As team leader, be sure to work on the right conditions where group tolerance is an important one.

Leading an innovation team is a challenge. Peter J. Denning and Robert Dunham identified 7 principles of innovative leadership in their book *The Innovator's Way*.

Leaders:[7]
1. ... look for opportunities to take care and produce value.
2. ... engage others with new narratives for the future.
3. ... make offers, take stands and engage with disagreements and resistance to their offers.
4. ... inspire followers to make and sustains commitments; in so build power for themselves and others.
5. ... initiate actions and conversations, accept the risks, and learn from the consequences.

6. ... build a presence, a voice, and identity to have their offers heard and accepted.
7. ... are continually learning and sharpening their own skills.

Based on these 7 principles they formulated 25 questions to assess if you are an innovation leader. Check out for yourself in chart 24 how many questions you can answer with a 'yes'.

CHOOSE THE RIGHT ROUTE

You can start innovation in several ways: with an idea, with a technology, with a customer problem or with a business challenge to innovate. To prevent you from getting lost be sure to choose the right route through the maze.

1. The idea route: You are starting with a new idea.
2. The technology route: You have discovered a new technology.
3. The customer issue route: You have identified an unsolved customer problem.
4. The business challenge route: Your business needs to innovate.

Each of the four innovation routes contains all 10 activities. The great news is that whether you start with an idea, a technology, a customer issue or a business challenge you can use the same activities and the same tools. The order in which the ten activities are undertaken depends on how you start innovation. Be aware that doing things in the right order at the start of innovation has a huge impact on the effectiveness of your innovation process.

KEY MESSAGES FROM THIS CHAPTER

1. **Choose the right moment to innovate; when it's time to explore.**
2. **Are you prepared to take the risk of failure, to go the extra mile and to get your innovation to market?**
3. **Choose a well-balanced diverse team and work on group tolerance.**
4. **Tension sparks creativity in a tolerant group.**
5. **Doing things in the right order at the start of innovation has a huge impact on the effectiveness of your innovation process. Choose the right route through the Maze.**

Notes

[1] www.innovationexcellence.com/blog/2014/10/28/the-2014-global-innovation-1000-study-from-strategy/.

[2] Max McKeown, *The Innovation Book*, Pearson, Harlow, United Kingdom, 2014, p. 4.

[3] Fortune Magazine, September 11, 1998.

[4] Game Changer: The Topology of Creativity, Mathijs de Vaan, Balazs Vedres, and David Stark, American Journal of Sociology, Vol. 120, No. 4 (January 2015), pp. 1144-1194

[5] *The Study of Product Team Performance*, Actuation Consulting, downloadable at http://www.actuationconsulting.com/the-study-of-product-team-performance/

[6] Tom Kelley & David Kelley, *Creative Confidence*, HarperCollins Publishers, 2013, pp. 2 -6.

[7] Peter J. Denning & Robert Dunham, *The Innovator's Way*, The MIT Press, Cambridge, Massachusetts, pp. 244, 251.

CHARACTERISTICS OF HIGH PERFORMANCE NEW PRODUCT TEAMS

An annual study conducted by Actuation Consulting among product develop teams from startups, SMEs and large corporations spanning 40 countries, researches the question: "What are the major characteristics of high performance new product teams?" High performance team is defined as product development teams consistently delivering on scope, schedule, costs and achieving their financial targets. Thus far they have identified 23 characteristics.

1

Unwavering executive team support – the key word is "team".

2

Strong product team alignment with strategy.

3

Post-Product development focus and accountability.

4

Assigning core product team members based upon the skills needed.

Bringing product team members on board.

The importance of successfully staffing and resourcing the product launch process.

Product manager role clarity.

Aligned product strategy with the company's overarching business strategy.

9

Business unit leader engagement.

10

Onboarding new product team members professionally.

11

Common goal or purpose.

12

Effective line management.

13

Availability of strong engineers and recognition of their importance.

14

Inclusion of user experience professionals.

15

Strong project manager or scrum master.

16

A collaborative relationship between product and project management.

17

Optimizing the product team's relationship with sales.

18

Product team understanding of their product's sales cycle.

19

Clear role delineation between product team and marketing.

20

Strategic decision-making aptitude.

21

High standup frequency.

22

Nimble problem recovery.

23

User Experience integration early into the product development process.

Source
The Study of Product Team Performance, Actuation Consulting
http://www.actuationconsulting.com/the-study-of-product-team-performance/

ARE YOU AN INNOVATION LEADER?

7+++++++++++++++++++++++
PRINCIPLES OF INNOVATION LEADERSHIP

1+++++++++++++++++++++++
LEADERS LOOK FOR OPPORTUNITIES TO TAKE CARE AND PRODUCE VALUE.

2+++++++++++++++++++++++
LEADERS ENGAGE OTHERS WITH NEW NARRATIVES FOR THE FUTURE.

3+++++++++++++++++++++++
LEADERS MAKE OFFERS, TAKE STANDS AND ENGAGE WITH DISAGREEMENTS AND RESISTANCE TO THEIR OFFERS.

25+++++++++++++++++++
Self-Study Questions for Innovation Leadership

1++++++++++++++++++++++
Can you state clearly what you care about?

2++++++++++++++++++++++
Can you state clearly what the people for whom you make your offer care about?

3++++++++++++++++++++++
Are they clear about what you care about?

4++++++++++++++++++++++
What do your adopters see as value?

5++++++++++++++++++++++
Do you listen to concerns?

6++++++++++++++++++++++
Do you have a narrative about your innovation?

7++++++++++++++++++++++
Does the narrative address a concern and reveal value?

8++++++++++++++++++++++
Are people making new commitments on account of your narrative?

9++++++++++++++++++++++
Are you building identity with it?

10+++++++++++++++++++++
Are you building a team?

11+++++++++++++++++++++
Are you and your team effectively spreading the narrative and generating new followers?

12+++++++++++++++++++++
Are you making offers?

13+++++++++++++++++++++
Are they seen as valuable?

14+++++++++++++++++++++
Are they being accepted?

15+++++++++++++++++++++
If not, are you listening to why not, and adjusting?

16+++++++++++++++++++++
Are you building satisfaction, value, identity, and power in fulfilling your offers? Do you take a strong stand for your offer? Do you productively engage with disagreement and resistance to your offer?

Source
Peter J. Denning & Robert Dunham, The Innovator's Way, The MIT Press, Cambridge, Massachusetts, pp. 244, 251.

4+++++++++++++++++++++++
LEADERS INSPIRE FOLLOWERS TO MAKE AND SUSTAIN COMMITMENTS; IN DOING SO BUILD POWER FOR THEMSELVES AND OTHERS.

17+++++++++++++++++++++
Are people committing to your offer – and not only initially but for the longer term?
18+++++++++++++++++++++
Are you building power: financial, know-how, symbolic? If not, what is missing?
19+++++++++++++++++++++
Are you building alliances? Networks of support? Value exchanges?

5+++++++++++++++++++++++
LEADERS INITIATE ACTIONS AND CONVERSATIONS, ACCEPT THE RISKS, AND LEARN FROM THE CONSEQUENCES.

20+++++++++++++++++++++
Are you disposed to map out action plans based on commitments, organize teams, initiate conversations, and build networks? Do you make grounded risks assessments and show people the risks can be managed?

6+++++++++++++++++++++++
LEADERS BUILD A PRESENCE, A VOICE, AND IDENTITY TO HAVE THEIR OFFERS HEARD AND ACCEPTED.

21+++++++++++++++++++++
Do you have a presence? A voice? An identity?
22+++++++++++++++++++++
Do people respond positively to you? If not, what learning and actions are needed?

7+++++++++++++++++++++++
LEADERS ARE CONTINUALLY LEARNING AND SHARPENING THEIR OWN SKILLS.

23+++++++++++++++++++++
What are your regular practices for renewal and learning? How do you continuously improve your competence in your area of expertise and as an innovation leader?
24+++++++++++++++++++++
Do you learn from your mistakes?
25+++++++++++++++++++++
Do you encourage those around you to do likewise?

QUOTE BY ELON MUSK

WHAT:
PAYPAL, TESLA MOTORS AND SPACEX

HOW TO BE SUCCESSFUL:
1. **WORK 80-100 HOURS A WEEK**
2. **PICK THE RIGHT TEAM**
3. **KNOW WHEN TO GROW**

Sources
1. http://blog.kissmetrics.com/the-mind-of-elon-musk/
2. http://www.slideshare.net/TimG1/advice-to-entrepreneurs-from-elon-musk-richard-branson
3. http://en.wikipedia.org/wiki/Elon_Musk
4. http://www.success.com/article/from-the-corner-office-elon-musk
5. http://www.businessnewsdaily.com/98-tips-for-business-success-from-entrepreneur-elon-musk-100802html.html

'YOU WANT TO HAVE A FUTURE
WHERE YOU'RE EXPECTING
THINGS TO BE BETTER,
NOT ONE WHERE YOU'RE
EXPECTING THINGS
TO BE WORSE.'

DIS
COVER

CS

No insights or inspirat

DISCOVER

Whichever way you start, _Discover_ is an essential activity on your innovation route as you have to take your blinders off to broaden your perspective and observe & learn. I will take you through 12 of the numerous sources of inspiration for innovation. The most important one is a deep understanding your potential customer's behavior. The goal is to avoid developing a new offering for which there is no need. That's why I will present 5 so-called voice-of-customer (VOC) methods. These constitute the top five best-rated methods out of 18 potential idea sources. Finally, we will discuss 3 techniques in depth: mapping your customer's journey, identifying customer frictions via focus groups and co-creating with lead users. They all will prove to be very useful on your innovation route through the maze.

THE INNOVATION MAGIC OFTEN OCCURS OUTSIDE YOUR OWN PERSONAL COMFORT ZONE.

Innovation is about breaking through patterns to discover new combinations. Being able to innovate means being able to learn from others. For this reason, it is important not to keep on looking for inspiration from behind your desk, but to go out and search for new inspiration and insights elsewhere. This is easier said than done. As a marketer, I used to have great difficulty in going out to explore. I was endlessly promising myself that I would go out to observe the customers; observe and learn in order to sense the right vibe. Long before I had children of my own, I was working as a marketer for a confectionary company and had every intention to visit school grounds for observation. Instead, I kept thinking up business excuses, meetings and emails to 'escape' from doing so.

Finally one Wednesday afternoon, three product managers and I actually took the leap and went on our 'marketing outing' to watch Disney's Aladdin at a cinema with hundreds of screaming children. While the children were watching the movie, we were watching them. I can imagine that you think you hardly have time for this in your job, but I do not have any sympathy for that. As an innovator, it is crucial to take off your blinders and the ones of your organization. You can only break through patterns in the market if you break through your own patterns: if you can't change, how can you expect it from others? So, get up and get out there! The innovation magic often happens outside your own personal comfort zone. Start wondering again and ask yourself the questions you haven't asked yourself for a long time. This is the way to challenge the status quo in the sector of your expertise.

EXPLORE 12 SOURCES OF INSPIRATION FOR INNOVATION

There are a lot of potential sources of inspiration for your innovation challenge out there. In their book _The Innovator's Way_, Peter J. Denning and Robert Dunham identified 12 sources of innovation, where innovators can find their inspiration.[1]

SOURCES OF INNOVATION

TYPE	EXPLANATION	ADVOCATE	EXAMPLE
Unexpected events	Unexpected successes or failures; outside events	Drucker	The failure of Apple's Newton. The success of Apple's iPod.
Incongruities	A gap between reality and common belief; disharmonies	Drucker	New business models emerge when the current system is attracting fewer customers.
Process needs	A bottleneck in a critical process	Drucker	Dell's user-driven Web interface to order computers eliminating delays, mistakes and excess inventory.
Change of industry structure	New business models, distribution channels, modes of business	Drucker	Starbucks offering a coffee experience replacing the office coffee pot.
Demographics	Changes in groups by age, politics, religion, income, etc.	Drucker	The influx of Latin American immigrants in the US fueled a booming market in Latino goods.
Change of mood or perception	Change in the way people see the world	Drucker	The financial crisis of 2008 to 2009 changed the public mood from consumption to savings.
New knowledge	Application of new knowledge, science advances	Drucker	The internet created a new communication structure gradually replacing telephone and broadcast media.

SOURCES OF INNOVATION

TYPE	EXPLANATION	ADVOCATE	EXAMPLE
Patent patterns	Identifying recurring patterns of invention analyzing millions of patents	Ideation International	Software analyzing 3 million worldwide patents of which 1000 patterns of invention have been extracted.
Value maximization	Simplifying all processes to support only the highest-value outcomes of the organization	Womack and Jones; Merrifield	Lean thinking to eliminate all actions and processes with low-value outcomes in an organization.
Marginal practices	Adapting practice to recognize what appears marginal to mainstream thinking or practice	Spinosa, Flores and Dreyfus	Noticing things around the "peripheries" for example, a new field like bioinformatics, a combination of biology and computer science.
"Dying Cows"	Discerning and responding to deep, strongly felt concerns within a community	Flores; Latour	Solve relevant issues for which communities will be receptive.
New games	Defining new rules of interaction and new objectives to be achieved	Kotler and Trias de Bes	Invent a new game, like Apple's iTunes music distribution service.

You have to decide for yourself which potential sources are the most relevant for your specific innovation assignment. In practice, a lot of people who start innovation begin exploring close to home on safe ground. But unfortunately the easy way won't bring you a lot of new insights. Like André Gide, a French writer said, "Man cannot discover new oceans unless he has the courage to lose sight of the shore." Products and services in your own industry from you and your competitors are often look-a-likes, as they are shaped by a common mindset where one copies the other. To break your pattern, scrutinizing trends and next practices in other sectors is quite refreshing. It is an excellent way to broaden your mind and spark creativity. Ramon Vullings & Marc Heleven challenge innovators in their book on cross-industry innovation to learn from other sectors[2]:

▸ What can a hospital learn from a hotel?
▸ What can a car manufacturer learn from the video game industry?
▸ What can a chemical company learn from a festival organizer?

Bear in mind that you learn the most from people and sectors who differ the most from you. From which other non-obvious sectors will you and your team learn the most?

THE IMPORTANCE OF UNDERSTANDING CUSTOMERS DEEPLY

Researchers of Strategy& stated in their study *The Customer Connection* that "companies can spend more money, hire the best engineers, develop the best technology, and conduct the best business market research, but unless their R&D efforts are driven by a thorough understanding of what their customers need and want, their performance may fall short." They tested this hypothesis and found that over a three-year period, companies that directly captured customer insights had three times the growth in operating income and twice the return on assets of industry peers that captured customer insights indirectly.[3] This is the best reason

for you to discover customer behavior already at the start of innovation.

Now connecting to customers does not mean merely asking customer what they want. Why? Because people don't know what they want. Henry Ford once said, "If I asked my customers what they wanted, they'd have told me "A faster horse." Another business icon, Steve Jobs said on this topic in an interview in 1998, "It's really hard to design products by focus groups. A lot of times people don't know what they want until you show it to them."[4] Customers tend to frame their answers based on what already exists. On what they know. They will always ask for better products and services. It's up to you to really innovate and come up with other offerings.

When you introduce a new offering, your customers will have to change their behavior to buy it. Why should they? Mostly because your new offering is a new solution for a problem they're experiencing and a need they have. That's why you should look out for relevant problems of your target groups and ideate a new offering bringing them a solution. As your innovation must be relevant for them to be adopted, you must first understand their pain points and dissatisfactions.

There are techniques which can help you in identifying needs, pain points and dissatisfiers. Based on a 1950s analysis of knowledge and learning, the Mayo Clinic Center for Innovation designed this practical helpful model.[5]

LEARNING MODE		Explicit	Tacit	Latent
ASK →				
OBSERVE →				
EXPERIENCE →				
	Customer need	Explicit	Tacit	Latent
		Articulated	Unarticulated	Unarticulated
		Codified	Cannot be codified	Unpredictable
		Concrete	Abstract	Abstract
		Readily	Experiential	Neo-experimental
		Accessible	"How to" knowledge	
	How identified	Focus Groups	Observation	Creation
		Surveys	Deep reflection	Exposure to something new
		Closes-ended questions	Dialogue	Open-ended questions

You identify explicit needs of your customers, ones which they can articulate well, in focus groups, surveys and asking closed-ended questions. Other needs are tacit, like riding a bicycle: you do it subconsciously and it's hard to convey it to another person. You explore these tacit needs by observing your customers closely and reflecting deeply on their behavior. Latent needs are subliminal. You will discover them by exposing your customers to something new and co-create new concepts with them. That's why experimenting with simple prototypes is so important when your aim is to radically innovate a sector.

The best sources for new ideas are directly related to customers as you will get new refreshing insights.[6] Five so called voice-of-customer (VOC) methods constitute the top five best-rated methods:

1. Ethnographic research. This involves camping out with and observing customers while they use products or services. I would love to inspire you with a great practical example of ethnographic research in chart 24. It's a case of Drägerwerk, an international leader in the field of medical and safety technology. When innovating breathalyzer testing devices a team of Drägerwerk camped out with police officers.
2. Customer-visit teams. Customers are visited and interviewed to uncover problems with products or services and their need and wants.
3. Customer-focus groups. Customers are invited to join a focus group to identify their frictions, needs, wants and suggestions concerning a product or service they use.
4. Lead-user analysis. This method reaches out to those users whose needs and preferences lead the market. It often combines both ethnographic research as focus groups. In chart 25, you can read a great story on connecting to lead users by 3M.
5. Customer or user designs. Customers are invited to take part in a contest to help the company find ideas for new products.

Now I would like to dig deeper into three techniques. With the first one you identify all the factors influencing the customer experience from the customer's perspective in a customer journey map. This is a great technique to use in service innovation, as a service is often so intangible and the user experience is actually your offering. The second technique identifies customer frictions via focus groups. This is a very practical technique which you can use in any innovation project to get to know a better understanding of your customers likes and dislikes. The third one is lead user research. Identifying the behavior of lead users and co-creating with them is intensive and time-consuming and especially useful when you want to discover unmet latent needs and create more revolutionary ideas.

MAPPING YOUR CUSTOMER'S JOURNEY GIVES YOU GREAT INSIGHT

A customer journey map is a visualization of the experience your offering your user with your product or service. It is a user-centered design technique. It provides a structured insight in how your offering is used from a customer's perspective. When you map the customer journey of all the present offerings in your market, you will get a great insight in the differences, which enables you to identify opportunities for innovation. So-called touchpoints play an essential role in your customer's journey: moments where the user interacts with your offering. Here's a practical 5-step method to draft a customer journey.

1. Characterize your users. First make so-called 'personas'. These are fictional characters you create to represent a certain user type. Make different personas for each user type. You can capture a persona in a 1-page description that includes personal characteristics, behavior pattern, product experience, attitudes, and his/her user environment. Be sure to fill in personal details to make the persona a realistic character. And add a picture too.
2. Identify the touchpoints. Discover how your persona is using your product and service by identifying the touchpoints. There

are several ways how to do it: by interviewing users, in focus groups with users fitting the same profile, by watching users while using your product/service. You can even involve users to document the way they use the products themselves in a blog or diary.

3. Draft the customer journey map. Here you are connecting all the touchpoints on a timeline in an attractive visual representation. A really effective format is putting the timeline on the x-axis and the emotions of the user on the y-axis. In this way you visually can see the pain points from a user perspective which identifies opportunities for innovation. Be sure to make a customer journey map for each persona.

In chart 26 you will find an example of a customer journey for a buyer of furniture at an IKEA store.

IDENTIFYING CUSTOMER'S FRICTIONS GENERATE GREAT WINDOWS OF OPPORTUNITIES FOR NEW OFFERINGS

A customer friction is a relevant pain point customers are experiencing which is not being met by existing offerings in the market. It is a problem or unfulfilled dream waiting for a new solution. Focus groups are a very effective way to identify them. In my innovation practice we usually invite six to eight people for the focus group in a place where there are good facilities for the innovation team to be able to join in the room to experience the emotions themselves. While a facilitator leads the group discussion your innovation team observes carefully, trying to spot relevant frictions in the discussions. The subject is defined by your innovation assignment. Products or services are not at the center of customer's minds; tasks are. For instance, consumers say "I need to clean the floor." They don't say "I need a floor cleaner." So an exhaustive assessment of the tasks to be done is essential in understanding consumer struggles and frustrations.

The facilitator asks open questions to start the discovery process:
▸ How relevant is this subject, task or product group for you?
▸ Can you describe your usage and buying behavior?
▸ What do you find important?
▸ With what are you struggling? Which problems do you encounter?

It is important to keep on asking: Why? How come? Can you tell us a bit more about it? It is quite remarkable to see how people open up and tell the story of their lives so openly, even in a business-to-business setting.

After the two-hour discussion, when your customers have left your innovation team, together with the facilitator, start dissecting the customer frictions mentioned. It is important to remember that it is not only about what has been said but also about what has not been said. Through this collective discussion and interpretation each focus group leads to about ten customer frictions at least. A practical example of a customer friction is described below. It always has 3 sections:

1. I am... (describe the persona: who am I?).
2. I need... (describe the need in plain user language).
3. But... (describe the problem as practical as possible).

After you described the friction, specify the target group and give the friction a catchy name. Here's an example of a customer friction for a regulatory council department
Name: Permission horror
Target group: People who have plans to build or renovate
customer friction:

▸ **I am** living in the same house for the past fifteen years. The children are growing up and the house is becoming fuller.
▸ **I need** permission from the local council to enlarge my house.
▸ **But** I hear from my friends and neighbors getting a permit is full of pitfalls and takes a very long time.

As you see, customer frictions are windows of opportunities for new innovative solutions. Besides focus groups you can also identify customer frictions by interviewing customers one-on-one, by observing them and even by doing online web searches on user forums, blogs, and social media like Twitter, Facebook or Pinterest.

CO-CREATING WITH LEAD-USERS GENERATES MORE REVOLUTIONARY NEW OFFERINGS

The lead-user research method reaches out to those users whose needs and preferences lead the market. They are so far ahead of the rest of the market that they modify products and create their own solutions to fit their own needs. 3M's scientist Mary Sonnack developed a practical methodology together with Joan Churchill and Eric von Hippel (the name-giver of the method).[7] All eight divisions of 3M were involved in lead-user research. The seven projects implemented at 3M showed that the annual sales of new product ideas generated were conservatively projected to be $146 million after five years, more than eight times higher than forecast sales for traditional idea-generation projects like brainstorming.

Lead-user research has, in my view, two key differences with other voice-of-the-customer research methods:

▸ Focus on needs of lead users, not regular users.
▸ Not only seeks insights but also user-developed solutions from users.

Lead-user research is designed to be completed in six to eight months with a cross functional project team of four to six people, all working part time. So it's more than only doing research, being applied as an innovation process in itself. You can conduct lead-user research in ten steps:

1. **Preparing**
   1. Draft a project plan schedule.
   2. Learn about the current marketplace.
   3. Shape the project focus.

2. **Identifying Key Trends and Needs**
   4. Seek out lead users to understand trends.
   5. Seek out lead users to gain deeper insight.
   6. Observe how lead users are innovating makeshift solutions.

3. **Explore Lead-Users Needs and Solutions**
   7. Visit lead users to observe and uncover tacit information.
   8. Generate preliminary solution concepts based on insights thus far.

4. **Improve Solution Concepts with Lead-Users**
   9. Improve solutions with lead users and experts in a 2.5 day workshop.
   10. Create a business case and present it to management.

The Discovery phase plays an essential role on every innovation route through the maze, as you connect to customers. It will generate windows of opportunities for new innovative solutions. Be sure to pick the voice-of-the-customer technique which fits your innovation challenge best. In the next chapter, I will dig deeper into how to create a new business model.

KEY MESSAGES FROM THIS CHAPTER

1. **Discover is an essential activity as you have to take your blinders off to broaden your perspective.**
2. **The innovation magic often happens outside your own personal comfort zone.**
3. **To break your pattern, scrutinizing trends and next practices in other sectors is quite refreshing.**
4. **The best sources for new ideas are directly related to customers as you will get new refreshing insights.**
5. **Co-creating with lead users generates more revolutionary new offerings.**

Notes

[1] Peter J. Denning & Robert Dunham, *The Innovator's Way*, The MIT Press, Cambridge, Massachusetts, p. 115.

[2] Ramon Vullings & Marc Heleven, *Not Invented Here*, Bis Publishers, Amsterdam, 2015, p. 12.

[3] www.innovationexcellence.com/blog/2014/10/28/the-2014-global-innovation-1000-study-from-strategy/

[4] Source: Cited in Rowan Gibson's *The 4 Lenses of Innovation*, Wiley, Hoboken, New Jersey, 2015, p. 182.

[5] Nicholas LaRusso, Barbara Spurrier, Gianrico Farrugia, *Think Big, Move Fast*, McGraw Hill, 2015 p. 107.

[6] Robert G. Cooper, Scott Edgett (March 2008). Ideation for Product Innovation: What are the Best Methods?, PDMA Visions.

[7] Source: Ivy Eisenberg, Lead-User Research for Breakthrough Innovation, Research-Technology Management, January - February 2011, pp. 50 - 58

ETHNOGRAPHY:
CAMPING OUT WITH POLICE OFFICERS

Source
Robert G. Cooper and Angelika Dreher, "Voice-of-Customer Methods: What is the Best Source of New Product Ideas", Marketing Management Magazine, Winter, 2010, p 41-42.

An example:

Drägerwerk is an international leader in the field of medical and safety technology. Its Dräger Safety subsidiary provides products, services and solutions for risk management for personal and facility protection. One of the company's product lines, breathalyzer testing devices, is used by police forces to test alcohol levels in suspected drunk drivers. The aim originally was to interview with police officers they suspect are drunk was, as always: "Remain in the car!" The breathalyzer test device was then passed through the driver's window by the officer (who wore latex gloves for fear of HIV), and the driver was instructed to blow into the mouthpiece. It took two minutes to get a full reading. Meanwhile, the other officer had also pulled over another car. Now they had to manage two cars full of people who they suspected were drunk. Quite clearly, observation was that, because of the dials on the U.K. version of the instrument, it could only be used on right-hand-side drivers. Thus, when a left-hand-side driver from France or Germany was pulled over in the U.K., the police could not conduct the test quite as quickly. And because of time pressures, they really had no other option but to simply wave the car through. This behavior was never revealed to their supervisors, nor in the formal interviews.

ETHNOGRAPHY INVOLVES CAMPING OUT WITH OR OBSERVING CUSTOMERS WHILE THEY USE PRODUCTS OR SERVICES

and their supervisors. But the real learning and insights came from their nighttime vigils—the camping out exercise—where the voice-of-customer (VoC) teams worked beside the police officers as they ran their night-time roadside spot checks on drivers. These insights provided the key to a new product with significant competitive advantage.

For example, the British VoC team soon realized how difficult a job the police officers have maintaining order and control over a car full of exuberant young drinkers fresh from the nearby pub. The command issued by police to those that the police officers were somewhat intimidated by the task of crowd control: They were outnumbered, and the lads in the cars were twice the size and half the age of the officers (who incidentally did not carry guns). Note that the officers never admitted to intimidation during the formal daytime interviews.

To overcome the problem of crowd control and intimidation, the team came up with one solution: Speed up the process. The aim was to substantially reduce the two-minute wait time that was creating the queue. This was achieved by developing a 10-second test device. A second

The solution here was to design an ambidextrous testing instrument: an arm with the mouthpiece attached that could be swung over the top of the test device depending on whether a right-hand or left-hand motor vehicle was pulled over.

These are just two of the 10 novel feature-ideas that made the new Dräger product line a huge success. Each idea was not, in itself, a breakthrough, but when each of the 10 new features and benefits were added together, the new product was indeed a blockbuster and absolutely delighted police forces.

A LEAD USER STORY FROM 3M

In 1998, I led a joint lead-user research project with 3M and Bell Atlantic (now Verizon), a major customer for 3M's telecommunication test equipment, Our charter was to look five years out and develop concepts for what the telecommunications field technician of the future would need. We were thinking along the lines of futuristic portable terminal devices and software components. Our initial focus was to understand the needs of advanced users (before we networked our way to lead users), in order to identify attributes of importance.

For my first visit, I rode along with Joe (not his real name), a telephone company field technician; he took me to one of the worst neighborhoods of Brooklyn. Responding to the first call, we walked into an apartment where a scantily clad, glazed-eyed young woman lounged on a mattress on the floor. Our troubleshooting found us climbing out her back bedroom window, into the backyard, across a thicket of thorns and weeds, and over to the pole at the far end of her yard, all the while being serenaded by a huge drooling, barking dog in the neighbor's yard. "I see the problem," Joe said. He climbed the pole, carrying an awkwardly worn, "hand-held" device that someone in our group had developed as a state-of-the-art field technician's tool. The terminal, which included 3M's test "brick", weighed about five pounds. Joe fixed the problem quickly. We had survived the thorns, the thugs, and the dogs, and I was ready to get back into the truck and lock the doors. But first, we had to climb back into the bedroom window, check the customer's dial tone, and use the customer's line to connect the hand-held to the service database and update the job details.

At our next call another field technician was standing out front, leaning against the building and drinking a soda. He had gotten a call for a different apartment in the same building. Why were there two technicians dispatched to the same building? The other guy was a novice. Joe was a super-technician, and Joe discovered that a cable had been clipped by neighborhood troublemakers, and its rubber melted so the copper could be sold. As it turned out, it was lucky that there were two field technicians at that one job. It made the activity of running the new cable much quicker, and the novice technician learned new troubleshooting and repair tips from Joe.

The findings from this site visit were echoed in numerous other site visits and interviews. A new "hand-held" terminal was but one of the future needs of field technicians. Technicians needed a better process to close out jobs, one that did not involve going into customers' houses. They needed better information about the equipment at the customer premises. New field technicians, of which there were growing numbers, needed to communicate with more-experienced technicians who could help them troubleshoot and clue them in to the realities of nonstandard telephone setups and a diverse, unpredictable client base. Dispatch rules needed to be overhauled. And as for the hand-held terminals, they needed to be designed ergonomically so that the technicians could climb poles and fences—and flee dogs. Any new hardware and software needed to keep pace with a new, rapidly changing set of multiple technologies, which meant upgrading and updating them had to be as cost-effective as possible.

Up to this point, our ethnographic research and trends analysis work did not distinguish the lead-user research method from other methods of identifying customer needs. When we began to tap into lead users our research changed. We identified which attributes of the technicians' needs were most important and began seeking out lead users in other industries with analogous needs and innovative solutions. Those attributes included the need to learn increasingly complex telecom equipment, the need to interact with colleagues, the need to work in cramped or uncomfortable quarters while fixing the customer's equipment, and the need to be able to respond to the strange and sometimes wild behaviors that human beings exhibited toward and around their telephone equipment.

We spoke to Julian Orr, a member of the Xerox Palo Alto Research Center and the author of Talking About Machines: An Ethnography of a Modern Job (1996). Orr's insights about Xerox copier repair technicians and their need for community, assistance in error diagnosis, and information sharing rang true for our telephone technicians. We met with someone at General Motors who had built an extensive expert-system database with 200,000 rules that could be presented to the technician to assist in diagnosis, based on the technician's level of knowledge and skill. We talked to Marc Prensky, a leading designer and developer of online training games. Prensky was using games to engage workers in order to help them learn. He had studied the vastly different reading and learning habits of the younger generation and had developed methods for corporations to train their younger workers.

We engaged Robert Weinreb, founder and president of the Tenba Bag Company, to give us insight on ergonomic design. Weinreb and his company had developed breakthrough innovations in ergonomically designed camera bags. He had been a photographer who desperately needed a malleable, special-purpose, lightweight, protective equipment bag to take with him on photo shoots. There was nothing like this on the market, so he designed and manufactured his own and had become a major seller of camera equipment bags. We worked with Dan Siewiorek, a Carnegie Mellon professor whose specialty was wearable computing. We also worked with people in the fields of learning and communications, human computer interaction, and virtual reality, as well as people from across the phone company: field technicians, supervisors, and management.

After five or so months of investigation, we brought top experts from this wide range of areas to a two-and-a-half-day solutions workshop, where participants worked on three carefully selected aspects of the solution space. Some of the features we listed: a smartphone; an off-the-shelf device that we could load applications on; a keyboard; a camera so that technicians could send each other pictures of what they had found in the field; the ability to store the device in a holster; and a device with hands-free, voice-activated capability. One of the concepts that emerged from that workshop bears an uncanny resemblance to the BlackBerry® CurveTM I use today.

The wealth of compelling insights and innovative concepts for the telecommunications field technician of the future came from working not only with current users, but with lead users, and from leaders not only from our own industry, but from related and very different fields, where users had the same attribute needs (such as a lightweight, malleable carrying case). 3M went on to develop a set of new telecommunications test equipment features that allowed physically isolated workers to work in virtual teams to resolve problems.

The Bell Atlantic team transferred seed ideas for process and tool improvements to the engineering and management teams. All team members involved in the process learned to look at users, lead users, and the innovation process itself in a new and exciting way.
Ivy Eisenberg

Source
Lead-User Research for Breakthrough Innovation, Ivy Eisenberg, Research - Technology Management, January -February 2011, p54-55.

CUSTOMER JOURNEY MAP

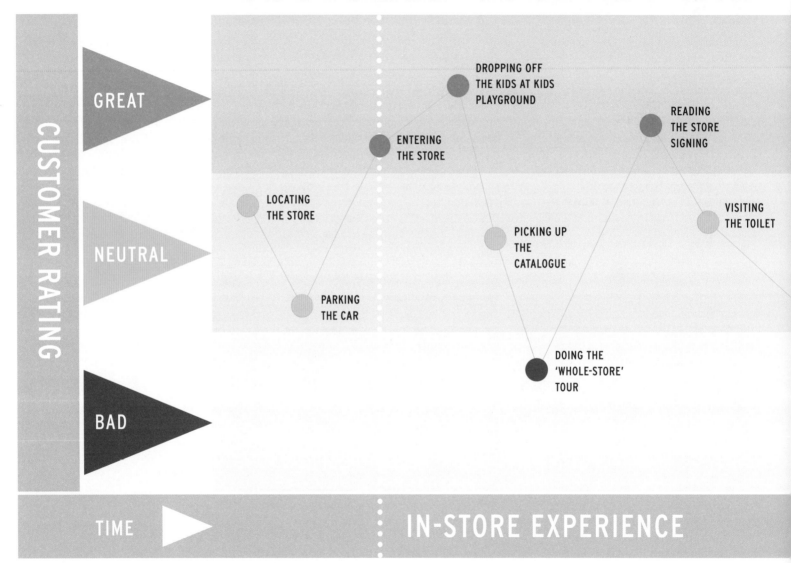

CUSTOMER RATING

GREAT

NEUTRAL

BAD

TIME

IN-STORE EXPERIENCE

LOCATING
THE STORE

PARKING
THE CAR

ENTERING
THE STORE

DROPPING OFF
THE KIDS AT KIDS
PLAYGROUND

PICKING UP
THE
CATALOGUE

DOING THE
'WHOLE-STORE'
TOUR

READING
THE STORE
SIGNING

VISITING
THE TOILET

FOR A BUYER OF FURNITURE AT AN IKEA STORE

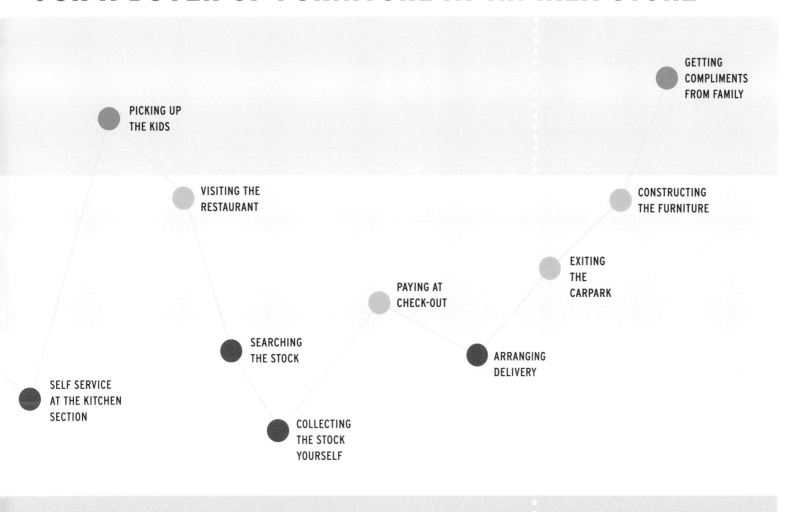

GETTING
COMPLIMENTS
FROM FAMILY

PICKING UP
THE KIDS

VISITING THE
RESTAURANT

CONSTRUCTING
THE FURNITURE

EXITING
THE
CARPARK

PAYING AT
CHECK-OUT

SEARCHING
THE STOCK

ARRANGING
DELIVERY

SELF SERVICE
AT THE KITCHEN
SECTION

COLLECTING
THE STOCK
YOURSELF

QUOTE BY JEFF BEZOS

WHAT:
FOUNDER OF AMAZON.COM

HOW TO BE SUCCESSFUL:
1. BE A THOROUGH RESEARCHER
2. BRING TOGETHER A DIVERSE GROUP OF TALENTED PEOPLE
3. FOCUS

Sources
1. Wikipedia: Jeff Bezos http://en.wikipedia.org/wiki/Jeff_Bezos)
2. http://www.businessinsider.com/jeff-bezoss-salary-is-only-14000-more-than-the-average-facebook-interns-2013-4
3. http://www.success.com/article/from-the-archives-jeff-bezos

'BE PREPARED TO TREAD INTO AREAS WHERE OTHERS HAVE NEVER TRODDEN BEFORE.'

CREATE
BUSINESS
MODEL

CREATE BUSINESS MODEL

A BUSINESS MODEL DESCRIBES THE WAY YOU CAPTURE VALUE

Product innovation or service innovation has a long history. Business model innovation, as such has only emerged recently and has created a new dimension to innovation.
My work as speaker on innovation & design thinking takes me around the world inspiring innovators how to start innovation more effectively. In every country I visited from Canada to India and from Japan to Brazil, the well-known Business Model Canvas, introduced by Osterwalder, Pigneur et al in 2010, with its nine business model building blocks was being used. Like everyone else, you probably also appreciate this canvas. It's most often used to analyze existing business models or business models of new entrants. It's also a great tool to capture your basic idea and communicate it to others in a simple way. You will find the model in chart 27.

A business model describes the rationale of how an organization creates, delivers and captures value.[1] Simply put, "It's the way you earn your money in a market." Sparked by digitalization, a lot of markets have been disrupted by new business models, often initiated by startups and new entrants:

- Airbnb disrupts the market for accommodation as you can rent unique lodgings online from local hosts in 190+ countries. In 2014, Airbnb had 25 million guests' bookings.
- Ted-Ed (the newest TED initiative) disrupts the traditional publishing market in education with free educational lessons-to-share from people all over the world in videos format.
- Streaming services like Netflix disrupt the traditional television market, as you can now watch TV shows & movies anytime, anywhere. Netflix has 65 million streaming subscribers as of 2015.
- Cloud-based solutions, like iCloud replace local infrastructure, hardware and software. By 2013, iCloud already had 320 million users.
- Uber, the 2009 startup, disrupts the license system that protects taxicab franchises in 58 countries. As of 2015, Uber has more than 160,000 active drivers in the US alone.

Even if you have ideated a real innovative product or service, it is still worthwhile to spend time coming up with an innovative business model as well. It will give another dimension to differentiate your offering from the existing ones in the industry where you're operating.

HOW TO CREATE AN INNOVATIVE BUSINESS MODEL?

Start-up entrepreneurs dream big about entering a huge market and overthrowing the incumbents with an innovative business model, like Uber or Airbnb. And as innovation professional or manager at a big corporation, you are well aware of the threats of new startups entering your market. Do you want to be an active innovator or a reactive one? That's the question. As an active innovator, the innovation challenge is to overturn the conventions of your own market before others do. The awareness to rethink your business models may be there. However, the main question is: "*How* do I come up with a new business model that disrupts my own market?"

I was very pleased when McKinsey recently published a new approach to business model innovation.[2] This will help you in coming up with new business models. It's a practical 5 step method meant to turn your present beliefs upside down. You will find it in chart 28.

Let's take a closer look at their five steps:
1. *Outline the dominant business model in your industry.* To start, you will answer the essential question: "What are the long-held core beliefs about how to create value?"
2. *Dissect the most important long-held belief into its supporting notions.* How do notions about customer needs and interactions, technology, regulation, business economics, and ways of operating underpin the core belief?
3. *Turn an underlying belief on its head.* Formulate a radical new hypothesis, one that no one wants to believe—at least no one currently in your industry. Ask yourself outside-the-box 'What-if' questions.
4. *Sanity test your reframe.* Many reframed beliefs will just be nonsense. Applying a reframe that has already proven itself in another industry greatly enhances your prospects of hitting on something that makes business sense.

5. *Translate the reframed belief into your industry's new business model.* Typically, once companies arrive at a reframe, the new mechanism for creating value suggests itself—a new way to interact with customers, organize your operating model, leverage your resources, or capture income.

Now, let's apply this approach to the car sector to come up with a new business model, where I will focus on 'car maintenance and repair'.
1. The dominant business model in 'car maintenance and repair'. When you buy a car, the dealer will give you a 1, 2 or even 5-year guarantee on some vital parts. The condition is often that you have to have your car serviced at your local dealer. After a certain number of miles/kilometers your car indicates it needs to go for a service check. You have to bring your car to the dealer and can pick it up later that day. As a service, they may give you a free replacement car. Afterwards, you will receive an invoice specifying all the service and necessary repair work and the payment will be due within two weeks.

2. The most important long-held 'car maintenance and repair' beliefs and their supporting notions.

   When you think deeply, you might identify the five following long-held 'car maintenance and repair' beliefs:
   1. Cars will break down.
   2. Cars might break down sooner if they are not serviced.
   3. Customers will pay for car maintenance in order to prevent expensive repairs.
   4. Cars must be serviced by professional mechanics.
   5. Cars must be serviced at professional garages

3. Turning an underlying 'car maintenance and repair' belief on its head.
   In this step you will do some breakthrough thinking by turning every belief on its head. This will lead to the following new assumptions:

1. What if cars would *never* break down?
2. What if cars were made *service-less*?
3. What if you would *get paid* when your car needs service or repair?
4. What if *anyone* or *anything* could repair the car?
5. What if a car could be repaired *anywhere*?

4. Sanity test our 'car maintenance and repair' reframes. Doing a quick sanity test on all five 'what-if' assumptions, you will have to admit that cars will still break down given the present state of technology. They will still need service, for example changing summer tires to winter tires as we do here in Northern Europe. As for the customer getting paid when his or her car needs service sounds like a very appealing promise. I would love for this one to come true soon. However, I have my doubts that you would you be willing to risk this cash-out as a car producer right now. Now, that leaves assumptions 4 and 5 both potentially passing the sanity test.

5. Translate our reframed 'car maintenance and repair' belief into a new business model.
   When you translate "anyone or anything can repair a car" into a business model and combine this with the fact that "cars can be repaired anywhere" you might come up with new concepts like:
   1. Join the Service Club. On special service days, which you can see on your app, a Service Truck will enter your street and you can get the service package you need and even professional help from a real mechanic. You pay a membership fee to the Service Club, which covers the professional help. So there will no surprise charges.
   2. A "McCar drive-thru service" at the drive thru of a McDonald's: have your car serviced while you wait for your hamburger order. Pay for both at the McDonald's check-out booth;
   3. App a service-drone if your car needs repair, which flies to you with a service-package which shows you on screen how you can do the service job yourself.

These five steps really make sense. In their approach you will of course recognize the creative process of divergent and convergent thinking. In my view, successfully applying this new approach to generate new disruptive business models is dependent on one thing: your ability and that of your colleagues/partners to postpone judgment and really implement outside-the-box thinking in formulating your 'What-if' questions. Be sure to practice this together upfront and create the right physical and mental environment for being creative together.

19 BASIC FORMS OF NEW BUSINESS MODELS

Now, how do you start coming up with a new business model completely out of the blue? I found a great list of basic business models which Mark Johnson identified in his book, *Seizing the White Space*.[3] I hope all 19 models will inspire you to find an innovative way to earn money for delivering value to your customers.

KEY MESSAGES FROM THIS CHAPTER

1. **A business model describes the rationale of how an organization creates, delivers and captures value.**
2. **Business model innovation has created another dimension to differentiate your offering from the existing ones in the industry where you're operating or entering.**
3. **New business models turn present beliefs in a sector upside down.**

Notes

[1] Alexander Osterwalder & Yves Pigneur, *Business Model Generation*, John Wiley & Sons, Hoboken, New Jersey, 2010, p. 14.
[2] Marc de Jong and Menno van Dijk *"Disrupting beliefs: A new approach to business-model innovation"*, McKinsey Quarterly, June 2015.
[3] Mark W. Johnson, *Seizing the White Space: Business Model Innovation for Growth and Renewal,* Harvard Business Press, 2010.

BUSINESS MODEL	HOW IT WORKS	EXAMPLES
Affinity Club	Pay royalties to some large organization for the right to sell your product exclusively to their customers	▸ MBNA
Brokerage	Bring together buyers and sellers, charging a fee per transaction to one or another party	▸ Century 21 ▸ Orbitz
Bundling	Package related goods and services together	▸ Fast-food value meals ▸ iPod/iTunes
Cell phone	Charge different rates for discrete levels of a service	▸ Sprint ▸ Better Place
Crowdsourcing	Get a large group of people to contribute content for free in exchange for access to other people's content	▸ Wikipedia ▸ YouTube
Disintermediation	Sell direct, sidestepping traditional middlemen	▸ Dell ▸ WebMD
Fractionalization	Sell partial use of something	▸ NetJets ▸ Time-shares
Freemium	Offer basic services for free, charge for premium service	▸ LinkedIn
Leasing	Rent, rather than sell high-margin, high-priced products	▸ Cars ▸ MachineryLink
Low-touch	Lower prices by decreasing service	▸ Walmart ▸ Ikea

BUSINESS MODEL	HOW IT WORKS	EXAMPLES
Negative operating cycle	Lower prices by receiving payment before delivering the offering	▸ Amazon
Pay as you go	Charge for actual metered usage	▸ Electric companies
Product to service	Rather than sell a product, sell the service the product performs	▸ Zipcar
Razor/blades	Offering the low-margin razor below cost to increase volume sales of the high-margin razor blades	▸ Printers and ink
Reverse razor/blades	Offer the low-margin item below cost to encourage sales of the high-margin companion product	▸ Kindle ▸ iPod/iTunes
Reverse auction	Set a ceiling price and have participants bid as the price drops	▸ Elance.com
Standardization	Standardize a previously personalized service to lower costs	▸ MinuteClinic
Subscription	Charge a subscription fee to gain access to a service	▸ Netflix
User communities	Grant members access to a network, charging both membership fees and advertising	▸ Angie's List

Source
Mark Johnson, *Seizing the White Space*.

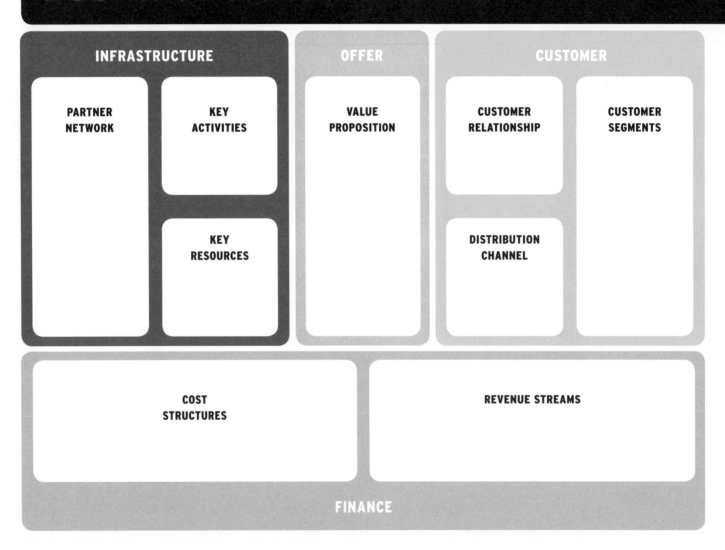

BUSINESS MODEL CANVAS

INFRASTRUCTURE

PARTNER NETWORK

KEY ACTIVITIES

KEY RESOURCES

OFFER

VALUE PROPOSITION

CUSTOMER

CUSTOMER RELATIONSHIP

CUSTOMER SEGMENTS

DISTRIBUTION CHANNEL

COST STRUCTURES

REVENUE STREAMS

FINANCE

THE BUSINESS MODEL CANVAS

(Business Model Generation, Alexander Osterwalder, Yves Pigneur, Wiley, 2010) is a management template for developing new or documenting existing business models. It is a visual chart with nine building blocks describing an organization's value proposition, infrastructure, customers and finances. A new business model starts with customer friction, i.e., any relevant need or wish from a specific customer segment that is not sufficiently satisfied. This is the basis for an innovative business model.

INFRASTRUCTURE

Key Activities:
The most important activities in executing a company's value proposition.

Key Resources:
The resources that are necessary to create value for the customer.

Partner Network:
The partners who optimize operations and reduce risks of a business model.

OFFER

Value Propositions:
The collection of products and services that serve the needs of its customers. A company's value proposition is what distinguishes the company from its competitors.

CUSTOMER

Customer Segments:
Various sets of customers can be segmented, based on specific needs.

Distribution Channels:
Fast, efficient and cost-effective ways to deliver a company's value proposition.

Customer Relationships:
The type of relationship the company wants to create with its customer segments (for example personal assistance, self-service or automated services).

FINANCE

Cost structure: The most important financial consequences under different business models.
Revenue Streams: The way a company makes income from each customer segment.

A NEW APPROACH TO BUSINESS-MODEL INNOVATION

5 STEPS TO TURN YOUR BELIEFS UPSIDE DOWN

OUTLINE THE DOMINANT BUSINESS MODEL IN YOUR INDUSTRY

To start, you will answer the essential question: "What are the long-held core beliefs about how to create value?"

DISSECT THE MOST IMPORTANT LONG-HELD BELIEF INTO ITS SUPPORTING NOTIONS

How do notions about customer needs and interactions, technology, regulation, business economics, and ways of operating underpin the core belief?

Source
Marc de Jong and Menno van Dijk *Disrupting beliefs: A new approach to business-model innovation*,
McKinsey Quarterly, June 2015.

TURN AN UNDERLYING BELIEF ON ITS HEAD

Formulate a radical new hypothesis, one that no one wants to believe—at least no one currently in your industry. Ask yourself outside-the-box 'What-if' questions.

SANITY TEST YOUR REFRAME

Many reframed beliefs will just be nonsense. Applying a reframe that has already proven itself in another industry greatly enhances your prospects of hitting on something that makes business sense.

TRANSLATE THE REFRAMED BELIEF INTO YOUR INDUSTRY'S NEW BUSINESS MODEL

Typically, once companies arrive at a reframe, the new mechanism for creating value suggests itself—a new way to interact with customers, organize your operating model, leverage your resources, or capture income.

QUOTE BY LARRY PAGE AND SERGEY BRIN

WHAT:
CO-FOUNDERS OF GOOGLE

HOW TO BE SUCCESSFUL:
1. IMPROVE THE LIVES OF AS MANY PEOPLE AS POSSIBLE
2. GIVE VALUE FOR FREE
3. DON'T TAKE YOURSELF TOO SERIOUSLY

'GREAT JUST ISN'T GOOD ENOUGH.'

Sources
1. http://www.entrepreneur.com/article/197848
2. http://www.businessinsider.com/history-sergey-brin-larry-page-and-google-strategy-2011-3?op=1
3. http://www.theregister.co.uk/2013/01/18/larry_page_dissing_facebook_apple/
4. http://www.gaebler.com/Larry-Page.htm
5. http://asianentrepreneurship.wordpress.com/2011/08/07/success-story-larry-page/
6. http://www.incomediary.com/google-follows-these-8-simple-rules-and-so-should-you

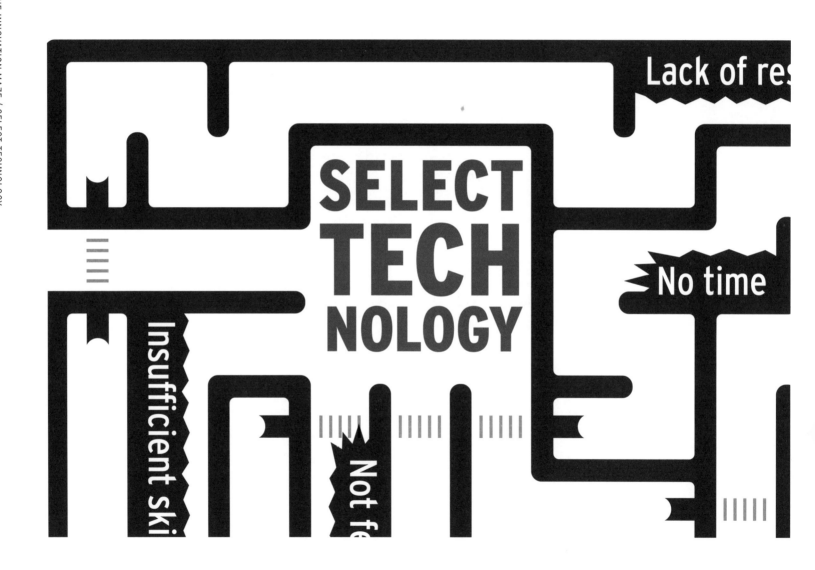

Lack of res

SELECT
TECH
NOLOGY

No time

Insufficient ski

Not f

SELECT TECHNOLOGY

Selecting the right technology focusses on *how* you are going to deliver your new concept to your target group. It's a crucial activity, which you should already include at the front end because the choices you make will have a huge impact on the feasibility of your new concept. Feasibility is crucial for convincing others to support and finance your new business case to take it from idea to market. New technology has great potential to create disruptive innovation. In this chapter I will present emerging technologies for the coming decades and a timeline of emerging science and technology in biotech, nanotech, neurotech, digitech and greentech.

WORK OUT HOW TO DELIVER YOUR NEW CONCEPT TO CHECK FEASIBILITY

The difference between a dream and an innovation is that you can turn the latter into reality. Does the technology deliver the value captured in your innovative idea from your as well as your customer's perspective? That's the question. The basics are covered by the building block 'Infrastructure' in the business model canvas in chart 27: key resources, key activities and partners network. You have to be more specific though, as it is my view that in broad sense technology affects the way you can make your concept become reality. It may cover:

- The way your offering is communicated;
- The way your offering is invoiced and paid;
- The way your client's order is processed;
- The way your offering is produced;
- The way your offering is serviced;
- The way your offering is used;
- The way your offering is disposed.

Of course you may choose for new technology to diversify your offering in the market. You have to be realistic though. Bill Buxton states in Business Week that, "The bulk of innovation is low-amplitude and takes place over a long period. Companies should focus on refining existing technologies as much as on creation".[1] Find the right balance in your organization between the existing technology you really master and new technology needed to be incorporated. He gives the wonderful example of the mouse. "Think of the mouse. First built around 1965 by William English and Doug Engelbart, by 1968 it was copied (with the originators' cooperation) for use in a music and animation system at the National Research Council of Canada. Around 1973, Xerox PARC adopted a version as the graphical input device for the Alto computer. In 1980, 3 Rivers Systems of Pittsburgh released their PERQ-1 workstation, which I believe to be the first commercially available computer that used a mouse. The Xerox Star 8010 workstation appeared a year later. In January 1984, the first Macintosh—the latter being the computer that brought the mouse to the attention of the general public. However, it was not until 1995, with the release of Windows 95, that the mouse became ubiquitous. On the surface it would seem that the benefits of the mouse should have been obvious—and therefore it's surprising that it took 30 years to go from its first demonstration to mainstream. But this 30-year gestation period turns out to be more typical than surprising."

You may be tempted to use new technology, but be aware though that proven technology makes your new concept more feasible and less risky.

When you pick the technology for the delivery of your innovative idea I would advise you to consider four different perspectives:

1. Performance. Which technology will provide the requested performance levels from a customer's perspective? Or, when the performance is new to the world (like the mouse), what is the chance the customer will like it?
2. Cost price. Technology is an important driver of your costs. Which technologies will provide you an acceptable cost price?
3. Cost related to value. How much extra is the end customer prepared to pay for it.
4. Operational risk. What is the risk that different technologies incorporate in delivering the expected performance to your customer?

It's wise in this early phase of innovation to consider several options. You may even work out three different concepts of your innovation, which vary in cost, complexity and risk. What would be in your case:

▸ A low-tech concept?
▸ A proven-tech concept?
▸ A new-tech concept?

In the activities 'Check Freedom to Operate' and 'Experiment' the different options will be checked and evaluated, after which you can make a sound decision on which tech-option to base your new business case.

NEW TECHNOLOGY HAS GREAT POTENTIAL TO CREATE DISRUPTIVE INNOVATION.

We live in exponential times. Every twelve to eighteen months, computers double their capabilities, and so do the information technologies that use them. Technology is progressing at a speed humanity has never seen before. Are you familiar with the 2002 science fiction film 'Minority Report' starring Tom Cruise and set in the year 2054? A specialized police department apprehends criminals based on the foreknowledge provided by three psychics. The film, featuring numerous fictional future technologies, has proven definitely prescient. Fifteen years after Minority Report, the world is closer to Steven Spielberg's vision of 2054 than anyone would've anticipated. Now, much of the science fiction technology imagined in 2002 is already a reality.

New technology has great potential to create disruptive innovation. It is one of the starting points for innovation. A great example is Google Glass (see chart 16) which started with this mission statement: "We think technology should work for you – to be there when you need it and get out of your way when you don't. A group of us from Google[x] started Project Glass to build this kind of technology, one that helps you explore and share your world, putting you back in the moment."[2] So, what's next? Business Insider selected 30 technologies that can change the world, like an inflatable seat belt, ovarian tissue transplants, microbes that can make energy, commercial space flight, a tiny microscope that attaches to a cell phone, lab-grown meat, or sub-retinal implants that restore sight to the blind (chart 29).

Which – and how fast- new technologies will become reality is dependent on many factors. An important one is the urgency of the problem it solves and the resources that are freed up for it. A great example of this, is the story of the race against time in getting the first man on the moon by the US. In 1957 the Soviet Union launched Sputnik, the world's first satellite, into orbit. This event created urgency in the United States. The Americans prioritized their Mercury program, which aimed to launch a man into space. On April 12, 1961 the Soviet Union stunned the world again when cosmonaut Yuri Gagarin became the first man in space. President JFK had to restore America's prestige and wanted to show American superiority. He declared, "I believe that this entire nation should commit itself to achieving the goal, before the decade is out, of landing a man on the Moon and returning him safely to Earth." The honor of a whole nation was at stake. Therefore, endless time and unlimited money were dedicated to the space program and everyone involved was prepared to think and act outside the box. On July 20, 1969 Neil Armstrong became the first to step onto the lunar surface. The total Apollo program costs were estimated to a shocking $23.9 billion[3], for what has been called the greatest technological achievement in human history. The Apollo program generated endless technological spin-offs we're using today ranging from moon boot material, which has revolutionized athletic footwear to renewable energy resource used on Earth and in space via solar panels.

AN INSPIRING TIMELINE OF EMERGING SCIENCE AND TECHNOLOGY[4]

What new technology can we expect in the coming decades as a starting point for innovative offerings? Richard Watson (Now and Next) and Alex Ayad (Imperial College) created a Timeline of Emerging Science and Technology to explore the future of five science fields. They explored which technologies, trends and big ideas lie downstream of breakthrough lab discoveries today. The Timeline covers the following five fields: biotech; nanotech; neurotech; digitech and greentech. They considered the future by first looking at weak signals from the present (defined as existing now or thereabouts with at least 1,000 occurrences existing where appropriate), and extrapolated from these to examine the probable future (defined as occurring between 2015-2030) and possible future (defined as potentially occurring thereafter). The timeline is depicted in chart 30. The predictions you see on their map were crowd sourced from Imperial College academics, PhD and Postgraduate students and industry delegates.

Developing new technology is one thing. Applying new technology as a base for your innovations is another one, which is dependent on the freedom you have or don't have to operate. This issue is the subject of the next chapter.

"But there's one more thing", Steve Jobs would have said. When you select a technology be sure to look at it from a customer point of view, like Steve Jobs did. Customers don't buy technology. They buy beautifully designed stuff and use new tech intuitively.

KEY MESSAGES FROM THIS CHAPTER

1. Work out how to deliver your new concept at an early stage.
2. New technology has great potential to create disruptive innovation.
3. You may be tempted to use new technology, but proven technology makes your new concept more feasible and less risky.
4. Work out alternative concepts, which vary in cost, complexity and risk: a low-tech option, a proven-tech option and a new-tech option.
5. When you select a technology be sure to look at it from a customer point of view, like Steve Jobs did.

Notes

[1] Bill Buxton, 'The Long Nose of Innovation', Business Week, January 2, 2008.
[2] http://glassalmanac.com/history-google-glass/#sthash.kdcsONvA.dpuf
[3] Wikipedia: http://en.wikipedia.org/wiki/Apollo_program#Program_cost
[4] http://www.imperialtechforesight.com/future-visions/87/vision/timeline-of-emerging-science-and-technology.html

30 TECHNOLOGIES THAT

Source
BUSINESS INSIDER, August 15, 2012
http://www.businessinsider.com/30-game-changing-innovations-2012-8?IR=T

Edible food packaging .1
Affordable DNA sequencing .2
An inflatable seat belt .3
Ovarian tissue transplants .4
Microbes that can make energy .5
Commercial space flight .6
A tiny microscope that attaches to a cell phone .7
Lab-grown meat .8
Subretinal implants that restore sight to the blind .9
Supersonic flight .10
The Water Recycling Shower .11
An inflatable abdominal tourniquet .12
An assisted walking device that senses your step .13
A fabric that generates electricity from body heat .14
A car engine that reduces emissions .15

CAN CHANGE THE WORLD

16. **A low-cost cooking stove for the developing world**
17. **A nanoparticle system that could cure cancer**
18. **Laser-guided bullets**
19. **Adaptive cruise control**
20. **Lab-grown organs**
21. **Robotic surgery**
22. **Augmented reality contact lenses**
23. **Life-saving oxygen foam**
24. **Printed skin cells**
25. **A sewage elimination system that could revolutionize air travel**
26. **A blood test that can predict heart attacks**
27. **An artificial 'brain' that can diagnose breast cancer**
28. **Concentrated solar cells that could power a city**
29. **A vaccine for drug addiction**
30. **A cure for paralysis**

TIMELINE OF EMERGING SCIENCE AND TECHNOLOGY

Legend

- BIO-TECH
- DIGITAL-TECH
- NANO-TECH
- NEURO-TECH
- GREEN-TECH

Innovation or event

PRESENT — Defined as existing now or thereabouts with at least 1,000 examples existing where appropriate

PROBABLE — Defined as occurring between 2015-2030

POSSIBLE — Defined as potentially occurring after 2030

Notes and acknowledgements

Conceived and created by Richard Watson and Alex Ayad with input from Chris Haley and additional input from Keeren Flora and the 'Smarties' at Imperial College London.

Note that whilst most entries on the timeline are deeply serious, a few are less so. High resolution files suitable for printing can be obtained free of charge from richard@nowandnext.com or techforesight@imperial.ac.uk

A3 and A1 printed wall charts can also be ordered via these addresses although a charge is applied purely to cover print, packing and postage costs.

Tech Foresight
Personal perspectives
Visionary talent

www.imperialtechforesight.com

What's **Next**
Stay ahead of the future"
www.nowandnext.com

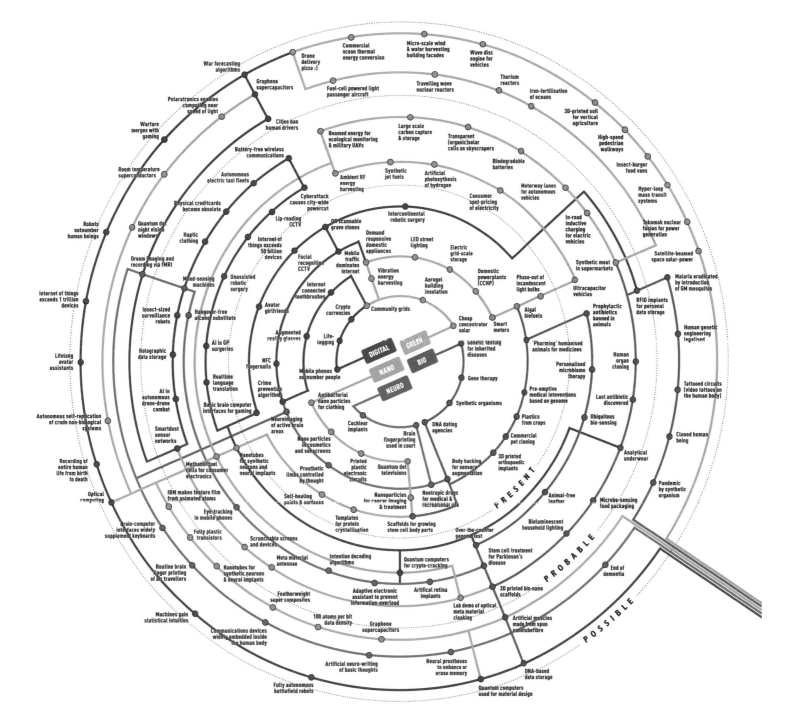

DIGITAL

GREEN

NANO

BIO

NEURO

PRESENT

PROBABLE

POSSIBLE

War forecasting algorithms

Drone delivery pizza :)

Commercial ocean thermal energy conversion

Micro-scale wind & water harvesting building facades

Wave disc engine for vehicles

Graphene supercapacitors

Polaratronics enables computing near speed of light

Fuel-cell powered light passenger aircraft

Travelling wave nuclear reactors

Thorium reactors

Iron-fertilisation of oceans

Warfare merges with gaming

Cities ban human drivers

3D-printed soil for vertical agriculture

Room temperature superconductors

Battery-free wireless communications

Beamed energy for ecological monitoring & military UAVs

Large scale carbon capture & storage

Transparent (organic)solar cells on skyscrapers

Biodegradable batteries

High-speed pedestrian walkways

Autonomous electric taxi fleets

Insect-burger food vans

Physical creditcards become obsolete

Cyberattack causes city-wide powercut

Ambient RF energy harvesting

Synthetic jet fuels

Artificial photosythesis of hydrogen

Motorway lanes for autonomous vehicles

Hyper-loop mass transit systems

Robots outnumber human beings

Quantum dot night vision windows

Lip-reading CCTV

QR-scannable grave stones

Intercontinental robotic surgery

Consumer spot-pricing of electricity

In-road inductive charging for electric vehicles

Tokomak nuclear fusion for power generation

Haptic clothing

Internet of things exceeds 50 billion devices

Demand responsive domestic appliances

LED street lighting

Electric grid-scale storage

Synthetic meat in supermarkets

Satellite-beamed space solar-power

Dream imaging and recording via fMRI

Facial recognition CCTV

Mobile traffic dominates internet

Domestic powerplants (CCHP)

Phase-out of incandescent light bulbs

Malaria eradicated by introduction of GM mosquitos

Internet of things exceeds 1 trillion devices

Mood-sensing machines

Unassisted robotic surgery

Internet connected toothbrushes

Vibration energy harvesting

Aerogel building insulation

Ultracapacitor vehicles

RFID implants for personal data storage

Insect-sized surveillance robots

Hangover-free alcohol substitute

Avatar girlfriends

Crypto currencies

Community grids

Cheap concentrator solar

Smart meters

Algal biofuels

Prophylactic antibiotics banned in animals

Human genetic engineering legalised

Holographic data storage

AI in GP surgeries

Augmented reality glasses

Life-logging

Genetic testing for inherited diseases

'Pharming' humanised animals for medicines

Human organ cloning

Lifelong avatar assistants

Realtime language translation

NFC fingernails

Mobile phones outnumber people

Gene therapy

Personalised microbiome therapy

Last antibiotic discovered

Tattooed circuits (video tattoos on the human body)

AI in autonomous drone-drone combat

Crime prevention algorithms

Antibacterial nano particles for clothing

Synthetic organisms

Pre-emptive medical inteventions based on genome

Autonomous self-replication of crude non-biological systems

Basic brain computer interfaces for gaming

Neuroimaging of active brain areas

Cochlear implants

DNA dating agencies

Plastics from crops

Ubiquitous bio-sensing

Cloned human being

Smartdust sensor networks

Nano particles in cosmetics and sunscreens

Brain fingerprinting used in court

Commercial pet cloning

Recording of entire human life from birth to death

Methanol/fuel cells for consumer electronics

Nanotubes for synthetic neurons and neural implants

Printed plastic electronic circuits

Quantum dot televisions

Body hacking for sensory augmentation

3D printed orthopaedic implants

Analytical underwear

Optical computing

IBM makes feature film from animated atoms

Prosthetic limbs controlled by thought

Nanoparticles for cancer imaging & treatment

Nootropic drugs for medical & recreational use

Animal-free leather

Microbe-sensing food packaging

Pandemic by synthetic organism

Brain-computer interfaces widely supplement keyboards

Eye-tracking in mobile phones

Self-healing paints & surfaces

Templates for protein crystallisation

Scaffolds for growing stem cell body parts

Over-the-counter genome test

Bioluminescent household lighting

Fully plastic transistors

Routine brain finger printing of air travellers

Scrunchable screens and devices

Intention decoding algorithms

Quantum computers for crypto-cracking

Stem cell treatment for Parkinson's disease

End of dementia

Meta material antennae

3D printed bio-nano scaffolds

Machines gain statistical intuition

Featherweight super composites

Adaptive electronic assistant to prevent information-overload

Artificial retina implants

Lab demo of optical meta material cloaking

Nanotubes for synthetic neurons & neural implants

100 atoms per bit data density

Graphene supercapacitors

Artificial muscles made from spun nanotubefibre

Communications devices widely embedded inside the human body

Artificial neuro-writing of basic thoughts

Neural prostheses to enhance or erase memory

DNA-based data storage

Fully autonomous battlefield robots

Quantum computers used for material design

QUOTE BY JAMES DYSON

WHAT:
FOUNDER OF THE DYSON COMPANY

HOW TO BE SUCCESSFUL:
1. BE CURIOUS
2. USE NEW TECHNOLOGY TO SOLVE COMMON EVERYDAY PROBLEMS
3. MAKE THE PERFECT PRODUCT

Sources
1. James Dyson on using failure to drive success: http://www.entrepreneur.com/blog/224855
2. http://www.famous-entrepreneurs.com/james-dyson
3. Knighthood for Dyson entrepreneur: http://news.bbc.co.uk/1/hi/business/6217291.stm

'YOU NEVER LEARN FROM SUCCESS, BUT YOU DO LEARN FROM FAILURE.'

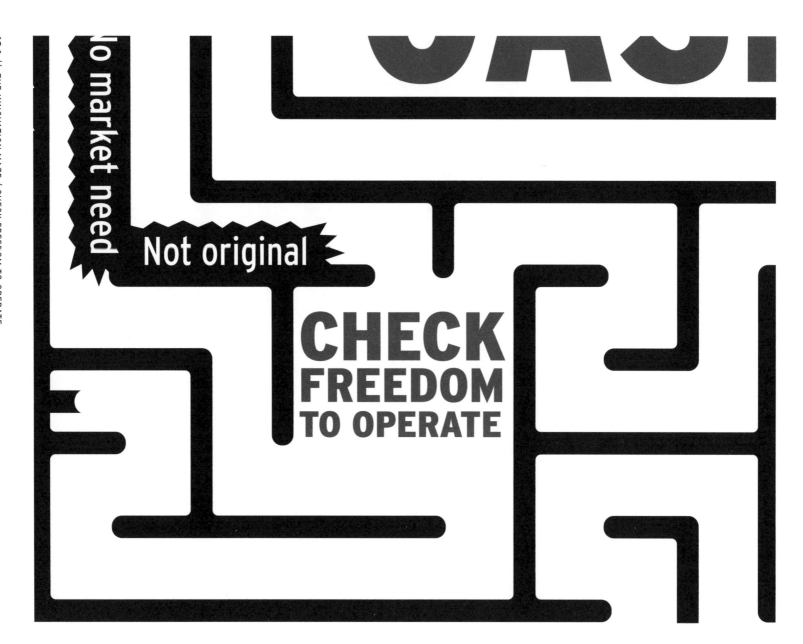

CHECK FREEDOM TO OPERATE

In this chapter you will enter the realm of intellectual property rights. Intellectual Property Rights (IPR) are a complex matter and are often overlooked by entrepreneurial people with great ideas without any legal background. That's why I have included this as an essential front-end activity. I hope to make you aware of the basic principle of checking your freedom to operate at a very early stage of your innovation process to reduce the risk of huge disappointments and costs down the road. Would you be able to say with certainty whether or not the core technology in your innovation is covered by intellectual property rights of others?

These days, when something new is invented or discovered with a lot of potential, you can be sure that a lot of patents will be filed. Just take a look at the new 'wonder material' graphene, which was discovered in a Manchester University physics lab in 2004. It's one atom thick, 200 times stronger than steel and an efficient conductor of both heat and electricity. Graphene has many possible applications: in hyper-fast computers, foldable mobile phones and super strong aircraft wings. Since its discovery, more than 11,000 graphene-related patents and patent applications have been filed globally.[1]

FREEDOM TO OPERATE IS THE ABILITY TO PROCEED WITHOUT INFRINGING THE RIGHTS OF OTHERS

Freedom to Operate (FTO) is the ability to proceed with the research, development and/or commercial production of a new product or process with a minimal risk of infringing the unlicensed intellectual property rights (IPR) of third parties.[2] A Freedom to Operate check addresses the question of "does my innovation infringe the IPR of others?"

According to the World Intellectual Property Organization (WIPO), intellectual property refers to creations of the mind: inventions; literary and artistic works; and symbols, names and images used in commerce. Intellectual property is divided into two categories:[3]
1. Industrial property, which includes patents for inventions, trademarks, industrial designs and geographical indications.
2. Copyright, covering literary works (such as novels, poems and plays), films, music, artistic works.

A patent is described as "an exclusive right granted for an invention: a product or process that provides a new way of doing something, or that offers a new technical solution to a problem." It provides patent owners with protection for their inventions for a limited period, generally 20 years for a utility patent. Patent rights are strictly territorial.

CHECK YOUR FREEDOM TO OPERATE IN THREE STEPS

A Freedom-To-Operate check is a risk management tool. The purpose is to assess the likelihood that you are infringing existing IPR with your innovation in specific countries where you are targeting. It is generally executed by internal or external patent specialists.

A FTO check usually consists of the following three steps:
1. Analysis of the technology and the potential product itself. The essential components must be clearly identified by you and the patent specialist as a starting point. As a rule, a separate search must be conducted for each unique component.
2. A patent specialist carries out a patent search collecting all accessible information about existing intellectual property rights, which are in force.
3. The patent specialist makes a technical comparison analysis and determines whether or not the technology or product that you want to develop infringes a patent. If this is the case, the next step is to examine in which countries the patents are valid and the expiry dates. Finally, the patent specialist will recommend how to pursue further.

A thorough analysis of the technology and the potential product in itself is essential. Finnegan, an IPR law firm, gives the example of a bicycle.[4] "For example, a bicycle, in its most rudimentary form, has at least six component parts: a frame, a seat, wheels, a steering mechanism, pedals, and a chain connected from the pedals to the rear wheel. Of course, many bicycles are far more complex. Some have more than one gear, which necessitates multiple chain-rings, a chain stay, and front and rear derailleurs. Further, even the rudimentary bicycle can have its parts subdivided into their individual hardware components (e.g., a wheel consists of a rim, hub, tube, and tire). Obviously, a search incorporating all of a bicycle's parts would be excessively time-consuming and costly. To keep it manageable, the company should focus on the components it anticipates to be novel or inventive."

In practice, you might want to watch out for the following risk. IP registrations are published 18 months after their filing date. The first 18 months are confidential. This means that your FTO check might not be complete, as there might be a patent pending that has not yet been published. So, it's wise to repeat an FTO check later on at the back end of the innovation process.

It's worth keeping in mind that there is no reason to immediately conclude that there is no Freedom to Operate when a patent application or patent in the database seems to relate to your innovation. Here are five reasons why a patent found could still be available to use.[5]

1. Patents may not have been applied for in multiple countries; the claimed matter is protected only where there is a patent.
2. Patents may not have been granted in some of the countries where applications were filed; laws about what is patentable vary between countries.
3. Patents that were issued may no longer be in force if the patentee has not met all patent fee obligations.
4. Patents are a limited monopoly and they do expire (check expiration dates!).
5. Some countries have exemptions for certain actions (for example, Germany is enacting a research exemption, and New Zealand has an exemption for certain types of clinical trials).

YOU CAN PATENT YOUR OWN NEW CONCEPT WHEN IT MEETS FOUR CRITERIA

In general, there are two kinds of patents you can file.
1. A utility patent for 20 years, for any process, machine, composition of matter or manufacture. Approximately 90% of the patent documents issued by the U.S. Patent and Trademark Office in recent years have been utility patents.
2. A design patent for 14 years, for any original and ornamental design for an article of manufacture.

A utility patent protects the way a product is used and works, while a design patent protects the way a product looks. The four requirements for a utility patent are:

1. It must be a machine, process, manufacture, composition, or any new or useful improvement.
2. It must be useful. You must demonstrate that your new invention works as intended and consequently you must prove its utility.
3. It must, of course, be novel.
4. It must be non-obvious. Is it non-obvious for people in your industry?

Protecting your innovation has become increasingly more important. One product manager in the displays industry explains this growing importance, "The importance of patents has trickled down from big companies to small and mid-size firms. Our industry has become more competitive so innovation has become more important to differentiate our products. We put more teeth into our IPR because we are an innovation leader and are often copied. We look at patentability so early because of this. All else being equal between new products, we will take the one with the best IPR potential."[6] Why is it in your interest to patent your innovations? Because this is how you can protect your innovation against infringement and misappropriation. This will also ensure your freedom to operate in your strategic target markets.

Filing a patent can be a tedious, lengthy and costly process. Should you consider to file a patent? Absolutely! A patent can become your company's most valuable asset if you're an inventor and startup-founder, whose future is tied to the success and failure of your innovation. The new business case which you draft at the end of your innovation route will provide you with an excellent decision paper to answer the question. When you don't file a patent, and your innovation is launched publicly, others will not be able to patent your new concept as it is 'public knowledge' from the moment you have launched.

Never start your back-end-of-innovation project without making sure that you have freedom to operate in the countries of your new business case. And if your project will last for a long time, be sure to monitor how the technology area is developing on a regular basis, as you don´t want unpleasant surprises when you´re almost done with your development.

When you've checked your Freedom to Operate, and the answer is 'yes', you can then proceed to the next crucial step: Experiment, which I will discuss in the next chapter.

KEY MESSAGES FROM THIS CHAPTER

1. **Check the Freedom to Operate to proceed without infringing the intellectual property right of others.**
2. **You can patent your own new concept when it's a new, useful and non-obvious machine, process, manufacture, composition, or any new or useful improvement.**
3. **Filing a patent makes sense when there's a valid new business case.**

Notes

1. http://www.ft.com/cms/s/0/4dfd6f86-4141-11e5-9abe-5b335da3a90e.html
2. ipHandbook of Best Practices, http://www.iphandbook.org/handbook/ch14/p02/
3. WIPO, What is Intellectual Property, p. 2 http://www.wipo.int/edocs/pubdocs/en/intproperty/450/wipo_pub_450.pdf
4. http://www.finnegan.com/resources/articles/articlesdetail.aspx?news=5ca04b7d-cfce-42a0-ab8b-1ada760f8887
5. http://www.bios.net/daisy/patentlens/2768.html
6. Whitepaper, Views of Inventors & Product Managers on Freedom-To-Operate & Portfolio Enhancement Work Products of Patent Law Firms, http://www.slwip.com/services/documents/SLWWhitePaperFTO_001.pdf

QUOTE BY
RICHARD BRANSON

WHAT:
FOUNDER OF VIRGIN GROUP

HOW TO BE SUCCESSFUL:
1. **STEP OUT OF YOUR COMFORT ZONE**
2. **MIX BUSINESS WITH PLEASURE**
3. **TAKE CALCULATED RISKS**

Sources
1. www.success.com/article/richard-branson-virgin-entrepreneur)
2. http://www.virgin.com/entrepreneur/10-inspirational-richard-branson-quotes
3. http://blog.iqmatrix.com/richard-branson
4. http://nl.wikipedia.org/wiki/Richard_Branson
5. http://www.businessinsider.com/richard-branson-taught-me-that-successful-people-start-before-theyre-ready-2013-8
6. http://www.entrepreneur.com/article/229510
7. http://www.biography.com/people/richard-branson-9224520

'THE CHALLENGE IS
TO FOLLOW THROUGH
ON A GREAT IDEA.'

EXPERIMENT

Experimenting at the start of innovation is crucial. It's in this activity that you verify if your new idea and business model is attractive. Inventors, startups and big corporations experiment by talking to customers, showing their new concept to customers or letting customers use their new concept. In this chapter I will discuss the concept of pretotyping and seven ways how to conduct an experiment. The chapter will conclude with three 'real-life stories' of experimenting by Xerox, Intuit and Tesla.

WHY EXPERIMENTING IS CRUCIAL AT THE START OF INNOVATION

What's the worst possible nightmare you could have as an innovator? It's launching a product or service nobody wants, making it an instant failure. The sooner you know your new innovation is attractive and be able show it the better. That's why you should experiment at the start of innovation. Don't wait until the delivery phase.

As you keep discussing your idea with others, it tends to evolve in your mind continuously. It's important that your innovative idea and business model be concrete so your fellow innovators or even more importantly potential customers know what you mean. That's why it's an important step to convert an abstract idea into a concrete offering. It helps you to materialize your idea for yourself and others. And it is a great way to test and improve your concept.

Experimenting means validating the adoption and attractiveness of your new product, service, process or experience through systematic research or testing. You test your new concept to learn if it

really delivers value to your customer and if the business model you came up with is valid. By doing so, you validate the future business potential of your new concept.

The goal of experimentation at the start of innovation is simply to learn and improve. I couldn't agree more with Davila & Epstein who state in their book *The Innovation Paradox* that: "Because breakthrough innovation is all about managing ignorance (rather than managing knowledge, as in incremental innovation), the way to learn is through confronting assumptions concerning a market with the reality of that market. The right technology and the right business model are discovered and shaped through smart experiments. A successful breakthrough innovation is not simply an ingenious idea, but an entire process of discovery and crafting."[1]

An important potential pitfall in this stage of innovation, might be your own perfectionism. It might be your own tendency to endlessly add new features and content to your concept, especially when you know that it will be judged by customers. By going about it this way though, you will be stuck in your innovation lab forever and your concept will never see the light of day. You know by now that a short time-to-market is more important than ever before. So, be sure to experiment with your concept in its early stages. Be inspired by Reid Hoffman, founder of LinkedIn, who said: "If you are not embarrassed by the first version of your product, you've launched too late."[2]

ONSET Ventures, a pioneer among accelerators to help early-stage startups, tried to identify which criteria were important to success by gathering information on 300 early-stage investments that had been funded by existing Silicon Valley venture capitalists. According to their research they found that the best predictor of failure was stubbornly sticking to the original business plan. The business models of successful startups, in contrast, nearly always underwent at least one major revision (and countless minor tweaks) before they were stabilized.[3] This insight underpins that innovation is 'learning by doing' and stresses the need for experimentation.

INVENTORS, STARTUPS AND BIG CORPORATIONS ALL EXPERIMENT

Did you know that the inventor James Dyson had made 5,127 prototypes of his famous Dual Cyclone bagless vacuum cleaner before settling on the model that would make him a billionaire?[4] I for one was surprised to learn this. It's surely an amazing example of the perseverance of a true innovator.

All that matters at the start of innovation is creating the right concept. This is emphasized in a quote by Airbnb's CEO Brian Chesky: "Create the perfect experience however you need to do it, and then scale that experience. Every company that makes something is just two things. It's creating an experience. And then it's multiplying them. We care about just two things: How great that one experience is and how many we make. Too many people start in technology with 'how many you sell' and then they try to make it better. A lot of movements start with a small set of evangelists."[5]

Inventors or startups aren't the only ones who are experimenting. Big organizations, like the Mayo Clinic in the US are also checking if they are on the right track in an early phase by doing something they call prototyping. The Mayo Clinic is a non-profit medical practice and medical research group based in Minnesota, USA. It is the first and largest integrated non-profit medical group practice in the world, employing more than 3,800 physicians and scientists and nearly 51,000 allied health staff. The Mayo Clinic is known for its innovation facilitated by their Mayo Clinic Center for Innovation, where experimentation plays a huge role: "We rely a lot on proto-

typing, and we believe we do prototyping well. Our prototypes are complete and realistic, yet fast to arise and fast to give us 'proof of concept'. We're not afraid to do a prototype a little 'rough' to get it out there and see how it works. We get real patients, real physicians, real staff, real facilities, and real systems involved in prototypes as quickly as possible, and we don't shy away from adjusting or tweaking the prototypes once they're set up. Our prototypes not only prove concepts, but they also become vehicles around which to collaborate and for demonstrating our programs."[6]

EXPERIMENT WITH PRETOTYPES INSTEAD OF PROTOTYPES

The outcome of an experiment is a decision based on the feedback to persevere with your new concept or to pivot it into something else. The ultimate deliverable of an experiment or several ones, is a solid 'proof of concept': a verification of the potential of your new concept. It serves as a solid base to build your new business case on.

The more realistic your experiment is, the more you will learn and the better you can assess the validity and attractiveness of your new concept. A real-life experiment with a working prototype, like the Google Glass Experiment (chart 16), would be the perfect building block for a convincing well-founded new business case. Unfortunately, at the start of innovation you sometimes lack the technology itself or you lack both the time and money to develop one. It might take you months or even years to develop a working prototype. In most cases you will need a new business case to raise the R&D budget from investors or your board to develop the technology.

So, it's time to improvise and be smart. I am very charmed by the work of Alberto Savoia, who led the development and launch of the original Google AdWords as well as coined the term: pretotypes,[7] a testing concept in which you pretend you have a real prototype. Savoia defines pretotyping as, "a way to test an idea quickly and inexpensively by creating extremely simplified, mocked or virtual versions of that product to help validate the premise that 'If we build it, they will use it.'" Pretotypes are what the Mayo Clinic innovators call "rough prototypes to get it out there and see how it works."

My favorite definition of Savoia's pretotyping is:
Make sure - as quickly and as cheaply as you can - that you are building the right it before you build it right.

It's a great motto for the Experimenting phase at the start of innovation, as pretotyping focuses on answering one very basic question: Is this the right thing to build?

SEVEN WAYS TO EXPERIMENT WITH PRETOTYPES

I can imagine that your time frame, your budget and also the innovativeness of your concept influence the way you test your new offering. However, be aware that the more innovative your concept is, the more you will have to show it to users and let them experience it, as customers have no point of reference.
Prototype experiments can come in many varieties. Here, you will find seven ways of pretotyping: [8]

- The Mechanical Turk - replace complex and expensive computers or machines with human beings.
- The Pinocchio - build a non-functional, "lifeless", version of the product.
- The Minimum Viable Product (or Stripped Tease) - create a functional version of it, but stripped down to its most basic functionality.
- The Provincial - before launching world-wide, run a test on a very small sample.
- The Fake Door - create a fake "entry" for a product that doesn't yet exist in any form.
- The Pretend-to-Own - before investing in buying whatever you need for your it, rent or borrow it first.
- The Re-label - put a different label on an existing product that looks like the product you want to create.

The basics of experimentation all come down to four steps. First, you design your test: you pick the test-type which fits your innovation project best and select a sufficient number of customers from all potential target groups. You might even include colleagues to get an idea how the new concept will be received internally. Secondly, you execute the test. You might facilitate it yourself or hire external professionals. It is my experience that at big firms, the latter will increase the credibility of the test results. Execute the test in a structured way. You might film it as well; to use parts of it later, for learning - or presentation purposes. As a third step, you analyze and evaluate the feedback with your team. As a final step, you make a decision to improve the concept, or to pivot it into a completely new direction. At this point, I would like to inspire you with three practical experiments by Xerox, Intuit, and Tesla.

EXPERIMENT 1: HOW Z'S PRETOTYPED NEW DOCUMENT MACHINE CONVINCED XEROX

John Seely Brown, former scientist of Xerox Corporation and director of Xerox Palo Alto Research Center (PARC) experienced how useful a pretotype could be in convincing top management to support a new idea: "Z Smith, a physicist, did one of the more dramatic examples of this [prototyping] in my tenure at Xerox PARC in the early 1990s around a radical new kind of document machine that could scan, think/interpret, and print the document. Z's prototype not only demonstrated the vision, it also became a powerful offer. His machine's 'thinking' was of many forms including summarizing, filing and distributing, and so on. It was a really cool, personal document machine that pushed the boundaries of what computing and imaging could do in those days. And it certainly pushed the concept of a printer or a copier to the extreme. We knew that getting this intelligent, multifunction device embraced within the culture of our copier company would be decidedly nontrivial. The company thought and breathed stand-alone, single-purpose devices, not devices that could actually interpret the documents they were being fed. Z's idea for moving the internal community adopting this idea was as ingenious as his invention. He built mockups of the machine and then designed, created and videoed three shorts skits of different uses of the device. At the end of the video he added a fourth skit by a professional comedian that ended with the comedian asking the viewers how they might use the capabilities of the device. We then invited senior officers of the company to watch the video and to storyboard out, with some artist help, how they might imagine using this device. The three main skits were meant to act as a sort of an intuition pump that would orient viewers and help them internalize what the device might mean to them. The comedian segment was designed to give some time for viewers to internalize the prior skits by providing a fun but purposeful distraction. And it provided a non-threatening transition for them to the activity of creating their own storyboard with which they could 'finish' the video. Finally, of course, the viewers' own storyboards served as the basis of new stories that they could then tell others in the company. Z titled the video 'More Than a Box', which was both what the comedic skit was about but more importantly was meant to provide a strategic nudge, suggesting that a copier could be much more than just a copier. Indeed, it was meant to nudge the company into seeing that it could be reconstituted as more than just a copier company. It could start to re-imagine itself not as a company that produced and sold 'boxes', but as *The Document Company* with the realization that documents are living, social artefacts that touch us and therein create meaning......Z's offer was successful. The Xerox company set up a division to manufacture and market Z's document machine."[9]

EXPERIMENT 2: HOW EXPERIMENTING INNOVATORS BUILT INTUIT'S PRICE-SMS-SERVICE IN INDIA

Intuit is an American financial - and tax software company with US $4 billion in annual revenues. Here's a story on experimentation in innovation from Intuit's founder and chairman of the executive committee Scott Cook.[10] "Our head of global asked our teams in India to figure out how we can improve the financial lives of people.

One team had the idea of focusing on farmers. They're half the population of India. We'd never done anything with farmers. Their bosses were uninterested. So the team went out, researched, spent time in the fields, time with the farmers, time in their homes, came up with a problem that they thought they could solve. These guys don't know where to take their goods when they harvest them. Do they take it to the town to the north? The south? The east? Which wholesaler will give them the best price? ... So our little team said, 'Why don't we collect prices and send them on SMS so they get them on their phones?' Well the bosses had all the reasons that it would not work. You know, farmers are often illiterate. Could they read it? Would they believe it? Would it change behavior? ... And would we even be able to get the price information from the wholesalers? ... Because of our culture of experimentation, the team didn't listen to the bosses. Instead they ran an experiment. In seven weeks they prototyped a product, went out and tried it. Two weeks later, they had proof it would work. One hundred and ten farmers, on average, reported 16 percent higher incomes. Twelve of the 14 wholesalers said they'd continue to give us data. Thirteen experiments later, we now have over 400,000 farmers who get price information on their phones in India. ... The bosses would have killed it. But because of experimentation - cheap experiments – that was an idea that could prove itself. This is a new kind of management, where instead of viewing the boss's role as the Caesar to make decisions, the boss's role is to put in a system whereby junior people can run fast and cheap experiments, so that the ideas can prove themselves."

EXPERIMENT 3: HOW TESLA USED A LOTUS ELISE TO INTEREST POTENTIAL BUYERS FOR THEIR ROADSTER

A Re-label pretotype puts a different label on an existing product that looks like the product you want to create. An excellent example comes from Tesla Motors.[11] In 2003, the founders of Tesla had an ambitious idea (an all-electric 2-door sports car) and a marketing challenge (Tesla was an unknown quantity as a carmaker). In order to convince potential buyers to order its car, Tesla created a pretotype of what the car would look like. The base for the pretotype was a Lotus Elise, the car whose chassis technology was ultimately licensed - and heavily modified - by Tesla to provide the basis for the Roadster chassis. Lotus supplied Tesla with a 'glider' Elise - a car without a powertrain - which was filled with models of key components like batteries and AC motors. This was not a prototype, because the vehicle didn't function, yet with a (relatively) trivial investment, Tesla was able to show prospective buyers a very close proxy for the final design. As if this were not canny enough, Tesla also deployed a Fake Door prototype to further validate demand. Instead of asking customers whether they "Would buy a Roadster" if Tesla built it, they asked "Will you put down a $5,000 deposit to have it built to order?" This is a true revealed-preference test, from which Tesla secured several hundred deposits, a non-trivial result to reassure Investors.

As a final remark on experimenting, I would like to quote Scott D. Anthony's 7 Rules of Thumb to maximize your flexibility and keep costs as low as possible in this phase:[12]

1. Prototype before you build.
2. Fake it before you make it.
3. Borrow before you buy.
4. Contract before you hire.
5. Test before you commit.
6. Research before you do it.
7. Outsource before you ramp up.

A successful experiment is a solid base to build your new business case on. Create a new business case is the final activity on every innovation route through the maze, which I will discuss in the next chapter.

KEY MESSAGES FROM THIS CHAPTER

1. **You validate the future business potential of your new concept by experimenting.**
2. **The right technology and the right business model are discovered and shaped through smart experiments.**
3. **The more realistic your experiment is, the more you will learn and the better you can assess the validity and attractiveness of your new concept.**
4. **Pretotyping is a way to test an idea quickly and inexpensively by creating extremely simplified, mocked or virtual versions of the new offering.**

Notes

1   Tony Davila & Marc J. Epstein, *The Innovation Paradox*, Berret-Koehler Inc., San Francisco, 2014, p. 52.
2   Alberto Savoia, *Pretotype It*, October 2011, p. 2.
3   Source: Donald Sull, McKinsey Quarterly, May 2015. http://www.mckinsey.com/insights/innovation/the_simple_rules_of_disciplined_innovation
4   "Life's Work: James Dyson", Harvard Business Review, https://hbr.org/2010/07/lifes-work-james-dyson
5   Thompson, "CEO Brian Chesky on Building a Company and Starting a 'Sharing' Revolution", The Atlantic, August 13, 2013.
6   Nicholas LaRusso, Barbara Spurrier, and Glanrico Farrugia, *Think Big, Move Fast*, Mc Graw Hill, 2015 p. 122.
7   Alberto Savoia, *Pretotype It*, October 2011, p. 4.
8   Alberto Savoia, *Pretotype It*, October 2011, p. 39.
9   Peter J. Denning & Robert Dunham, *The Innovator's Way*, The MIT Press, Cambridge, Masachusetts, pp. x –xi.
10 Michael Schrage, *The Innovator's Hypothesis*, The MIT Press, Cambridge, Massachusetts, 2014, pp. 57-58.
11 pretotyping@work, Jeremy Clark, 2012, pp. 25 -26.
12 Scott D. Anthony, *The First Mile*, Harvard Business Review Press, Boston, Massachusetts, 2014, pp. 92-93.

QUOTE BY STEVE JOBS

WHAT:
CO-FOUNDER OF APPLE

HOW TO BE SUCCESSFUL:
1. BE COMMITTED TO PERFECTION
2. SAY 'NO' TO 1,000 THINGS
3. SELL DREAMS, NOT PRODUCTS

Sources
1. http://wallstcheatsheet.com/stocks/20-most-memorable-quotes-from-steve-jobs.html/?a=viewall
2. http://www.entrepreneur.com/article/220515: Steve Jobs and the seven rules of success
3. http://www.entrepreneur.com/article/197538: Steven Jobs an extraordinary career
4. http://abcnews.go.com/Technology/steve-jobs-successful/story?id=11890666
5. http://en.wikipedia.org/wiki/Steve_Jobs

'INNOVATION DISTINGUISHES
BETWEEN A LEADER
AND A FOLLOWER.'

Fear of failure

CREATE NEW BUSINESS CASE

CREATE NEW BUSINESS CASE

I have seen a lot of innovative people presenting ideas in very original ways. Playing a movie. Doing a dance. Making a painting. Writing one huge post-it. Making a newspaper. And even by doing a flash mob. Although it's very creative, the essence of presenting your new concept is to get approval from decision makers or financers so you can go ahead to the development phase. That's why the concrete deliverable of your innovation route, next to the insights, ideas and prototype, is a well-founded convincing business case for your new product, service, process or experience. It's the end of the beginning. In this chapter, I will describe why you need a new business case and how you can draft a convincing one. I will give you a recent example of a new business case for a business-to-business service, as a source of inspiration.

YOU NEED A CONVINCING BUSINESS CASE TO GET THE DEVELOPMENT OF YOUR NEW OFFERING FUNDED

Does a great idea automatically sell itself? Can a top executive recognize the potential of a great idea? That's the question. You may be familiar with the story of Kodak, "A Kodak engineer, asked by his supervisor, invented the first digital camera. They combined a new semiconductor with a television and data cassette to take a 0.01 megapixel photo. It took Kodak 16 years to get a single dollar from the invention: a one-off sale of a spy camera after a request from the US government. Kodak ignored the new idea because it didn't play nicely with its existing beliefs. Apple was first to market with a digital camera that worked with home computers. Kodak was second to market, and created a network to popularize the digital camera. Microsoft built the kiosks. Kinko's served customers. IBM created a photo network. HP invented color inkjets for printers. Yet, Kodak refused to give up its old idea and so could not adapt to the new idea as fast as its competitors."[1]

History has shown us that a lot of wise people haven't been able to recognize the potential of a great idea, as you can read in Chart 19: "10 Great Ideas that Were Originally Rejected." Even when it's the top management of your company who ask you to be innovative and expect you to break patterns, it is still wise to keep in mind that they are as conservative as ever. So the question is; how will you be able to help your colleague, your top manager, your shareholder or your venture capitalist to support your idea and fund the development and execution of it? As you're proposing an innovation to them, you have to be aware that these decision makers who are assessing your new concept might know very little about the new target market, the new product and business model or the new technology. They would like as much tangible proof as they can get before making a decision. As long as they haven't decided anything they don't run any risk. Once they say yes, they will be in it up to their necks.

The most essential question is, "Why should we fund the development of this new product or service?"

YOUR IDEA WILL BE EVALUATED FROM AT LEAST FIVE PERSPECTIVES

Jennifer Mueller of the University of San Diego, Jeff Loewenstein of the University of Illinois at Urbana-Champaign, and Jennifer Deal of the Center for Creative Leadership studied a company that was considering dozens of new product ideas. The researchers asked middle managers, C-suite executives, idea generators, and other stakeholders to rate each idea on its creativity, feasibility, and profitability. Then they asked customers how desirable each idea was. The team found that the customers wanted the most creative ideas, but not the ideas that people in the firm thought would be most profitable or feasible.[2] Jennifer Mueller states, "We believe that the major reason novelty and feasibility are thought to be at odds is that new ideas involve more unknowns. CEOs want to see metrics, such as ROI, to determine the viability of ideas, but for the newest ideas, such metrics are hard to produce, if not impossible. If decision makers are more tolerant of uncertainty—if they focus on the 'why' or consider that there are many possible solutions—it may mitigate their tendency to reject creative ideas."

In a new business case it is your challenge to be convincing. The more radical your innovation is, the bigger the challenge as there will be more uncertainties. In the boardroom your idea will be evaluated from at least five perspectives:
1. The Customer: will they buy it?
2. The Technology: can we deliver it?
3. The Business model: will it pay off?
4. The Risk: what do we risk? What if it's a failure? What if it's a huge success?
5. The Fit: Why should we do it? What's the strategic perspective?

When the front end of innovation is finished, a lot is still unknown. The figures in your business case will be estimations, extrapolations, best guesses and hard results from small-scale experiments. It is the potential risk of failure that makes managers and investors so prudent. Gilbert and Eyring found it useful to think in three broad, sometimes overlapping categories of risks starting up a new venture: deal-killer risks, path-dependent risks, and easy-win, high-ROI risks.[3] Deal-killer risks are uncertainties that, if left unresolved, could undermine the entire venture. Path-dependent risks arise when pursuing the wrong path would involve wasting large sums of money or time or both. The remaining risks are risks that can be resolved without spending a lot of time and money. When you fail to spot a deal-killer risk, your innovation is doomed, so it's of extreme importance to identify and address the most important uncertainties in your new business case.

A PRACTICAL FRAMEWORK FOR YOUR NEW BUSINESS CASE COVERS 7 SUBJECTS

For more than 10 years, I have been using and giving instructions on a handy, practical framework for a new business case. My advice was to just use PowerPoint (or keynote) instead of writing a full written report, as nobody will read it anyway. Here's the framework of a 7-paged new business case, which you can present in 20 minutes at the most.

Slide 1. The Customer Friction.
▸ The customer situation.
▸ The customer need.
▸ The customer friction (problem/challenge).

Slide 2. Our New Concept.
▸ The customer target group (qualitative and quantitative).
▸ The marketing mix of the new product, service or business model.
▸ New for.... (the world, the market, our company).

Slide 3. This Makes our Concept Unique.
- Buying arguments for the customer.
- Current solutions and competitors.
- Our positioning.

Slide 4. It will be Feasible.
- We are able to develop it.
- We are able to produce it.
- The development process.

Slide 5. What's in it for us.
- The number of customers (in year three).
- The projected revenues (in year three).
- The projected profits (in year three).

Slide 6. Why now?
- Why develop it now.
- What if we say 'no'.

Slide 7. The Decision to Proceed.
- The major uncertainties.
- The development team,
- The process, costs and planning.

An original way of presenting your idea gets you attention. By making a new business case according to this format, you strengthen the persuasiveness of your proposal. It increases the chance you will get a 'Yes', especially if you also have a prototype which makes your new concept tangible and easy to understand. Be serious. Remember: "Nobody buys innovation from a clown."

In chart 31 you will find a 'real-life' new business case of Bruil, a Dutch supplier of building materials, on a new concept for applying tiles: the tile-adhesive silo service.

Presenting a new business case is a different kind of sales pitch. Of course you need to convince your board or investors. Beware of being too 'salesy' though. In this phase of the innovation process there are still so many uncertainties. It will increase your trustworthiness if you make the uncertainties very explicit. In the innovation delivery process, there are plenty possibilities to be eliminated. With a 'yes' on your new business case you managed to find your way through the innovation maze successfully. I hope the four routes will be quite useful to you in your daily work. Once you have gotten approval you can start in the delivery phase. I will describe this in the next chapter, "We have a business case. Now what?"

KEY MESSAGES FROM THIS CHAPTER

1. **A lot of wise people haven't been able to recognize the potential of a great idea.**
2. **You need a convincing business case to get the development of your new offering funded.**
3. **Your idea will be evaluated from at least five perspectives**
4. **The more radical your innovation is, the bigger the challenge to convince, as there will be more uncertainties.**
5. **Be serious. Remember: "nobody buys innovation from a clown."**

Notes
[1] Max McKeown, *The Innovation Book*, Pearson, Harlow, United Kingdom, 2014, p. 24.
[2] Jennifer Mueller, Harvard Business Review, July 2014.
[3] Jennifer Mueller, Harvard Business Review, July 2014.

A NEW BUSINESS CASE FOR BRUIL: THE TILE-ADHESIVE SILO SERVICE

THE INNOVATION CHALLENGE OF BRUIL

Bruil is a leading supplier in the Netherlands of cement-based building materials like concrete, mortar, prefab concrete products, and adhesives. It's a family owned company founded in 1906. Today, Bruil is a medium sized company employing 350 people with a revenue of around € 100 million.

In recent years, the Dutch construction market has been in a huge crisis. The entire market had to adapt by undergoing structural changes to its processes and methods. Consequently, in order to 'play to win' again in this market, Bruil needed to innovate. That's why they started an innovation process to create new products and services which are new to Bruil and distinctive in the market. Bruil will focus its innovation efforts on the Dutch construction market with a possible spin-off abroad. The goal of their innovation process is to generate new business cases which will meet the following criteria:

1. Substantial revenues for Bruil, in year three after introduction.
2. A profit margin of at least 10 percent.
3. Break-even within three years.
4. An investment budget is available when a return on investment (ROI) of 7 percent is met.
5. The new offering will be sustainable.
6. The new offering may be co-created with other parties.

THE INNOVATION PROCESS OF BRUIL

Bruil used the FORTH innovation method to start innovation (www.forth-innovation.com). This structured methodology follows the innovation maze via the business challenge route. All 10 activities are accommodated in five steps: Full Steam Ahead, Observe & Learn, Raise Ideas, Test Ideas and Homecoming. A core team of twelve people and an extended team with four top managers joined this innovation expedition of fifteen weeks. The project was led by Oscar Dekkers, one of their directors. The deliverables of their innovation process were six new business cases. Here, I will focus on the so-called new business case for the tile-adhesive silo service under the Coba brand. This new business case was developed by Benno van Dijk and Theo Voogd, who I would like to thank for making it available for this book.

THE NEW BUSINESS CASE FOR THE TILE-ADHESIVE SILO SERVICE

1. **The customer friction:** as a professional tiler my profit margin is squeezed.
   The new offering's target group are professional tiler companies, hired by their clients, such as large retailers who wish to have their new shop floor tiled.
   The customer situation: I am the director of a tiler company. Tiling floors is a real profession. Our work mainly consists of cutting the tiles, mixing the dry adhesive with water and tiling the tiles to the floor.
   The customer need: I am looking for opportunities to improve my competitive position for large tiling assignments. Now that the market sentiment is improving, I would like to increase my revenues and margin as well.

The customer friction: There's a lot of competition for tiling large floors and margins are low. There's a lot of time pressure and my productivity must be huge to be able to generate a profit on these projects.

2. **Our new concept:** the Coba tile-adhesive Silo Service for large tiling companies

To solve this relevant customer friction Coba introduces a new-to-the-world offering. It's the VTA180, a tile-adhesive for flooring which can be applied mechanically with the tile-adhesive silo service. With one push of the button, the adhesive is mixed mechanically and then pumped to the place of application. Coba offers a silo with powdered adhesive, including a mix/pump installation. Coba has pumping tubes available for tile works larger than 200 m². As a tiler, the silo service will cost you € 150 per day, excluding the adhesive.

The target group consists of the top 300 tiling companies in the Netherlands, which all regularly tile floors larger than 200m². Their customers are mainly healthcare institutions, schools and retailers.

3. **This makes our concept unique:**

"You can cut back one man to mix and transport the adhesive."

A large floor tiling project is around 1,200 m². For this you will need 6,000 kilos of powdered adhesive, which is 6 pallets with 240 bags, and a man mixing the adhesive with water. It means a lot of dust, packaging waste and manual labor.

Our main competitors are all major suppliers of dry tile adhesives like Ardal, Schonox and Omnicol Laticrete. With the introduction of our new silo service with a mixing/pumping system customers can reduce the tiling crew from 4 to 3 people and eliminate the dust, waste and heavy carrying. Our market positioning will be: "You can cut back one man making the adhesive" with the Coba tile-adhesive silo service. Currently, there is hardly any difference among the dry tile-adhesives. The Coba adhesive silo system can change this fundamentally. The concept is unique.

4. **It will be feasible:** our development time will be short.

We will parallel develop both a mechanically pumpable tile-adhesive and the mixing and pumping system.

The adhesive must be:

▸ Quickly solvable.
▸ Pumpable (10 kg per minute).
▸ Specific for flooring.
▸ Application possible without floating and buttering.
▸ C2E S1 quality.

The mixing and pumping system:
▸ Be fitted to the scale and building phase of the tiler.
▸ Can be co-developed with partners, like: PFT, m-Tec or Collomix

In the development process we will need to develop the tile-adhesive, develop and test the equipment internally and finally do some 'live-tests' at customer sites.

5. **What's in it for Bruil:** A significant additional profit margin of € 613,000 in year 3.
The market share for ready-mixed dispersion-adhesives for Coba is about 18 percent. The market share for dry cementitious adhesives for Coba is about 6 percent.

Our market assumptions:
▸ We will gain market share due the unique concept and grow from 6% to 18% in 5 years. This prognosis is supported by the enthusiastic response to the concept by the owner of one of the biggest tilers of the Netherlands, saying: "If you can make this happen, we are in business!" Large tilers will be very interested in using the Coba silo service.
▸ A large tiler, tiles around 120,000 m² yearly.
▸ Coba VTA180 will be priced at € 550. - per ton
▸ On average, the rent for the silo system will be € 150, per day for 2 days.

PROJECTED REVENUES IN €	2016	2017	2018
Adhesive	360,000	720,000	1,440,000
Rent	40,000	80,000	160,000
Total revenues	400,000	800,000	1,600,000

PROJECTED COSTS IN €	2016	2017	2018
Maintenance & transport	75,000	150,000	225,000
Sales	60,000	90,000	120,000
Marketing	50,000	50,000	50,000
Cost price adhesive	148,000	296,000	592,000
Total costs	333,000	586,000	987,000

PROJECTED PROFIT MARGIN IN €	2016	2017	2018
Total profit margin	67,000	214,000	613,000

PROJECTED INVESTMENTS IN €	2015	2016	2017
Product development	100,000		
20 silos and pumps	120,000	120,000	120,000
Unforeseen	25,000	20,000	5,000
Total investment in 3 years	510,000		

PROJECTED ROI IN %	2016	2017	2018	Total
Investment	245,000	140,000	125,000	510,000
Margin	67,000	214,000	613,000	894,000
ROI	27%	153%	490%	175%

6. **Why now?:** It will triple our market share in floor tile adhesives
There are four reasons to say 'yes' to the development of the Coba tile-adhesive silo system:
   1. It will boost our market share in floor tile adhesives from 6% to 18%.
   2. Everybody has bags; nobody has silos.
   3. Relatively low investment costs.
   4. The silo system has great scores when assessing the sustainability factor.

7. **The decision to proceed:** start as soon as possible
The major uncertainties are:
   ▸ The number of large machines on construction sites will be reduced.
   ▸ How can we clean and maintain the pumping tubes and system?
   ▸ How can we clean the system environmentally friendly?
   ▸ Competitors will react with lower prices for their adhesives.
   ▸ The system must be 100% reliable.

Theo, Aart, Benno and Reinier are members of the innovation delivery team and will start product development as soon as possible. The market introduction is planned for January 2016
Post script. Bruil has developed the system in reality and launched it successfully at the time this book was published in 2016.

QUOTE BY FEODOR KAMPRAD

WHAT:
FOUNDER OF IKEA

HOW TO BE SUCCESSFUL:
1. **BREAK THE PATTERN**
2. **SIMPLIFY**
3. **PERSIST**

Sources
1. http://news.investors.com/management-leaders-in-success/100899-359181-ikea-founder-ingvar-kamprad. htm#ixzz2sSqG1HER
2. Challenges faced by Ingvar Kamprad, great lesson from IKEA: http://testervn.hubpages.com/hub/Challenges-faced-by-Ingvar-Kamprad-great-lesson-from-IKEA
3. http://en.wikipedia.org/wiki/Ingvar_Kamprad
4. "He lives in a bungalow, flies easyJet and 'dries out' three times a year... the man who founded Ikea and is worth £15bn". Daily Mail (London). April 14, 2008

'ONLY THOSE WHO ARE ASLEEP MAKE NO MISTAKES.'

WE HAVE A NEW BUSINESS CASE: NOW WHAT?

In his book *David & Goliath*, Malcolm Gladwell quotes the psychologist Jordan Peterson who argues that innovators and revolutionaries tend to have a very particular mix of personality traits.[1] "Innovators have to be open. They have to be able to imagine things that others cannot and to be willing to challenge their own preconceptions. They also need to be conscientious. An innovator who has brilliant ideas but lacks the discipline to carry them out is merely a dreamer. That, too, is obvious. But crucially, innovators need to be disagreeable. ... They are people willing to take social risks – to do things that others might disapprove of."
I recognize these words so much in the daily practice of an innovator, having a new business case and looking for a speedy way to develop the new product or service and launch it on the market. In this chapter I will show you six fallacies in developing new products and I will share ten insights with you to execute innovation effectively. The chapter ends with the story of how the Finnish start-up Rovio developed and launched Angry Birds, the most downloaded app of all time (Chart 34).

INNOVATION DOES NOT STOP AT THE FIRST 'NO'; THAT'S THE MOMENT IT REALLY STARTS

When you presented your new business case and you got a go from your management, your financers or your partners it's not the end of a journey. It's only the start of it. When you share your innovative idea with others in the development - and launch phase you will probably get a lot of negative reactions like:

1. No, it's always done this way...
2. No, customers won't like that!
3. No, we don't have time for this...
4. No, it's not possible...
5. No, it's too expensive!
6. No, let's be realistic...
7. No, that's not logical...
8. No, we need to do more research...
9. No, there's no budget...
10. No, the finance department won't agree...
11. No, the market is not ready yet...

12. No, it might work in other places but not here...
13. No, that's way too risky...
14. No, it doesn't fit our strategy...
15. No, that's for the future...

The single biggest obstacle in innovation is one small word: 'no'. Real innovators turn the 'Noes' into 'Yesses' on their way, as innovation does not stop at the first 'no'; that's the moment it really starts. As an innovator you have to be prepared to do things others won't approve and don't want to be bothered with it.

Once you have passed the start of innovation, your new initiative has entered "Death Valley", as you can see in chart 32. My best advice: persevere at great will and full speed. In 1928 it was the famous economist Joseph Schumpeter who wrote, "Successful innovation is a feat not of intellect but of will. Its difficulty consists in the resistance and uncertainties incident to doing what has not been done before." Overcoming resistance and managing uncertainty is determining, according to Schumpeter, the innovation outcomes. I could not agree more with him![2]

A great example of someone crossing Death Valley with great will is Ingvar Kamprad, the founder of IKEA, the Swedish furniture retailer. Malcolm Gladwell mentions the story of how he got started: "His great innovation was to realize that much of the cost of furniture was tied up in its assembly: putting the legs on the table not only costs money but also makes shipping the table really expensive. So he sold furniture that hadn't been assembled, shipped it cheaply in flat boxes, and undersold all his competitors. In the mid-1950s however, Kamprad ran into trouble. Swedish furniture manufacturers launched a boycott against IKEA. They were angry about his low prices, and they stopped filling his orders. IKEA faced ruin. Desperate for a solution, Kamprad looked south and realized just across the Baltic Sea from Sweden was Poland, a country with much cheaper labor and plenty of wood. That's Kamprad's openness: few companies were outsourcing like that in the early 1960s. Then Kamprad focused his attention on making the Polish connection work. It wasn't easy. Poland in the 1960s was a mess. It was a communist country. It had none of the infrastructure or machinery or trained workforce or legal protections of a Western country. But Kamprad pulled it off. "He is a micromanager," says Anders Aslund, a fellow at the Peterson Institute for International Economics. "That's why he succeeded where others failed. He went out to these unpleasant places, and made sure things worked. He's this extremely stubborn character. That's conscientiousness. But what was the most striking fact about Kamprad's decision? It's the year he went to Poland: 1961. The Berlin Wall was going up. The Cold War was at its peak. Within a year, East and West would come to the brink of nuclear war during the Cuban Missile Crisis. The equivalent today would be Walmart setting up shop in North Korea. Most people wouldn't even think of doing business in the land of the enemy for fear of being branded a traitor. Not Kamprad. He didn't care a whit for what others thought of him. That's disagreeableness."

SIX FALLACIES IN DEVELOPING NEW PRODUCTS

In product and service development you're always struggling to bring in innovation projects on time and on budget. This is actually quite normal as many tasks you do are unique both for you and your company. The innovation delivery phase is also a learning process for many. In product development, I came across six fallacies, identified by Stefan Thomke and Donald Reinertsen,[3] which I would like to share with you:

Fallacy 1: High utilization of resources will improve performance.

Untrue. The speed of innovation projects and their quality inevitably decrease when you completely fill the capacity of your product-development employees. How many projects need to be managed? What kind of development work is needed? How long will it take before they are done? There are so many uncertainties, that planning on full capacity will lead to huge delays and frustration.

Fallacy 2: Processing work in large batches improves the economics of the development process.

Untrue. Thomke and Reinertsen teach us that the reduction of batch sizes is a critical principle of lean manufacturing: "Small batches allow manufacturers to slash work in process and accelerate feedback, which, in turn, improves cycle times, quality, and efficiency." They give the example of a new product that is composed of 200 components. "You could choose to design and build all 200 parts before you test any of them. If you instead designed and built only 20 components before you began testing, the batch size would be 90% smaller. That would have a profound effect on queue time, because the average queue in a process is directly proportional to batch size." So, do small batches to keep the speed high in your project.

Fallacy 3: Our development plan is great; we just need to stick to it.

Untrue. Of course your new business case is great, but it contains a number of major uncertainties and risks. A classic study of technical problem solving done by Thomas Allen showed that, "engineers developing an aerospace subsystem conceived of and evaluated a number of design alternatives before selecting one that they judged to be the best. Along the way their preferences changed frequently, as they tested and refined competing technical solutions." Only by experimenting will you find out what works and what doesn't. This is not only typical in technical innovation projects. Also in service design and development, testing and experimentation reveal what does and doesn't work. Use the feedback and learnings to deviate from your original plan whenever appropriate.

Fallacy 4: The sooner the project is started; the sooner it will be finished.

Untrue. When you are in a hurry and you start quickly before having the right people and resources on board, developing your innovation will go slowly. You might even have to stop and wait a while. This can be detrimental, as assumptions about technologies and the market can quickly become obsolete. The slower development advances the higher the chance that it will have to be reviewed. So, even when you're in a hurry, only start when you're ready for it.

Fallacy 5: The more features we put into a product, the more customers will like it.

Untrue. During product development, a lot of people all with the best intentions like to add stuff to your initial offering. I coined this as "building a Christmas tree." All the add-ons will often only detract the customer from the real value. Customers just want a product or service which solves their 'customer friction' in a simple practical effective way. Be sure to focus on it, while building your product or service.

Fallacy 6: We will be more successful if we get it right the first time.

Untrue. When you want to get it right the first time you tend to choose the less risky and safer way. Now developing a new-to-the-sector - or even new-to-the-world product requires news of getting things done. This indeed creates the risk that it will not be right the first time. It's well worth the effort though.

In trying to spark innovation, bigger organizations are founding innovation centers to help overcome these fallacies in product development. A recent study shows that four types of innovation centers are popular: in-house innovation labs (Walmart) university residences (Volkswagen), community anchors (Allianz) and innovation outposts Nestlé (see chart 33).

TEN INSIGHTS HOW TO EXECUTE INNOVATION EFFECTIVELY

At the end of the front end of innovation, the way in which new products and services are developed in so many sectors diverge enormously. Developing a new pharmaceutical product is in almost every aspect different from developing a web-based platform for car sharing, for example. I would like to conclude this chapter though sharing ten insights with you that I have gained in my practice as a manager consultant and innovation facilitator which might help you in improving your effectiveness at the back end of innovation.

1. Only start developing an innovation, when you yourself are 100% convinced of it- and committed to it.
2. Communicate to everyone a clear vision on the 'why' and the 'what', not ten, not hundred but a thousand times if necessary.
3. Keep the pressure on while knowing that it takes a long breath to get it ready for launch.
4. Use the original new business case of the front end of innovation as a hypothesis in the back end and pivot your offering under development swiftly when necessary.
5. Instead of working with a steering committee of top managers, you get them directly involved as godfathers of your new creation.
6. As speed is more important than ever, do fewer projects faster.
7. Be sure that a structured innovation process helps your innovators to get to launch at a high speed instead of frustrating them with endless reviews.
8. Reach out to customers regularly during the development process with prototypes and real-life tests to confirm you're still on the right track.
9. Open up your development process and co-create with committed passionate partners.
10. Keep it simple: an innovation is a straightforward new simple offering that solves a relevant customer friction or dream.

Although it's all about perseverance, in some cases you are better off abandoning your idea, especially when the gap between ideation and adoption in the market is unbridgeable. There's the story for example of Stephen Tang, who took his clean energy startup Millennium Cell, Inc., all the way from launch to IPO to eventual failure – and got fired along the way. At Millennium Cell, he tried to anticipate market demand for hydrogen-powered cars. He describes it the following way, "Even though we had a proprietary process to store, generate and deliver hydrogen on demand, it was a premature model. We had a great idea, but were well ahead of the market. Despite a $30 million initial public offering (IPO), groundbreaking technology and President George W. Bush's proposal to invest more than $1 billion in research on developing a clean, hydrogen-powered car, we could not successfully diffuse our innovation through to the market adoption stage. The gap between ideation and adoption was ultimately unbridgeable.[4] You just can't win them all.

I wish you lots of success at the back end of your innovation endeavors. In the next chapter I will summarize the major learnings from this book in an innovation checklist.

KEY MESSAGES FROM THIS CHAPTER

1. The single biggest obstacle in innovation is one small word: 'no'. Real innovators turn the Noes into Yesses.
2. Communicate to everyone a clear vision on the 'why' and the 'what', not ten, not hundred but a thousand times if necessary.
3. Use the original new business case of the front end of innovation as a hypothesis in the back end and pivot your offering under development swiftly when necessary.
4. Reach out to customers regularly during the development process with prototypes and real-life tests to confirm you're still on the right track.
5. Open up your development process and co-create with committed passionate partners.

Notes

[1] Malcolm Gladwell, *David & Goliath*, Penguin Books, 2014, pp. 116 – 118.
[2] Michael Schrage, *The Innovator's Hypothesis*, The MIT Press, Cambridge, Massachusetts, 2014, pp. 23-24.
[3] Stefan Thomke and Donald Reinertsen, *Six Myths of Product Development*, Harvard Business Review, May 2012, https://hbr.org/2012/05/six-myths-of-product-development
[4] Stephen Tang, *3 Signs You're Better Off Abandoning Your Idea*, Entrepreneur, http://www.entrepreneur.com/article/249468

BEWARE OF 'DEATH VALLEY'

During your front-end innovation project, when the ideas are born, there's a lot of enthusiasm. The excitement of a new idea, the positive feedback from customers and a very convincing new business case, all lead to great excitement. When the new business case is approved, it's time to pop open a bottle of champagne.

In the days that follow though a (partly) new innovation team will come in to oversee the delivery. More often than not, new facts will pop up:
"Gee, the market segment appears to be smaller than we projected initially....."

"Hmmm, technology development is not as easy as we thought...."

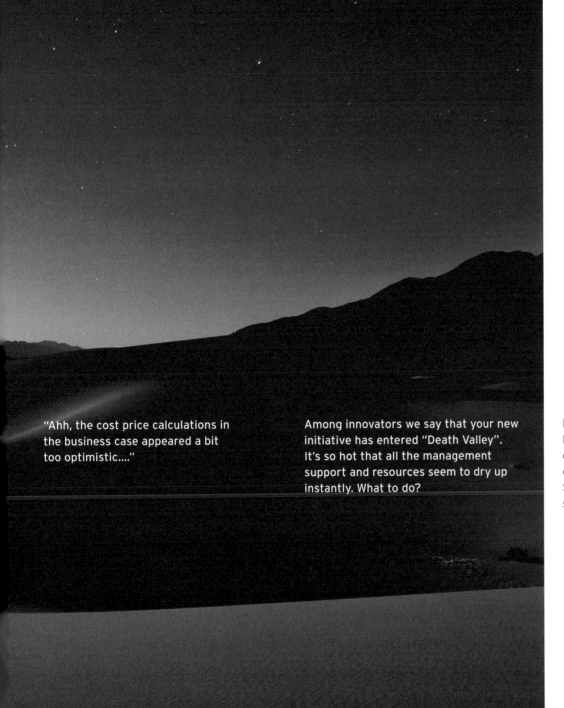

"Ahh, the cost price calculations in the business case appeared a bit too optimistic...."

Among innovators we say that your new initiative has entered "Death Valley". It's so hot that all the management support and resources seem to dry up instantly. What to do?

My best advice: persevere at full speed. Don't hesitate. Cross it as fast as you can. Take comfort in the knowledge that every project has its own "Death Valley". Stay confident: windfalls will come sooner or later.

4 TYPES OF INNOVATION CENTERS

Nowadays, there is a growing trend for companies to tap into new technologies, developments, products, and media by investing in various types of innovation centers.

In-house Innovation Labs

The innovation engine for their companies, these centers perform all innovation activities from inception to prototyping using an in-house approach. Given this in-house focus, these centers are typically large in size, with hundreds of staff. Walmart Labs, for example, is part of the Walmart Global eCommerce team, which runs Walmart's global websites. The two teams work in tandem so that e-commerce innovations can be seamlessly plugged into the websites.

University Residence

In this model, companies invest to set up a center at a university campus to drive innovation through university researchers.

One such center is the Volkswagen Automotive Innovation Lab (VAIL) established by Volkswagen and Stanford University's School of Engineering to drive innovation in automotive development. The Volkswagen Group has donated $5.75 million to the creation of VAIL, including $2 million for building construction and another $750,000 a year for five years to fund research. Stanford researchers and international visiting scholars will work with automotive equipment manufacturers and Silicon Valley experts.

Community Anchor

These innovation centers actively identify mentors and provide opportunities to startups to work actively with the company to test the startup's products. The startups also gain from mentoring and the availability of mature processes to test their innovations. In its role as an anchor, Allianz Digital Labs invites early-stage companies, students and innovators to run proof-of-concept pilots with the possibility of eventual licensing, development and commercialization on a large scale in areas such as Big Data, social media and mobile. Additionally, organizations might take an equity position in startups.

Innovation Outpost

Innovation outposts are small teams that are based in technology hubs, typically Silicon Valley. For large organizations, the idea is to be involved in the tech community, without committing significant investment. As time progresses, organizations can then choose to grow these innovation outposts to other forms of innovation centers. Take the case of Renault-Nissan. The company initially set up a small Silicon Valley Research Office in 2011 focusing on vehicle IT, advanced engineering research and technology recruitment. By 2013, the office was expanded to specialize in autonomous driving and connected vehicles. Similarly, Nestlé set up a Silicon Valley innovation outpost in 2013 with the aim of understanding customers better and work with large technology companies. The company has just announced that they intend to strengthen this team with more investment by Spring 2016.

Source
Capgemini Consulting, "The Innovation Game: Why and How Businesses are Investing in Innovation Centers", 2015. https://www.capgemini-consulting.com/resource-file-access/resource/pdf/innovation_center_v14.pdf

ANGRY BIRDS: THE MOST DOWNLOADED APP OF ALL TIME

After developing more than 50 games in the first six years they were still struggling to survive financially as the mobile operators controlled the market for mobile gaming. The success of Apple's App Store marketplace made Rovio decide to focus all efforts on developing a game for the iPhone; one that would make an impact and stand out. Game designer Jaakko Iisalo, was working on a number of ideas, one of which was the wingless, legless bird-like characters with thick eyebrows. In the beginning, he simply titled them 'Birds' and they were instantly liked.

From the positive reactions to early proto-types of Angry Birds, the Rovio team knew they were onto something special. When Rovio needed additional funding to complete the development of Angry Birds, Kaj Hed, the father of Rovio's young CEO Mikael Hed, struggled to find a solution to keep the company running. In an interview, Mikael Hed recalls, "He told me that he wanted to mortgage my grandparents' flat so he could put some more money in the company to keep it afloat. Now I am glad he did, but it was a big gamble."

The design and fine-tuning of Angry Birds took an eight-month development period. Gradually, many of the current features were added, including the pigs and slingshot as well as showing the flight path of the birds after being catapulted. The basic aim of the Angry Birds game is to knock out as many green pigs as possible by catapulting birds at them. The birds are angry at the pigs for stealing their eggs and the pigs take cover by hiding in various obstructions made of wood, glass, or rock. The first game published had 63 levels.

At the time the Angry Birds game was released in December 2009, it had to compete with 120,000 other paid apps, which was really a challenge. To draw attention to the game Rovio created a cinematic trailer that was launched on YouTube. Nevertheless, Angry Birds did not sell well at first. Rovio then decided to focus primarily on smaller markets. It was when their app became a best-seller in Finland, Sweden and Greece, that the App Store took interest in the game and supported it by featuring it more prominently. Immediately in the UK, the app became the best-selling app and a few months later it went to number one in the US and other markets around the world as well.

Along the way, Rovio learned how to keep the game at the top of the download-lists, as Petri Järvilehto, head of Rovio's gaming division explains, "When Angry Birds came out, we noticed that we got ranked highly in some countries and then rather rapidly started dropping off the top lists. But when we updated the apps with free content and levels, and we shot back to the top of the list in some countries almost immediately, we knew that that's what we needed to gradually repeat in other countries."

The Angry Birds brand and franchise successfully catapulted Rovio to great heights. In December 2010, one year after the launch, Angry Birds was downloaded 13 million times and had 10 million active users in 71 countries. Backed by this success, Rovio started a round of investment, raising US $ 42 million to expand its operations. For 2011, two years after the launch of the first Angry Birds game, Rovio revealed that it had booked revenue of € 75.4 million and earned € 48 million, before tax.

The popularity of Angry Birds allowed Rovio to franchise the characters for a range of items including toys, cups, key-chains, clothing, books, soft drinks, candies and other collectables. "With Angry Birds, we have successfully launched not only a strong new brand, but also a whole new entertainment franchise," said co-founder, Niklas Hed. Since 2009, Rovio has launched numerous successful games under the Angry Birds brand for different platforms: Angry Birds, Angry Birds Seasons, Angry Birds Rio, Angry Birds Space, Angry Birds Friends, Amazing Alex, Bad Piggies, Angry Birds Star Wars, Angry Birds Star Wars II, Angry Birds GO, Angry Birds Stella and Angry Birds Transformers. Rovio's focus on Angry Birds is part of the reason for its success. As Jami Laes, EVP Games at Rovio explained, "Our focus on that one brand resonated so well – taking that to different places, different platforms, different forms of entertainment and different products completely, rather than purely focusing on being a games developer (...) I think that less than half of our employees are working on games now. Games however will always be at the core of Rovio. That's our heritage."

As of January 2014, there have been over two billion downloads of Angry Birds across all platforms and including both regular and special editions, which makes Angry Birds the highest downloaded freemium series of games of all time.

"Download figures tell you nothing about engagement, but we still have 200 million people playing Angry Birds every month, the size of the Twitter audience," said Rovio CMO Peter Vesterbacka, speaking at Pocket Gamer Connects in London.

Without doubt Rovio has been extremely successful with Angry Birds, but as Jami Laes explains there will always be new challenges in the gaming market. "For us, the biggest challenge is that we want to build bigger games that have higher fidelity, but represent a bigger download. It's about the limitations of the mobile connection, when people are on the subway or in an elevator and want to continue to have a seamless experience. Before we get to a point where the cloud is always available, always reachable with high bandwidth, we're limited on the kind of gaming experiences we can build on mobile."

To date, the global gaming market is steadily booming. Over the past decade interactive entertainment has almost tripled in size into a $ 74 billion market. Smartphones have elevated mobile gaming to unprecedented heights, improved broadband speeds and infrastructure have propelled online gaming forward, and novel revenue models and digital distribution have greatly expanded the addressable market.

www.angrybirds.com
www.rovio.com

Sources

1. www.rovio.com.
2. "Angry Birds downloaded 2 billion times, has as many MAUs as Twitter", https://www.vg247.com/2014/01/22/angry-birds-downloaded-2-billion-times-has-as-many-maus-as-twitter/.
3. "Rovio's Jami Laes on keeping Angry Birds in the entertainment vortex", Venturebeat.com, Dean Rakahashi, January 14, 2014, http://venturebeat.com/2014/01/14/rovios-jami-laes-on-keeping-angry-birds-in-the-entertainment-vortex-interview/2/
4. INSEAD Case 04/2014-6044, "Rovio Entertainment: A Case Study of How Rovio Derived "Place Surplus" in the Finnish City of Espoo", Sami Mahroum, 2014.
5. "Playable media is the next big thing in $74B global games market", May 20, 2015, https://www.superdataresearch.com/blog/global-games-market-2015/.
6. Angry Birds: a Case Study in App Publishing https://www.youtube.com/watch?v=f0Lx4-3LPgw
7. "How the Angry Birds Almost Died Before the First Level", Ina Fried, February 23, 2012, http://allthingsd.com/20120223/how-the-angry-birds-almost-died-before-the-first-level/.
8. "Inside the nest: After 3 years of Angry Birds, what's next for Rovio?", Robin Wauters, December 21, 2012, http://thenextweb.com/insider/2012/12/21/inside-the-nest-how-angry-birds-catapulted-rovio-to-the-starsand-what-happens-next/4/
9. "$42M SERIES A INVESTMENT IN ROVIO", rovio.com, March 10, 2011.

THE INNOVATION CHECKLIST

The start of innovation is fuzzy. It's the messy getting-started period of a new product development process. The early phases of innovation are said to have the highest impact on the whole process and the outcome, since they extremely influence the design and total costs of the innovation. The high failure rate and the frustrations shared by many managers and innovation professionals, all lead to the conclusion that the start of innovation is not just some informal phase; there are also many potential pitfalls that need to be avoided. That's why I would like to provide you with a practical checklist to lead you through the innovation maze.

1. Pick one of the two sweet-spot moments for innovation: the moment you want to innovate or the moment you need to innovate.
2. Focus as an innovator on reducing the uncertainty to acceptable levels for yourself and your organization, as you always start at 100%.
3. Pick one of the four routes to guide you through the innovation maze: the Idea Route, The Technology Route, The Customer Issue Route or the Business Challenge Route.

PERSEVERE, ABANDON OR PIVOT YOUR IDEA INTO SOMETHING BETTER

4. Include at the front end of innovation at least these ten activities: Ideate, Focus, Check Fit, Create Conditions, Discover, Create Business Model, Select Technology, Check Freedom to Operate, Experiment and Create New Business Case.
5. On your innovation journey as startup, highlight both Discover and Experiment because you have created a new product or service under conditions of extreme uncertainty.
6. Risk failing and going the extra mile which is all essential in getting your innovation to market.
7. Use all your learnings to decide at any moment on your innovation journey whether to persevere with your idea or to abandon your idea and pivot it into something new and better than the original.

PICK A CLEAR FOCUS

8. Identify innovative quick-wins and prioritize them, as they will build trust among your company, when you're innovating after a crisis.
9. Pick a clear focus for innovation, otherwise your efforts will be all over the place and you will endlessly hesitate to pick the right idea.

10. Find a good balance between incremental innovations and radical innovations in your organization. They are both indispensable.

CREATE THE RIGHT CONDITIONS: MOMENT, TEAM, LEADER, AND ROUTE

11. Draft an innovation assignment where your senior management is explicit about their expectations on the results.
12. Be ambitious when you quantify your innovation goals.
13. Pick a well-balanced diverse team and work on group tolerance.

DISCOVER TO BREAK YOUR PATTERNS AND TO LEARN

14. Embrace tension in the team, as it sparks creativity in a tolerant group.
15. Discover, as it will take your blinders off and broaden your perspective.
16. Move beyond your personal comfort zone, as that is where the innovation magic happens.
17. Scrutinize trends and connect to innovators in other sectors to help you break your pattern.

IDEATE RELEVANT IDEAS DEFERRING YOUR JUDGMENT

18. Identify customers' pain points as they create an entry for new solutions you might develop for them.
19. Mingle among customers as they will give you new, refreshing insights which are the best stepping stones for innovative ideas.
20. Be open to ideas which come to you as slow hunches.
21. Create slack time, as your best ideas will pop up in your mind at these moments.
22. Co-create with lead users to generate revolutionary new offerings.
23. Defer your judgment, most of the time, or you will kill everything.

CREATE A BUSINESS MODEL TO DESCRIBE THE WAY YOU CAPTURE VALUE

24. Describe the rationale of how your organization creates, delivers and captures value in a practical business model.
25. Turn present beliefs in your sector upside down by creating new business models.
26. At an early stage, work out how to deliver your new concept.
27. At the start of innovation, incorporate an activity to match your new technology with relevant market needs.

SELECT THE TECHNOLOGY TO WORK OUT HOW TO DELIVER YOUR NEW CONCEPT

28. Experiment with tangible prototypes among potential customers to accelerate the pace of learning when you start with new technology.
29. Work out alternative concepts, which vary in cost, complexity and risk: a low-tech option, a proven-tech option and a new-tech option.
30. Use proven technology when it's essential to make your new concept more feasible and less risky.
31. Select a technology from a customer point of view, like Steve Jobs did.

CHECK IF YOUR INNOVATION FITS YOUR COMPANY

32. Be aware that the single biggest obstacle in innovation is one small word: 'no'.
33. Even be prepared to quit your present job to make your idea become reality.
34. Check if your innovation fits your organization at the front end, as it will be killed sooner or later if it doesn't.
35. Leave your organization when there's no match between your idea and them, and approach others with a better match or startup yourself.

CHECK YOUR FREEDOM TO OPERATE TO PROCEED WITHOUT INFRINGING THE RIGHT OF OTHERS

36. Don't spend time on ideas that don't have any chance of becoming reality.
37. Check the 'Freedom to Operate' to proceed without infringing the intellectual property right of others.
38. Consider a patent when your own new concept is a new, useful and non-obvious machine, process, manufacture, composition.
39. File a patent when there's a valid new business case.

EXPERIMENT AT THE START OF INNOVATION TO VALIDATE THE FUTURE BUSINESS POTENTIAL

40. Tweak the right technology and the right business model through smart experiments.
41. Validate the future business potential of your new concept by experimenting.
42. Make your experiments as realistic as possible, as the more you learn the better you will be able to assess the validity and attractiveness of your new concept.
43. Pretotype to test an idea quickly and inexpensively by creating extremely simplified, mocked or virtual versions of the new offering.

CREATE A CONVINCING NEW BUSINESS CASE TO GET YOUR INNOVATION FUNDED

44. Keep in mind that a lot of wise people aren't able to recognize the potential of a great idea.
45. To get the development of your new offering funded, you require a convincing new business case.
46. Convincing decision makers of more radical innovations is a bigger challenge as the uncertainties are bigger.
47. Be serious when you pitch your new business case, as "nobody buys innovation from a clown."
48. Only start implementing an innovation, when you yourself are 100% convinced - and committed to it.

PIVOT YOUR NEW OFFERING SWIFTLY WHENEVER NECESSARY DURING DEVELOPMENT

49. Communicate to everyone in a clear vision on the 'why' and the 'what'. Do this, not ten, not hundred but a thousand times if necessary.
50. Keep the pressure on while developing, while knowing that it takes a long breath to get it ready for launch.
51. Use the original new business case of the front end of innovation as a hypothesis in the back end and pivot your offering under development swiftly when necessary.
52. Ban a steering committee of top managers. Instead, get them directly involved as godfathers of your new creation.
53. Do fewer projects faster, as speed is more important than ever.
54. Adopt an innovation process which helps you and your innovators get to launch as quickly as possible instead of frustrating them with endless reviews.
55. Reach out to customers regularly during the development process with prototypes and real-life tests to confirm you're still on the right track.
56. Open up your development process and co-create with committed passionate partners.
57. Keep it simple as an innovation is a feasible relevant offering with a viable business model that is perceived as new and is adopted by customers.

IDEATION TECHNIQUES

In every route through the Innovation Maze, ideation is an essential activity towards a successful new business case. In essence, ideation is a two-step process of first generating ideas and then selecting the best ones. Your first goal is to generate an abundance of original ideas for your challenge. Outside-the-box thinking is required here for the best results. Secondly, you'll have to sift through all the ideas and choose the ones that best fit your goals. Both steps are necessary and equally important. What often happens in practice though is that groups spend hours generating new ideas and only leave themselves a half-hour to choose the best ones. This simply can't be done! Keep in mind that the most challenging aspect of a brainstorm is not simply getting lots of ideas, it's picking the right ones. To help you along, I have selected 21 ideation techniques to guide you through your ideation process. Also accompanying each technique you'll find a procedure explaining how to proceed step-by-step with a time-estimation. To brainstorm professionally be sure to appoint someone other than yourself as the manager, project leader or start-up founder to act as the facilitator. Mixing these roles will not only confuse you but also the rest of the group. As manager, project leader or start-up founder you should be the decision-maker and not the facilitator.

IDEA GENERATION TOOLS (DIVERGENCE)

1. Brain Dump

2. Innovation Opportunities

3. Customer Frictions

4. Presumptions

5. SCAMPER

6. Flower Association

7. Biomimicry

8. Comic Book Hero

9. Silly Things

10. The Insight Game

11. Crawl into the Skin of

12. What Would Apple Do?

13. Trends Dance

IDEA SELECTION TOOLS (CONVERGENCE)

14. Pinpoint Ideation Directions

15. Select Ideation Directions

16. Idea Mind Mapping

17. With Ketchup?

18. Salt and Pepper

19. Pros and Cons

20. Multi-criteria Selection of Concept Boards

21. My Valentine

1. Brain Dump

The brain dump is the starting technique for idea generation: to unleash the first spontaneous ideas. The participants 'brain dump' whatever comes to mind first and the facilitator then harvests these ideas.
Duration: 30 minutes.

Procedure:
- The facilitator reads the innovation assignment and asks the participants to write down their first ideas (in a few key words) in silence on a post-it. One idea per post-it.
- The facilitator invites two participants at a time to the front of the group to read their ideas aloud, quickly one after another, and to post them on the idea wall.
- The facilitator asks the rest of the participants to listen well and write any new ideas on a post-it.
- This is repeated until all the participants have come to the front in pairs to read their ideas aloud before adding their post-its to the idea wall and there are no more new ideas left.

2. Innovation Opportunities

Innovation opportunities are a wonderful source of inspiration for innovative ideas. Use them early in the idea generation phase.
Duration: 45 minutes as a separate tool; 20 minutes as part of the brain dump.

Procedure A: as a separate tool.
- The inspiration of the six to ten innovation opportunities are posted on the wall.
- The facilitator asks the 'owner' of the innovation opportunity to make an inspirational pitch to the group on what he or she has discovered and what lessons have been learned. Top innovation opportunities are allowed a three-minute pitch. The other innovation opportunities are only given one minute.
- Listening to the opportunities, participants are invited to jot down their ideas (in a few key words) in silence on a post-it. One idea per post-it.
- Afterwards, the facilitator invites two participants at a time to come to the front of the group to read their ideas aloud, quickly one after another, and to post them onto the idea wall. This is repeated until all the participants have added their post-its to the wall and there are no more new ideas left.

Procedure B: as part of the brain dump.
- To shorten the process, you can integrate the innovation opportunities with the ideas produced in the brain dump.
- After the participants in the brain dump have jotted down their first ideas (in a few key words) in silence on a post-it, the facilitator proceeds to facilitate the innovation opportunities tool by integrating the ideas harvested from the brain dump and the innovation opportunities in one shift. It is my experience that you will win much more time this way, without compromising the effectiveness.

3. Customer Frictions

Meeting customers in person and finding out the frictions of the customer provide a wonderful source of inspiration for innovative ideas. Use them like innovation opportunities early on in the idea generation phase.
Duration: 45 minutes as a separate tool.

Procedure:
- All the boards with relevant customer frictions are at the workshop venue.
- In the previous Observe & Learn workshop, the innovation team has selected the five most promising frictions. The participants should therefore be divided into five groups.

- Allow each group ten minutes to generate as many solutions as possible for these customer frictions and to write down their ideas (in a few key words) on a post-it. One idea per post-it. Add them to the board.
- Let the groups switch from table to table to brainstorm for a maximum of three minutes generating additional ideas for each of the other remaining customer frictions.
- Afterwards, the facilitator invites the participants of each sub-group to come to the front of the whole group to read their ideas aloud, quickly one after another, and add them to the idea wall.
- This is repeated until all the sub-groups and participants have added their post-its to the idea wall and there are no more ideas left.

4. Presumptions

This is a creative technique whereby the presumptions implied by the assignment or challenge are identified, discussed and eliminated. The presumption technique can be applied best at the beginning of the divergence phase in order to reverse the habitual conventions in the product market or within the company.
Duration: 45 minutes.

Procedure:
- The facilitator starts by asking "What are the key concepts of the assignment?"
  - ▷ The participants are instructed to write down the key concepts for themselves.
  - ▷ The participants are asked to read these key concepts aloud.
  - ▷ The facilitator chooses the most important three to five key concepts.
- Generate ideas by eliminating the presumptions from each key concept.
  - ▷ The facilitator makes a list of the presumptions for each key concept.

- ▷ The facilitator asks the participants to eliminate the presumptions.
- ▷ The facilitator then asks the participants to invent new ideas without the presumptions and write them on post-its.
- ▷ The facilitator repeats this for each key concept until there are no more new ideas and the harvest has been exhausted.
- The facilitator invites the participants in pairs to come to the front of the group to read their ideas aloud, quickly one after another, and add them to the idea wall. This is repeated until all the participants have added their post-its to the idea wall and there are no more ideas left.

5. SCAMPER

SCAMPER is a technique developed by Bob Eberle. It is an acronym consisting of the first letters of seven different approaches useful for changing a product or service. It can also be very useful when brainstorming for new products. It is comparable to the presumptions technique, but easier to apply for new products.
Duration: 1 hour.

Procedure:
- SCAMPER identifies seven main approaches:
  - ▷ S = Substitute. What can I replace in the composition, the material, the appearance and the size etc. of the product?
  - ▷ C = Combine. What can I combine with the product to improve it?
  - ▷ A = Adapt. Can I adapt the product to something else or can I copy something from other sectors?
  - ▷ M = Magnify/Minimize/Modify? What can I magnify, minimize or modify about the product?
  - ▷ P = Put to other uses. Can I use the product for something else?
  - ▷ E = Eliminate. What can I eliminate?
  - ▷ R = Reverse/Rearrange. Is there anything I can reverse, turn inside out or do in a different order?

- Generate ideas by tackling the questions one by one presented in the seven approaches of SCAMPER.
  - ▷ The facilitator recites all the questions for each approach.
  - ▷ The facilitator asks the participants to create new ideas and write them down on a post-it.
  - ▷ The facilitator invites the participants in pairs to come to the front of the group to read their ideas aloud, quickly one after another, and add them to the idea wall. This is repeated until all the participants have added their post-its to the idea wall and there are no more ideas left.

6. Flower Association

The basic principle of association is that one thought conjures up another thought. A flower association is the first investigation into the context of a specific word in the assignment. The associations are put down on paper around the central word like the petals of a flower. A flower association is usually one of the first creative techniques.
Duration: 30 - 45 minutes.

Procedure:
- Determine the core concepts.
  - ▷ What are the core concepts in the assignment or in the market?
  - ▷ Allow the participants to write down the core concepts.
  - ▷ Allow the participants to name the core concepts.
  - ▷ Choose the most important three to five core concepts.
- Do the flower association.
  - ▷ Questions:
    - - What do you associate with this concept?
    - - What type of aspects does the concept have?
    - - What does the concept remind you of?
  - ▷ With the concept in the center, write down all the associated words around it like petals of a flower.
  - ▷ The facilitator asks the participants to create new ideas based on the associations and write them down on a post-it.

- ▷ The facilitator invites the participants in pairs to come to the front of the group to read their ideas aloud, quickly one after another, and add them to the idea wall. This is repeated until all the participants have added their post-its to the idea wall and there are no more ideas left.
- The facilitator repeats these steps of the flower association for the remaining concepts.

7. Biomimicry

Biomimicry is a relatively young science derived from the words bios (life) and mimesis (imitate, copy). It uses nature as a source of inspiration for the challenges people are confronted with in modern society. Biomimicry is commonly used to solve technical (design) problems. Janine Benyus, the promoter of Biomimicry, writes about this in her book *Biomimicry: Innovation Inspired by Nature* published in 1997.
Duration: 30 minutes.

Procedure:
- The facilitator starts by asking, "If you take the assignment (or the product, or the customer) as the starting point, which animal or object does it resemble in your mind?"
- The facilitator writes down the names of these animals or objects.
- The facilitator then chooses one animal or object. Choose one that is most familiar and gives the most inspiration.
- Relate back to new product ideas based on some of the charac-teristics.
  - ▷ What are the characteristics of the animal or object?
  - ▷ Use these characteristics as a source of inspiration for new product ideas and ask the participants to write them down on a post-it.
- The facilitator repeats this procedure until there are no more new ideas and then proceeds to the remaining characteristic until all have been completed.

8. Comic Book Hero

In comic books anything is possible. The heroes are not bothered by the fixed patterns of reality. And this is exactly what we are trying to attain when we brainstorm. We stimulate our own fantasies by 'crawling into the skin' of our favorite childhood comic book heroes.
Duration: 30 minutes.

Procedure:

▸ The facilitator starts by asking, "What was your favorite childhood comic book hero?"
▸ Relate back to the innovation assignment from the perspective of the comic book hero.
▸ Place yourself in the character of the comic book hero. Which new product ideas would Asterix or Donald Duck create?
▸ Ask the participants to write these ideas down on post-its.
▸ The facilitator repeats this procedure until there are no more new ideas.

Tip: If the participants cannot name any specific comic book heroes, then you can ask them to come up with their favorite childhood fairy tale figure or a movie star.

9. Silly Things

You confront the participants with a random object, which lies completely outside the context or theme of the brainstorming session, such as a garden gnome, baby rattle or binoculars. The object strikes everyone as so oddly random that it leads to inspiration for new ideas.
Duration: 30 minutes.

Procedure:

▸ The facilitator passes around a completely random object, which has nothing to do with the product or the market.
▸ The participants study the object and are then asked to think about the specific characteristics of it.
▸ Relate back to the assignment based on these characteristics.

▷ What are the characteristics of this object?
▷ Use the characteristics as a source of inspiration for new product ideas and ask the participants to write them down on post-its.
▷ The facilitator repeats this procedure until there are no more new ideas.

10. The Insight Game

The Insight Game is a divergence technique whereby new ideas are generated around the most important customer frictions (which were discovered during the focus groups in the Observe and Learn stage) in combination with the strengths of the organization. For this technique you can make a board game that might need to be adapted to fit the circumstances. The participants work in groups of three or four.
Duration: 90 minutes.

Procedure:

▸ All the customer friction boards from the Observe and Learn stage are on display in the brainstorming room. Choose the most relevant customer frictions. Each participant receives four stickers and places them on the customer frictions considered most favorable with reference to the assignment. During the FORTH method this takes place in the final Observe & Learn workshop.
▸ Choose the strengths of the organization.
Each participant receives green post-its where they write down a maximum of four strengths of the company that are considered a competitive advantage relevant to the assignment. The facilitator then adds the post-its to the wall. Each participant receives four stickers and places them on the strengths considered most favorable with reference to the assignment.
▸ Play the game.
Each group is given a four-by-four matrix with the client frictions in the rows and the strengths of the company in the

columns. Number each box from one to sixteen. Fill in the customer frictions and strengths.
- Play the board game.
  - ▷ The facilitator divides the participants in groups of three or four. Each group receives a board game, a die and a pawn.
  - ▷ Player one rolls the die and moves the number of squares indicated. The player then lands on a square, which is a combination of a customer friction and a strength. The player's group then brainstorms over the combination and jots down their ideas on a post-it.
  - ▷ Once the group has finished brainstorming, player two rolls the die and the game is repeated.
  - ▷ The combinations which have already been used, are crossed out and you continue until all sixteen squares have been played.
- At the end of the game the players choose the three squares, which have generated product ideas with the most potential. These are then shared with the group when the facilitator invites participants of each sub-group to come to the front of the whole group to read their ideas aloud, quickly one after another, and add them to the idea wall. This is repeated until all the sub-groups and participants have added their post-its to the wall and there are no more new ideas.

11. Crawl into the skin of
With this brainstorming technique, ideas are generated by crawling into the skin of someone fitting the profile of the target group. When the participants imagine themselves in their new role as 'this other person' new ideas are then created.
Duration: 45 minutes.

Procedure:
- Ask the participants, perhaps using the flower association technique, to distinguish the 'types' or 'characters' in the target group.
- For the consumer market:

- ▷ the seemingly uninterested adolescent
- ▷ the energetic 70-year-old who is traveling the world
- ▷ the 24/7 X-Box gamer
- ▷ the beer-drinking neighborhood biker (with all due respect).
- For the business-to-business market, for example the energy market:
  - ▷ the desperate buyer who is taking great risks with rising energy prices
  - ▷ the manufacturing manager for whom continuity is the most important aspect
  - ▷ the controller who does not want to deviate when it comes to cost price calculations
  - ▷ the director who won't spend a penny extra on energy.
- Instruct the individual participants or the groups of three or four, to crawl into the skin of an actual person by giving as many details as possible for the fullest possible effect including a name, address, daily activity, work, hobby etc. Stimulate them to imitate their chosen 'type'. By using caricatures it eases the imagining process, gives great pleasure and by exaggerating features, it also generates effective perspectives for new ideas.
- Ask the individual participants (after they have finished laughing) to create new ideas through this 'new person' and to write them down on a post-it.
- Harvest the post-its.

12. What would Apple do?
With this brainstorming technique ideas are generated by crawling into the skin of another company, organization or group like Apple, IKEA, McDonald's or Toyota. When the participants imagine themselves as working for this company, ideas are created in their new role.
Duration: 45 minutes.

Procedure:
- Select the organizations. Choose the ones you suspect will add new perspectives to your innovation challenge.

▸ Ask the groups of three or four to crawl into the skin of these organizations. Encourage them to exaggerate their imitations of their chosen 'type'. Exaggerating the caricatures makes the perspectives more effective, stimulates the imagination, adds lots of fun and contributes to generating many new ideas.

▸ Ask the individual participants (after they have finished laughing) to create new ideas for their innovation assignment from the perspective of being the other organization and to write them down on a post-it. What would Apple do?

▸ Harvest the post-its.

13. Trends Dance

This energizing brainstorming technique will take you far outside the box combining various future trends. It gets people up on their feet, moving and dancing, and is very well-suited as the final idea generation tool.
Duration: 60 minutes.

Procedure:

▸ Select as many future trends as there are participants and write down each one separately on a stringed card.

▸ Try to match the trends to the interests and expertise of each participant and have the participants hang the cards around their necks giving them free use of their hands to write down ideas on the post-its.

▸ Step one: everyone is asked to individually come up with as many new ideas as possible based on the trend on his or her card and jot these down on the post-its.

▸ Step two: turn on dancing music at a high volume. When the music plays, have the participants start dancing and moving around the room. When the music stops, instruct the participants to stop dancing and team up in pairs. Their assignment is to come up with as many ideas as possible based on the trends on both cards and jots these down on the post-its.

▸ This is repeated several times.

▸ Step three: play dancing music at a high volume. The participants start dancing. This time when the music stops playing, the participants form groups of three. Their assignment is to come up with as many ideas as possible based on each of the three trends.

▸ This is repeated several times until the idea flow stagnates.

▸ The facilitator invites two participants to come up to the front of the group to read their ideas aloud, quickly one after another, and add their post-its to the idea wall. The facilitator instructs the rest of the participants to listen well and write down any new ideas on a post-it. This is repeated until all the participants have added their ideas to the wall and there are no more new ideas.

IDEA SELECTION TOOLS

14. Pinpoint Ideation Directions

The convergence phase starts with pinpointing the directions that our ideas take. Day One of a brainstorming session can generate anywhere between 500 – 750 post-its on the idea wall. This technique will help you make the transition from the post-its linking them to specific directions and grouping them together accordingly.
Duration: 45 minutes, depending on the number of post-its.

Procedure:

▸ The facilitator starts by asking the participants to closely examine the post-its wall. The facilitator explains that, for now, the participants need to focus on choosing the two post-its they consider the most promising. The remaining ideas will be held onto, as part of the brainstorming session at the end of this stage. Allow five to ten minutes for everyone to carefully study the impressive idea wall. Ask them to choose one post-it which is 'close to home' and a second one which is 'far from home'. This will give you a good mix of feasible solutions and outside-the-box ideas.

- The facilitator asks the participants to read the selected post-its to the group one after another. Subsequently, the group chooses a title to give to each ideation direction. The facilitator follows the same procedure for each selected post-it. Post-its which are linked to the same direction are placed together on the idea wall. This is repeated until the facilitator has the impression that the group has exhausted all possible ideation directions. It is common that a new product brainstorming session can produce up to 30 or 40 different ideation directions.
- In past brainstorming sessions, we would group all 500+ post-its under different titles of ideation direction. However, this turned out to be a very time-intensive procedure. Nowadays, we proceed directly to selecting the most promising ideation directions. We have found in practice that doing it this way does not compromise the quality of the final concepts.

15. Select ideation directions

This technique often follows the previous phase where 30 to 40 ideation directions are titled and categorized into groups. In this technique you proceed to select the twelve directions with the most potential and develop them further in the next stage using idea mind maps.
Duration: 30 minutes, depending on the number of directions.

Procedure:
- The facilitator hands out stickers and asks the participants to stick them on the ideation direction they believe to have the most potential. In other words, they must choose the ideation direction, which they would like to develop into a new concrete product or service idea. Each participant is only allowed to put one sticker on an ideation direction.
- After this step is completed, the most promising directions are selected by the facilitator determines in collaboration with the internal client and the project leader. The principle that works best is; the ones with the most stickers have the most potential. I would recommend giving the internal client a 'wild card' so

that he or she can also make a choice; this just might give a 'hidden gem' a second chance.
- The selected twelve ideation directions are then developed into idea mind maps.

Tip: The number of stickers depends on the number of directions. It is my experience that giving each participant seven stickers to distribute over 30 to 40 ideation directions, gives a good representation of the stronger and weaker ideation directions.

16. Idea mind mapping

Mind mapping is a well-known brainstorming technique made popular by Tony Buzan, an English psychologist. To make a mind map, place the main theme in the center enclosed in a circle. Key words associated with the central theme are added around it. It's common to use different colors and add drawings. It's a simple technique and the fact that it is very visual makes it easier and quicker for everybody to see the connections between the ideas related to the central theme.
Duration: 45 minutes.

Procedure:
- The facilitator explains how mind mapping works and discusses the mind map sheet. On a flip-over page, the ideation direction is written on a post-it and placed in the center. It already has three sub-divisions: 'what?', 'for whom?', and 'how?'. There are twelve blank mind map sheets, one for each ideation direction.
- The facilitator gives the participants a marker and asks them to write down or draw everything they associate with the central idea. Judgment, of course, should be deferred until a later stage.
- The participants are given 30 minutes to enrich the twelve idea mind maps with their ideas about its development.
- As soon as everyone has completed this, the facilitator asks the participants to each read their idea mind map to the group.

Doing this exercise gives everybody a good image of the possible developments for each idea.

17. With ketchup?
New concepts are presented one by one in a sales pitch or three-minute verbal explanation. The purpose of this technique is to improve the concepts.
Duration: 5 minutes per product idea.

Procedure:
- The facilitator asks one of the participants to present the concept to the whole group in three minutes.
- The facilitator asks the rest of the participants if they have any ideas how to strengthen the concept and to write these ideas down on a post-it.
- After the facilitator discusses the additional ideas, they are added to the concept board.
- The facilitator continues with the next concept board and the procedure is repeated until all the concepts have been presented.

18. Salt and Pepper
The purpose of this technique is to improve a good basic idea, by adding salt and pepper seasoning in the form of fresh ideas.
Duration: 20 minutes for each new concept.

Procedure:
- The facilitator in consultation with each group singles out one developed concept that by consensus still needs much improvement. One of the participants is asked to explain the idea.
- The facilitator then asks all the participants to walk up to the original idea wall and choose one idea which can function as 'salt and pepper' for the original concept. In other words: 'Choose the idea which can make this concept better.'

- Each participant then explains his or her 'salt and pepper idea'. The group discusses this and chooses which elements to add.
- The procedure is repeated with the next idea, group by group.

Tip: The group that has developed the concept board has final say which ideas will be added and which ideas will not. In this way the group retains ownership of the idea.

19. Pros and cons
With the help of this technique you can improve an idea by quickly summing up its pros and cons and brainstorming new solutions for its negative aspects. This technique is similar to the 'salt and pepper', but in this case the positive and negative aspects are discussed explicitly.
Timing: 60 minutes for each new concept.

Procedure:
- The facilitator in consultation with the group chooses which developed product ideas are eligible for further development. The finding of the qualitative research in the Test Ideas stage will provide an immediate answer.
- The facilitator divides the participants into groups of two or three and in consultation with the project leader then divides the product concepts among the groups. In this way, the groups can simultaneously improve four to eight concepts. The improvements are immediately adapted to the description of the original concept.
- The participants present the improved concepts to each other. More additions from the group might be added.
- The procedure is repeated until all eligible concepts have been discussed.

20. Multi-criteria selection of concept boards

The purpose of this technique is to determine the final rank order of the completed new concepts. Which one scores best?
Duration: 60 minutes.

Procedure:

▸ The facilitator has prepared evaluation charts beforehand. All boards with the concepts and evaluation charts are displayed on the tables along the wall. The facilitator shows the evaluation chart and discusses the evaluation procedure. This is an important phase, so make sure to allow enough time. It is also good to emphasize to the participants that a lot of thought has gone into the evaluation procedure and that the criteria have been selected in close consultation with the project leader and internal client and are based on the innovation assignment.

▸ The facilitator explains that for each developed product idea there are five evaluation criteria. For each criterion the participants have the possibility to give the idea 0 to 5 points (stickers): 0 = low and 5 = high. The categories for each criterion are explained with the help of the evaluation board.

▸ The facilitator hands out the sticker sheets with the task to evaluate each product idea according to the five criteria.

▸ After the participants have completed their evaluations of all the concept boards, the facilitator signals that it's time to tally the stickers for each board. The facilitator is the first to know the rank order of the most attractive developed product ideas. The results will be kept secret until the facilitator presents them to the group during the grand finale.

21. My Valentine

This is a nice technique to add some 'passion' to the final evaluation. With a red, heart-shaped 'I love you' sticker the participants can now give their favorite idea an extra boost with this final evaluation.

Procedure:

▸ The facilitator hands out one 'I love you' sticker to each participant with the request to openly declare which developed product or service idea has stolen his or her heart.

▸ The participants then stick their heart and evaluation stickers onto the selection boards of their choice.

▸ At the presentation of the final rank order the facilitator makes a note of how many stickers the concepts received in the previous technique compared to how many hearts the concepts received in this technique.

Tip: In most cases, the hearts go to the concepts which end high in the rank order. If that is not the case, then this striking difference should be pointed out to the group to see if they can find an explanation for this. How is it possible that the concept boards, which received the most hearts, scored so low in the rank order? The participants are allowed to alter the rank order on the basis of a contextual discussion; and should certainly do so if it is justified.

CUSTOMERS ARE SCARY CLIFFS

ALSO AVAILABLE

THE
INNOVATION
EXPEDITION

A VISUAL TOOLKIT
TO START INNOVATION

BUSY BUSY BUSY
ESCAPE HARBOUR

OUR OWN BLIND SPOTS

MARVELOUS BOOKS ON INNOVATION

Clayton M. Christensen (1997), *The Innovator's Dilemma*, Boston, MA: Harvard Business School Press.

Harvard Business Review (1997), *On Innovation*, Boston, MA: Harvard Business School Press.

Ernest Gundling (2000), *The 3M Way to Innovation, Balancing People and Profit*, Tokyo: Kodansha International.

Robert Jones (2001), *The Big Idea*, London: HarperCollins Publishers.

Shira White (2002), *New Ideas about New Ideas*, New York, NY: Perseus Publishing

Jonathan Cagan & Craig M. Vogel (2002), *Creating Breakthrough Products Innovation from Product Planning to Program Approval*, Upper Saddle River, NJ: FT Press.

W. Chan Kim & Renee Mauborgne (2005), *Blue Ocean Strategy*, Boston, MA, Harvard Business School Publishing Corporation.

Anthony Ulwick (2005), *What Customers Want*, New York, NY McGraw-Hill.

Chris Barez-Brown (2006), *How to Have Kick-Ass Ideas*, London: HarperCollins Publishers.

David Nichols (2007), *Return On Ideas – A Practical Guide to Make Innovation Pay*, New York, NY: John Wiley & Sons.

Henry Chesbrough, Wim Vanhaverbeke, Joel West (2008), *Open Innovation*, Oxford: Oxford University Press.

Marc Stickdorn & Jakob Schneider (2010), *This is Service Design Thinking*, Amsterdam: BIS Publishers.

Peter J. Denning, Robert Dunham (2010), *The Innovator's Way*, Cambridge: The MIT Press.

Alexander Osterwalder, Yves Pigneur (2010), *Business Model Generation*, Hoboken, NJ: John Wiley & Sons.

Steven Johnson (2010), *Where Good Ideas Come From*, London: Penguin Books.

Robert Cooper (2011), *Winning at New Products*, New York, NY: Basic Books.

Henry Chesbrough (2011), *Open Services Innovation*, San Francisco, CA: Jossey-Bass.

Eric Ries (2012), *The Lean Startup*, London: Penguin Books.

Noam Wasserman (2012), *The Founder's Dilemmas*, Princeton, New Jersey: Princeton University Press.

Tom Kelley, David Kelley (2013). *Creative Confidence*. London: William Collins.

Malcolm Gladwell (2013). *David & Goliath*. London: Penguin Books.

Larry Keeley, Ryan Pikkel, Brian Quinn, Helen Walters (2013). Ten Types of Innovation. Hoboken, NJ: John Wiley & Sons.

Gijs van Wulfen (2013). *The Innovation Expedition*. Amsterdam: Amsterdam: BIS Publishers.

Max McKeown (2014). *The Innovation Book*. Harlow, England: Pearson.

Peter Thiel (2014). *Zero to One*. London: Penguin Random House UK.

Tony Davila, Marc J. Epstein (2014). *The Innovation Paradox*. San Francisco, Ca: Berret-Koehler Publishers Inc.

Michael Schrage (2014). *The Innovator's Hypothesis*. Cambridge: The MIT Press.

Dave Richards (2014). *The Seven Sins of Innovation*. Houndmills, Basingstoke, Hampshire: Palgrave Macmillan.

Rowan Gibson (2015). *The 4 Lenses of Innovation*. Hoboken, New Jersey: John Wiley & Sons.

Duncan D. Bruce, Dr. Geoff Crook (2015). *The Dream Café*. Chichester, United Kingdom: John Wiley & Sons.

Nicholas LaRusso, Barbara Spurrier, Gianrico Farrugia. *Think Big, Start Small, Move Fast*. New York: McGraw-Hill Education.

Ramon Vullings, Marc Heleven (2015). *Not Invented Here, cross-industry innovation*. Amsterdam: BIS Publishers.

◄ Check out Gijs van Wulfen's innovation bestseller HOW TO START INNOVATION on the proven FORTH innovation method to start innovation effectively.

GLOSSARY

Active Innovators

Organizations and people who want to innovate; giving innovation priority at the end of the growth stage and not waiting until they get hit by a crisis.

Back End of Innovation

The innovation process of the new business case until market launch.

Biomimicry

A relatively young science derived from the words bios (life) and mimesis (imitate, copy). It uses nature as a source of inspiration for the challenges people are confronted with in modern society.

Brainstorming

A way of thinking whereby individuals or groups can create new ideas for a problem or a challenge according to certain guidelines. The founder of the brainstorming technique, who also introduced the term in 1941 was Alex Osborn.

Brain Dump

A technique with which the divergence phase of a brainstorm starts to 'catch' the first spontaneous ideas. The participants 'dump' their first ideas.

Brain Writing

A creative technique in the divergence phase of a brainstorm where you first get the opportunity to start generating new ideas in complete silence before sharing them.

Breakthrough Innovation

A feasible relevant offering such as a product, service, process or experience with a viable business model that is perceived as radically new and is adopted by customers, changing their behavior considerably. It's a big jump for customers.

Business Model

A description of how an organization creates, delivers and captures value. To put it in plain English: "It's the way you earn your money in a market."

Check Fit

Checking if your idea, technology, customer issue or business challenge fits your personal and corporate priorities.

Check Freedom to Operate

Checking if you do not infringe intellectual property rights of others.

Comic Book Hero

A creative technique in the divergence phase of a brainstorm, where you stimulate your imagination by 'crawling into the skin' of your favorite childhood comic book heroes.

Concept

A practical description of a new product or service which includes: a description of the situation and need of the customer, the customer friction, the solution brought about by the new idea, arguments as to why it provides the right solution and an advertising slogan.

Convergence Phase

A phase during a brainstorming session when the best ideas are selected according to certain criteria based on a brainstorm or innovation assignment.

Crawl into the Skin of

A "funny creativity technique" in the divergence phase of a brainstorm, generating new ideas, whereby you identify yourself with the "product or service you are innovating."

Create Conditions

Organizing the right moment, the right team, the right pace and the right funding for your innovation initiative.

Create New Business Case

Creating a well-founded convincing business case for your new product, service, process or experience.

Creativity

A way of observing and thinking using different angles and combinations which cause a breakthrough in your existing thinking patterns. It is stimulated by postponing your judgement.

Customer or User Designs

Customers are invited to take part in a contest to help the organization find ideas for new products.

Customer Friction

A relevant concrete need from a target group in a recognizable situation, which is not met and which we use as a stepping stone for a new distinctive product or service. Also called a customer pain point.

Customer Insight

A new and unique insight into the motives, wishes and behavior of the customer, which forms the basis for an appealing and relevant new idea.

Customer Journey Map

A user-centered design technique, which provides a structured insight in how your offering is used from a customer's perspective.

Customer Touchpoints

Moments where the user interacts with your offering on their customer journey.

Design Patent

A patent for 14 years, for any original and ornamental design for an article of manufacture.

Discover

Discovering new trends, markets, technologies and customer insights.

Divergence Phase

A phase during a brainstorming session where, with the help of creative techniques, as many new appealing ideas as possible are generated.

Ethnographic Research
Camping out with and observing customers while they use products or services.

Experiment
Carrying out a systematic research or test which validates the adoption and attractiveness of your new product, service, process or experience.

Facilitator
The guide of an innovation process. He/she also functions as partner and confidant of the project leader of the innovation team.

Flower Association
The basic principle of association is that one thought conjures up another thought. A flower association is a technique for divergence: the first investigation into the context of a specific word in the assignment. The associations are put down on paper around the central word like the petals of a flower.

Focus
Defining your innovation center-of-interest including all the boundary conditions.

Focus Group
A common term in customer research, meaning a conversation with about eight people from the target group under the direction of a facilitator to investigate their motives, behavior and needs. The purpose is to highlight relevant customer frictions.

FORTH Innovation Method
An inspiring practical innovation method in five stages with which you create and develop new products and services with the help of a team. FORTH is an acronym for: Full Steam Ahead, Observe and Learn, Raise Ideas, Test Ideas and Homecoming. This scientifically proven method effectively combines business best practices with design thinking techniques in a structured way (www.forth-innovation.com).

Freedom to Operate (FTO)
The ability to proceed with the research, development and/or commercial production of a new product or process with minimal risk of infringing the unlicensed intellectual property rights (IPR) of third parties.

Freedom-To-Operate Check
A risk management tool to assess the likelihood that you are infringing existing IPR with your innovation in the specific countries you are targeting.

Front End of Innovation
The front end of the innovation process prior to the new business case. It's usually associated with the starting phase where ideas are created. As this usually occurs with great difficulty and is unclear, it is also known as 'fuzzy front end'.

Ideate
Generating and choosing original relevant ideas for a product, service, process or experience.

Incremental Innovation
A feasible relevant offering such as a product, service, process or experience with a viable business model that is perceived as slightly new and is adopted by customers, not changing their behavior at all. It's a small step for customers.

Insight Game
A creative technique in the divergence phase whereby new ideas are generated around the most important customer frictions (which were discovered during the focus groups in the Observe and Learn activity) in combination with the strengths of the organization.

Innovation
A feasible relevant offering such as a product, service, process or experience with a viable business model that is perceived as new and is adopted by customers.

Innovation Assignment
A concrete description of the innovation mission of an organization, which gives direction to the type of innovation expected, the degree of newness, the target group for whom the ideas are developed and which specifies which criteria the new concepts must meet.

Innovation Opportunities
A subject, theme, technology, trend, area or target group which provides great opportunity to create innovations.

Innovation Maze
The front end of the innovation process prior to the new business case, which for many is a journey into unknown territory where you can so easily run into obstacles and lose your way.

Innovation Process
The process whereby concrete new products, services, processes or experiences are created, developed and introduced in the market. This process is usually divided into various steps. One of the most used processes for innovation is the Stage-Gate process by Robert G. Cooper.

Intellectual Property Rights (IPR)
Creations of the mind: inventions; literary and artistic works; and symbols, names and images used in commerce.

In the Box
To think within existing patterns and conventions.

Lead User Research
Reaching out to those users whose needs and preferences lead the market. It often combines both ethnographic research as focus groups.

Mind Mapping
A well-known visual brainstorming technique, to see the connections between the ideas related to the central theme, made popular by Tony Buzan, an English psychologist.

Multi-Criteria Selection

A creative technique in the converging phase of the brainstorm to assess ideas more rationally, based on the criteria of your innovation assignment.

My Valentine

A creative technique in the converging phase of the brainstorm to add some 'passion' to the final evaluation. With a red, heart-shaped 'I love you' sticker you give your favorite idea an extra boost.

New Business Case

A small business plan for a newly developed concept consisting of seven to ten sheets where a strategic, commercial, professional and financial foundation is presented.

Offering

A product, service, process or experience offered to customers.

Outside the Box

To be able to think outside existing patterns and conventions.

Patent

An exclusive right granted for an invention: a product or process that provides a new way of doing something or that offers a new technical solution to a problem.

Personas

Fictional characters you create to represent a certain user type.

Pinpoint Ideation Directions

A creative technique to start the convergence phase, which pinpoints the directions that your ideas take.

Presumptions

A creative technique in the divergence phase whereby the presumptions implied by the assignment or challenge are identified, discussed and eliminated.

Pretotype

A way to test an idea quickly and inexpensively by creating extremely simplified, mocked or virtual versions of that product to help validate the premise that "If we build it, they will use it."

Product Idea

A concrete idea about a new offering for customers.

Pros and Cons

A creative technique in the converging phase of the brainstorm to improve an idea by quickly summing up its pros and cons and brainstorming new solutions for its negative aspects.

Reactive Innovators

Those organizations and people who wait until they get hit by a crisis when their markets saturate or get disrupted by new technologies and/or business models.

Salt and Pepper

A creative technique in the converging phase of the brainstorm to improve a good basic idea, by adding salt and pepper seasoning in the form of fresh ideas.

SCAMPER

A creative technique developed by Bob Eberle for the divergence phase. It is an acronym consisting of the first letters of seven different approaches useful for changing a product or service.

Select Ideation Directions

A converging creative technique to select idea directions with the most potential and develop them further in the next stage using idea mind maps.

Select Technology

Identifying and selecting the right technology to deliver your new product, service, process or experience.

Silly Things

A creative technique in de divergence phase, where you confront the participants with a random object, which lies completely outside the context or theme of the brainstorming session, such as a garden gnome, baby rattle or binoculars. The object strikes everyone as so oddly random that it leads to inspiration for new ideas.

Stage-Gate Process

A blueprint for the product development process which was developed by Robert G. Cooper. In the original Full Stage-Gate model it is divided into five stages. Each stage ends with a gateway which serves as a quality control and as a go/no-go moment of decision for the management. The suitability as well as the effectiveness regarding additional insights (fuzzy gates), the number of stages in the project result (newness, complexity) and dependability has been enlarged. Nevertheless, the use of it is still open for discussion.

Start-Up

A new risky venture of entrepreneurs getting a new product or service idea to market.

The Business Challenge Route

A structured route to a New Business Case through the Innovation Maze of 10 activities, based on the challenge that you are at a point where you have to innovate as an organization.

The Customer Issue Route

A structured route to a well-founded convincing new business case through the Innovation Maze of 10 activities, starting with a customer pain point or frustration.

The Idea Route

A structured route through the Innovation Maze of 10 activities, starting with an idea and answering the question: "How do you develop your idea or opportunity into a well-founded convincing new business case?"

The Technology Route

A structured route to a well-founded convincing new business case through the Innovation Maze of 10 activities, starting with a new technology.

Trends Dance

An energizing brainstorming technique in the divergence phase which will take you far outside the box by confronting various future trends where several rounds are interspersed with dancing to loud music.

TRIZ

A technique for systematic innovation. TRIZ is a Russian acronym for 'Teoriya Resheniya Izobreatatelskikh Zadatch' which in English is: the Theory of Inventive Problem Solving. The founder of the TRIZ technique is the Russian engineer Genrich Altshuller. According to the TRIZ theory all innovations can be converted to 40 principles. Furthermore, it seems as if the evolution of technological progress follows predictable patterns.

Utility patent

A patent for 20 years, for any process, machine, composition of matter or manufacture.

"What Would Apple Do?"

A creativity technique in the divergence phase where ideas are generated by crawling into the skin of another company, organization or group like Apple, IKEA, McDonald's or Toyota.

With Ketchup?

A creative technique in the converging phase of the brainstorm to improve concepts.

INDEX

PHOTO CREDITS

I would like to thank all the photographers on Flickr (www.flickr.com) who granted permission to copy, distribute, transmit (and adapt) their work under Creative Commons.

Page 5	This photo is used under Creative Commons from Michael Ocampo.
Page 8	This photo is used under Creative Commons from chrstphre ☺ campbell.
Page 44	This photo is used under Creative Commons from George Lane.
Page 64	This photo is used under Creative Commons from wplynn.
Page 70	Photo credits: Airbnb.
Page 76	This photo is used under Creative Commons from Beth Jusino.
Page 82	This photo is used under Creative Commons from Brian B Sorensen.
Page 86	This photo is used under Creative Commons from Tim Green.
Page 92	Photo credits: Hövding.
Page 94	This photo is used under Creative Commons from Kitty DuKane.
Page 100	Photo credits: LEGO.
Page 116	Photo credits: Dell Inc.
Page 122	This photo is used under Creative Commons from Bro. Jeffrey Pioquinto SJ.
Page 124	This photo is used under Creative Commons from OROZ Studio.
Page 130	This photo is used under Creative Commons from Skoll World Forum.
Page 142	This photo is used under Creative Commons from Thomas Hawk.
Page 154	This photo is used under Creative Commons from Ken Walton.
Page 160	This photo is used under Creative Commons from Ali Asaria.
Page 172	Photo credits: Google.
Page 182	This photo is used under Creative Commons from Conservatives.
Page 188	This photo is used under Creative Commons from Kris Krueg.
Page 196	This photo is used under Creative Commons from Jon Snyder/Wiredcom.
Page 202	Photo credits: Bruil Groep.
Page 204	Photo credits: Bruil Groep.
Page 208	This photo is used under Creative Commons from Jack Dorsey.
Page 214	This photo is used under Creative Commons from Mr Jason Hayes.
Page 217	This photo is used under Creative Commons from Juhan Sonin.
Page 218	This photo is used under Creative Commons from Lepidoptorologic beauty*.
Page 222	This photo is used under Creative Commons from Michael.
Page 226	This photo is used under Creative Commons from Cassandra Rae.